Analyzing the Nexus of Big Data and International Trade

Rizwan Khan
Chandigarh University, India

Mohd Taqi
Bahrain Polytechnic, Bahrain

Khaled Hussainey
University of Portsmouth, UK

IGI Global
Scientific Publishing
Publishing Tomorrow's Research Today

Vice President of Editorial	Melissa Wagner
Director of Acquisitions	Mikaela Felty
Director of Book Development	Jocelynn Hessler
Production Manager	Mike Brehm
Cover Design	Phillip Shickler

Published in the United States of America by
IGI Global Scientific Publishing
701 East Chocolate Avenue
Hershey, PA, 17033, USA
Tel: 717-533-8845
Fax: 717-533-7115
Website: https://www.igi-global.com E-mail: cust@igi-global.com

Library of Congress Cataloging-in-Publication Data

Names: Khan, Rizwan, 1990- editor. | Taqi, Mohd, 1988- editor. | Hussainey, Khaled, 1972- editor.
Title: Analyzing the nexus of big data and international trade / edited by: Rizwan Khan, Mohd Taqi, Khaled Hussainey.
Description: Hershey, PA : IGI Global Scientific Publishing, [2025] | Includes bibliographical references and index. | Summary: "This book investigates the mutually beneficial relationship between data analytics and global business, highlighting the transformational possibilities inherent in their convergence"-- Provided by publisher.
Identifiers: LCCN 2024055554 (print) | LCCN 2024055555 (ebook) | ISBN 9798369365922 (hardcover) | ISBN 9798369365939 (paperback) | ISBN 9798369365946 (ebook)
Subjects: LCSH: International trade--Data processing. | Big data.
Classification: LCC HF1379 .A6958 2025 (print) | LCC HF1379 (ebook) | DDC 382.0285/57--dc23/eng/20250214
LC record available at https://lccn.loc.gov/2024055554
LC ebook record available at https://lccn.loc.gov/2024055555

British Cataloguing in Publication Data
A Cataloguing in Publication record for this book is available from the British Library.

Table of Contents

Detailed Table of Contents

Technological innovation has played a crucial role in addressing important contemporary issues in the 21st century, including promoting sustainable development, preserving vital natural resources, and fighting climate change. The combination of technological progress and the expansion of global trade has the capacity to greatly improve operational efficiency, promote international partnerships, and encourage economic prosperity and progress in both developed and developing countries. The chapter contributes to the existing knowledge by providing a well-organized strategy or roadmap for incorporating digital infrastructure and big data into international trade processes. The current framework focuses on using the potential of digital infrastructure and big data to facilitate international business.

Big data technologies are transforming business operations and decision-making, recognized for enhancing firm competitiveness. Over 80% of firms believe big data will change the competitive landscape, seeing its adoption as vital for gaining market share. Big data analytics can revamp production standardization, operation networks, and service precision. Firms are accelerating big data initiatives to gain critical insights for competitive advantage. However, only 25% of firms report significant improvements in outcomes from big data analytics, with many lacking deep understanding and necessary conditions for generating insights. Understanding how to effectively use big data analytics to improve decision-making quality is crucial for competitive advantage.

With the rapid technology augmentation, it becomes necessary to find complementary emerging computing technologies. This chapter highlights future computing technologies, emerging trends and industry buzz to identify most prominent technologies in India. In the emerging technologies, the market is perceiving the entry of local vendors covering such areas as the Internet of Things (IoT), Robotic Process Automation offerings and Machine Learning based technologies. Some technologies are of transformational nature and result in the foundation of new ecosystem; these are "Internet of Things" with its associated applications and "Machine Learning". Technologies on innovation trigger take more time for wide market acceptance. The main objective of this paper is to present a future vision for a smart environment which can provide knowledge accumulation and new directions to new researchers in the related field.

In recent years, experts have focused on oil, agricultural, and commodity import changes. The G7 nations have used various economic tactics to adjust import levels according to oil, agricultural, and commodity price swings throughout the previous four decades. Several variables directly affect national economic policies. First, most G7 nations import oil. Second, global warming and population expansion generate unanticipated price changes for agricultural products. Finally, iron, copper, and aluminum costs, which affect many everyday items, are always changing. This study examines whether industrialized G7 oil, agricultural, and commodity import shocks are permanent or temporary. The sudden swings in oil, agricultural, and commodity imports are examined using 1980–2020 annual data. Enders and Lee (2012) recommended using the Fourier ADF (FADF) structural break unit root test to assess the series' stationarity. If the series remains stationary, import shocks will last. Based on the outcomes, a conclusion and policy proposal will be prepared.

Technological advancements in recent decades have significantly transformed the global economy, leading to remarkable growth, enhanced productivity, and increased innovation. This shift has been marked by the widespread use of information and communication technologies (ICT), the emergence of the internet, and the incorporation of cutting-edge technologies like big data, artificial intelligence (AI) and blockchain. These developments have brought about a revolution in multiple industries, including manufacturing, finance, logistics, healthcare, and education, promoting a more interconnected and streamlined global economic environment. Businesses have been able to leverage big data to analyze large volumes of data and extract valuable insights on market trends, consumer behavior, and operational efficiency. Accordingly, this chapter provides an overview of Big Data and its applications in international trade. It is important to understand the implications of big data on global trade in order to effectively navigate the ever-changing realm of international trade.

In the dynamic landscape of global commerce, the nexus of trade finance and risk management emerges as a critical domain for businesses seeking resilience and sustainability. This chapter delves into the multifaceted interplay between trade finance practices and risk management strategies, elucidating their symbiotic relationship in navigating the complexities of international trade. At its core, trade finance serves as the lifeblood of commerce, facilitating transactions across borders by mitigating financial risks inherent in cross-border trade. However, in an era fraught with geopolitical uncertainties, economic volatility, and disruptive technological advancements, the landscape of risk has evolved exponentially. Furthermore, the chapter delves into emerging trends and innovations reshaping the trade finance and risk management landscape, including the digitization of trade finance processes, the rise of blockchain technology, and the advent of predictive analytics.

This abstract presents a thorough method for improving trade analysis by combining data visualization strategies with decision support technologies. This chapter's first section addresses the value of trade analysis in the modern, globalized economy. It emphasizes how crucial data-driven insights are for supply chain optimization, spotting developing markets, and boosting competitiveness. It also highlights the necessity of creative approaches to effectively manage the enormous volume of trade data. Then it explores data visualization's function in trade analysis. Charts, graphs, and maps are examples of visual representations that provide easy ways to study large, complex datasets and spot patterns that might not be seen in raw data. Users can dynamically filter, dive down, and examine trade data from several viewpoints by utilizing interactive visualization tools, which facilitates more informed decision-making. At the core of effective trade analysis lies the ability to process and interpret vast amounts of data.

Based on the presumption that individuals make fair predictions about the future and make rational decisions, the subject of finance has developed during the past few decades. Different behavioral biases have a significant impact on investors' decision-making processes. The study's major goal is to identify the cognitive and emotional biases that influence investor decisions and to ascertain whether there is a connection between behavioral biases and investment choices. The major goal of the study is to identify and rank the behavioral aspects that affect investors' decision-making processes. The study also explores how using big data can prevent bias in decision making. Through a survey, information was gathered from 396 people in Northern India, which was then examined. The results of this study suggest that emotional and cognitive biases might affect investing decisions. Both constructs have significant effects and is important for the development of attitudes towards investment decisions as well as for investment intentions.

Technological advancements are set to redefine industries and societal norms, heralding an era of unprecedented innovation and interconnectedness. Leading this transformation are artificial intelligence (AI), quantum computing, and biotechnology. AI is revolutionizing healthcare and finance through predictive analytics and autonomous systems. Quantum computing promises breakthroughs in cryptography, materials science, and drug discovery. Simultaneously, the Internet of Things (IoT) is creating a hyper-connected world, enhancing efficiency and generating new data-driven insights. Biotechnology advances, such as CRISPR, offer groundbreaking medical treatments and agricultural innovations, tackling disease and food security. The convergence of these technologies will spur new interdisciplinary fields and applications.

Preface

In an era defined by rapid technological advancement and unprecedented global interconnectedness, the intersection of big data and international trade represents a pivotal frontier. *Analyzing the Nexus of Big Data and International Trade* explores this dynamic relationship, uncovering the profound ways in which data-driven insights are reshaping global commerce. As editors, we are honored to present this comprehensive reference work, which brings together leading voices from academia, policy, and industry to offer a multifaceted understanding of how big data is transforming trade dynamics, policy frameworks, and business strategies.

The idea for this book emerged from our shared recognition of a growing gap in the literature on the practical and strategic implications of big data for international trade. While the rise of big data has already transformed industries such as finance, healthcare, and marketing, its impact on international trade has yet to be fully explored in a systematic and interdisciplinary manner. This book addresses that gap, providing a detailed exploration of how data analytics is influencing trade policy development, supply chain optimization, market intelligence, and beyond.

Our objective with this volume is threefold. First, we aim to offer readers a deep understanding of how big data is shaping the global trade landscape—from policy formulation and trade finance to compliance and market decision-making. Second, we seek to highlight the opportunities and challenges presented by the integration of predictive analytics and machine learning into trade ecosystems, equipping readers with the tools to leverage these advancements. Finally, we strive to provide actionable insights and strategies that can help businesses, policymakers, and researchers harness big data to foster competitiveness, drive innovation, and promote sustainable global trade.

This book is structured to address the key dimensions of data-driven trade. The chapters cover a wide range of topics, including big data applications for trade policy development, supply chain optimization, trade finance, cross-border e-commerce, and the regulatory and ethical challenges surrounding data privacy and security. Special attention is given to the environmental and social sustainability implications of big data in trade, as well as future trends and emerging technologies that are poised to shape the next era of global commerce.

CHAPTER OVERVIEW

Chapter 1: A Roadmap for Unlocking the Potential of Big Data and Digital Infrastructure to Accelerate International Trade

In this opening chapter, the authors present a strategic framework for integrating big data and digital infrastructure into international trade processes. The chapter explores how technological innovation has become a crucial driver of sustainable development, resource preservation, and climate change mitigation. By examining the intersection of technological progress and global trade, the authors highlight how operational efficiency, international partnerships, and economic growth can be significantly enhanced. This chapter provides a well-structured roadmap for harnessing the potential of big data and digital infrastructure to facilitate international business, offering valuable insights for policymakers, business leaders, and researchers.

Chapter 2: Analysing the Nexus of Big Data and International Trade: Evaluating the Economic Impact of Big Data

This chapter delves into the transformative power of big data technologies on business operations and competitive strategy. It explores the growing consensus among firms that big data is essential for maintaining a competitive edge, with over 80% of firms recognizing its potential to reshape market dynamics. However, the chapter also identifies a gap between big data adoption and measurable business outcomes, with only 25% of firms reporting significant improvements. The authors provide a thorough analysis of the challenges businesses face in leveraging big data for decision-making and competitive advantage, offering practical insights into overcoming these barriers.

Chapter 3: Analyzing the Nexus of Big Data and International Trade: Future Trends and Emerging Technologies

In this forward-looking chapter, the authors examine the role of emerging technologies in shaping the future of international trade. Key technologies such as the Internet of Things (IoT), Robotic Process Automation (RPA), and Machine Learning (ML) are highlighted as transformative forces poised to establish new trade ecosystems. The chapter discusses how these technologies are expected to gain market acceptance over time and outlines their potential to create a smart environment for knowledge accumulation and strategic decision-making. This chapter serves as a guide for understanding and leveraging future technological trends in global trade.

Chapter 4: Are Shocks in Import Temporary? Permanent? Evidence from Fourier ADF Unit Root Test

This chapter addresses the volatility of imports in developed economies, particularly among G7 nations. The authors examine how price fluctuations in oil, agricultural products, and key commodities like iron and copper have influenced national economic policies over the past four decades.

Using annual data from 1980 to 2020, the chapter employs the Fourier ADF (FADF) structural break unit root test to determine whether these import shocks are temporary or permanent. The findings provide valuable insights for policymakers on designing adaptive economic strategies in response to global market shocks.

Chapter 5: Big Data and International Trade: What is it and Why it Matters?

In this foundational chapter, the authors provide a comprehensive overview of big data and its transformative impact on international trade. The chapter examines how technological advancements—such as the rise of information and communication technologies (ICT), artificial intelligence (AI), and blockchain—have revolutionized global business operations. By analyzing how big data enhances market intelligence, operational efficiency, and strategic decision-making, the authors offer readers a clear understanding of why big data is critical for navigating the complexities of modern international trade.

Chapter 6: Cultivating Resilience: The Intersection of Trade Finance and Risk Management

This chapter explores the intricate relationship between trade finance and risk management in the context of global commerce. The authors argue that trade finance is essential for enabling cross-border transactions and mitigating financial risks. However, the chapter also acknowledges the evolving nature of trade-related risks due to geopolitical uncertainties, economic instability, and technological disruptions. Emerging trends such as the digitization of trade finance, the application of blockchain technology, and the use of predictive analytics are examined as strategies for building resilience and fostering sustainable trade practices.

Chapter 7: Data Visualization and Decision Support Tools for Trade Analysis

In this chapter, the authors explore the value of data visualization and decision support tools in trade analysis. The chapter highlights how visual representations of trade data—through charts, graphs, and maps—can simplify complex datasets and reveal hidden patterns. The authors discuss how interactive tools enable users to filter and analyze trade data dynamically, facilitating more informed and strategic decision-making. The chapter underscores the importance of developing innovative approaches to managing large volumes of trade data to enhance competitiveness and supply chain efficiency.

Chapter 8: Effect of Behavioral Biases on Investment Decisions Using Big Data to Avoid Bias

This chapter investigates the impact of cognitive and emotional biases on investment decisions and explores how big data can mitigate these biases. Based on a survey of 396 individuals in Northern India, the authors identify key behavioral biases influencing investment choices and examine how predictive analytics can improve decision-making accuracy. The chapter provides a framework for understanding and addressing behavioral biases through data-driven insights, helping investors make more rational and strategic decisions.

Chapter 9: Enhance Trade Analysis with Data Visualization and Decision Support Tools

This chapter builds on the themes of Chapter 7, offering a deeper exploration of how data visualization and decision support systems enhance trade analysis. The authors examine how integrating advanced analytics, machine learning, and predictive modeling into decision support tools can improve business intelligence and risk assessment. Real-world examples, including Bloomberg Terminal and Thomson Reuters Eikon, are presented to demonstrate how these tools are used to interpret market trends and inform strategic decisions. The chapter also discusses challenges related to data quality and integration, offering solutions for improving analytical accuracy and business outcomes.

Chapter 10: Exploring the Environmental and Social Sustainability of the Coffee Industry in South Asia: A Case Study of Starbucks Coffee in India, Bangladesh, and Sri Lanka

This chapter examines the intersection of environmental and social sustainability in the coffee industry, focusing on Starbucks' operations in South Asia. The authors highlight Starbucks' commitment to sustainable sourcing, gender equality, and social responsibility. The chapter discusses the challenges faced by the company in implementing sustainability practices and explores the innovative strategies used to overcome them. The case study illustrates how businesses can balance profitability with social and environmental responsibility, offering valuable lessons for other global brands.

Chapter 11: Future Trends and Emerging Technology

In the final chapter, the authors provide a broad perspective on the future of technology and its impact on global trade. The chapter explores how artificial intelligence (AI), quantum computing, biotechnology, and the Internet of Things (IoT) are reshaping industries and creating new opportunities for innovation. The authors discuss how these technologies are expected to drive the next wave of industrial transformation, offering insights into how businesses and policymakers can adapt to a rapidly evolving technological landscape. This chapter sets the stage for future research and strategic planning in the era of technological convergence.

As editors of *Analyzing the Nexus of Big Data and International Trade*, we are proud to present this comprehensive exploration of how big data and digital infrastructure are transforming the global trade landscape. The chapters in this volume reflect the collective expertise and insights of leading scholars and practitioners, providing a rich tapestry of perspectives on the challenges and opportunities at the intersection of data and international commerce.

Through the diverse contributions featured in this book, readers will gain a deeper understanding of how big data is reshaping trade policy, supply chain management, market intelligence, and decision-making. From the strategic roadmap for integrating digital infrastructure into global trade to the exploration of future technological trends and behavioral insights, this book equips policymakers, business leaders, academics, and students with the knowledge and tools needed to navigate the complexities of modern trade.

We hope that this work serves not only as a valuable resource for understanding the transformative impact of big data on international trade but also as a catalyst for further research and innovation in the field. The rapidly evolving nature of global commerce demands adaptive and forward-thinking strategies, and it is our belief that the insights contained in this volume will inspire new approaches to enhancing competitiveness, driving innovation, and fostering sustainable growth.

We extend our sincere gratitude to all the contributing authors for their insightful and thought-provoking research, as well as to the reviewers and publishing team for their dedication and support. It is our hope that this book will serve as a guiding light for navigating the future of data-driven trade and contribute to a more prosperous and interconnected global economy.

Rizwan Khan

Chandigarh University, India

Mohd Taqi

Bahrain Polytechnic, Bahrain

Khaled Hussainey

University of Portsmouth, UK

Chapter 1
A Roadmap for Unlocking the Potential of Big Data and Digital Infrastructure to Accelerate International Trade

Karima T. Sayari
Al Zahra College for Women, Oman

ABSTRACT

Technological innovation has played a crucial role in addressing important contemporary issues in the 21st century, including promoting sustainable development, preserving vital natural resources, and fighting climate change. The combination of technological progress and the expansion of global trade has the capacity to greatly improve operational efficiency, promote international partnerships, and encourage economic prosperity and progress in both developed and developing countries. The chapter contributes to the existing knowledge by providing a well-organized strategy or roadmap for incorporating digital infrastructure and big data into international trade processes. The current framework focuses on using the potential of digital infrastructure and big data to facilitate international

DOI: 10.4018/979-8-3693-6592-2.ch001

business.

INTRODUCTION

The importance of the impending digital economy, which is based on information, computation, and communication, has long been emphasized by developmentalist economists. They have also spoken about the linkages between the local and the global, as well as the enormous influence that the internet and web have on how organizations are structured (Brynjolfsson & Kahin, 2002). Twenty years ago, professionals are having open conversations about the internet and web economy, quantifying interconnectivities in crowdsourcing, smart energy design, and the reconstruction of the global value chain in order to study "intelligent capitalism." The focus has shifted to financialization and the development of next-generation strategic digital technologies like deep learning, artificial intelligence, quantum computing, 5G/6G, and bioinformatics in order to propel technological convergence and steer the next stage of globalization (Peters, 2020).

To support these activities, data sharing, storage, and analysis costs have decreased in lockstep with the growth of cloud computing. The digital economy is claimed to create a new architecture for a labor market shift based on job growth, competences, and skills.

As global markets and trade opportunities grow, emerging digital technologies may foster innovation, efficiency, and productivity; safeguard supply chains; markedly improve product transparency; and elevate customer experiences. Technological innovation and increased commerce may enhance global partners' perspectives, streamline processes, and foster growth in both the Global North and South. At the onset of the Fourth Industrial Revolution, it remains uncertain whether technologies can effectively enhance global living standards and promote inclusive commerce by broadening opportunities for the Global South (Ezell and Koester, 2023).

Several studies dealt with the importance of the existence of digital infrastructure and achievement of economic development. Pradhan et al. (2018) examined the causal link between international trade openness, four main macro-indicators, economic growth, and development of the telecommunications infrastructure. Research findings show for both industrialized and emerging nations a bi-directional causal link between the expansion of telecommunications infrastructure and long-term economic growth. Toader et al. (2018) investigated the impact of ICT infrastructure on economic growth in the European Union. The result indicates that using ICT infrastructure has a favorable and sizable effect on economic growth in EU member states; the impact differs depending on the kind of technology examined. In the study of Amiroz and Avazov (2023), the macroeconomic climate and digital infrastructure's effects on economic growth are evaluated. The model's findings indicate that trade openness and foreign direct investment have a substantial positive correlation with economic growth. Although mobile, broadband, and secure internet servers have a negative impact on economic development, measures of digital infrastructure, such as internet and phone customers, have a favorable effect.

As Peter (2023) indicates modern reassessment of the digital economy depends on the emergence of digital commerce, where the internet functions as a trading platform that introduces new challenges related to the unrestricted flow of data across borders, security and privacy concerns, source code protection, and digital localization. This included the removal of digital customs duties and obligatory technology transfers, the assurance of fair and non-discriminatory network competition, the improvement of cybersecurity collaboration, the advancement of innovative encryption and authentication, the guarantee of global interoperability, and the implementation of rigorous patent and copyright protections, alongside measures to prevent trade secret theft.

Social networks and service ecosystems are becoming more and more important as we go into a time of linked intelligence and demand-driven predictive modeling. The enormous $30 trillion global capital markets landscape is being dominated by giant asset management businesses, giant investment banks, hedge fund juggernauts, new wave of autonomous investors, and trailblazers driving the financial digital revolution.

The chapter answer to the following research questions:

1- What are the key barriers to the successful adoption and use of digital infrastructure and big data analytics in the global commerce ecosystem?
2- How can big data analytics promote the transparency and openness of global trade flows, facilitate business, and improve supply chain effectiveness?
3- What fundamental components and best practices need to be part of a comprehensive framework or roadmap for successfully integrating big data and digital infrastructure into cross-border business processes?
4- What are the potential economic, operational, and competitive benefits that companies and nations may expect from using big data and state-of-the-art digital capabilities to expedite and facilitate global trade?

DEFINITION OF BIG DATA AND DIGITAL INFRASTRUCTURE

In the last ten years, Big Data surged across most sectors. Large-scale, high-volume, high-velocity, and/or high-variety information assets that need creative, economical information processing techniques to provide improved insight, decision-making, and process automation are referred to as big data by Gartner. Large amounts of paperwork and digital data are produced every minute by international trade transactions from a variety of sources, including customs, shipping lines, borders, warehouses, distributing logistics hubs, port terminals, dockyards, and others.

Figure 1. The 5 vs. characterizing big data

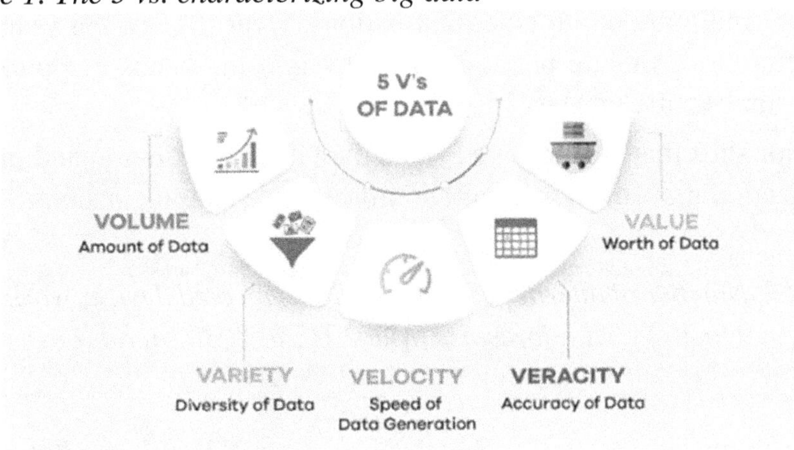

Source: Gartner Information Technology, Glossary

In the current Digital Age, vast amounts of data are routinely created and flowing from diverse sources, via multiple channels, every minute. In the past, this data was only accessible through a restricted number of channels. The data flood is made up of two factors: the increase in the quantity and diversity of sources from which data is released and transferred, and the speed and frequency with which it does so.

The revolution has produced a wide range of characteristics. There is an increasing quantity of data accessible, with less than a minute old. A portion of this data is generated and made accessible there in real-time. Another change in information is the emergence of social media and the expansion of mobile phone services. Most of this data might be better described as "data exhaust," or more precisely, as "the digitally trackable or People make storable decisions, behaviors, and preferences as they go about their daily lives."10 thousands of people may have access to such data at any one moment and location, offering a figurative way to measure the health of a community (Big Data for development, 2012).

It is important to underline the relevance of these characteristics once again: the transition is very recent, having been ongoing for more than ten years, developing swiftly, and having substantial implications for society, with emerging nations benefiting much from it.

The data revolution is not limited to developed nations; it is also occurring, and more so, in emerging nations. Over the last ten years, the proliferation of mobile phone technology into the hands of billions of people may be the greatest.

major shift that has occurred since the Green Revolution and the decolonization movement and has an impact on developing nations.

Figure 2. Number of internet of things (IoT) connected devices worldwide from 2019 to 2023, with forecasts from 2022 to 2030 (in billions)

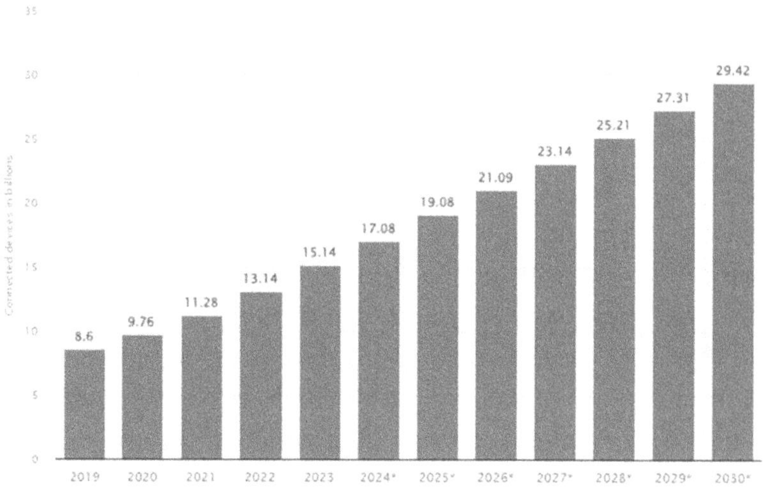

Source: Statista, 2023

According to Statista, it is projected that by 2030, there will be over 29 billion Internet of Things (IoT) devices globally, almost doubling from 15.1 billion in 2020. China will have almost 8 billion consumer IoT devices by 2030, making it the country with the most of any country.

IoT devices are used in a wide range of consumer markets and industrial verticals; by 2020, almost 60% of all IoT-connected devices will be in the consumer sector. Over the next 10 years, this proportion is expected to remain at this level. Globalization has reached a new phase, characterized by increased digitization of international commerce. Data flows serve as the conveyor belt for this change. New opportunities for trade, innovation, and productivity development are emerging, but there are also threats. In my chapter in the recently released book "Growth in a Time of Change," I discuss new prospects and policy problems.

Access and utilization of data may stimulate commerce, innovation, and productivity development. Data is fueling innovation, with the potential for a new wave of productivity development. Currently, almost half of the globe is online. Between 2005 and 2021, worldwide internet traffic will expand 127 times. The 5G network's implementation will assist the "internet of things" (IoT), with the number of internet-connected gadgets expected to treble the world population by 2021.

The capacity to transmit data effortlessly and worldwide is enabling new business models, accelerating R&D, promoting international cooperation, and revolutionizing international commerce. International e-commerce now accounts for around 12% of global goods trade. E-commerce presents a potentially large opportunity to boost small firms' involvement in international trade since having a website offers them an immediate worldwide presence, and e-commerce platforms provide integrated services such as financial payments and logistical assistance. In Korea, for example, 100% of companies on eBay have cross-border sales, compared to 20% of offline businesses.

Data centers were once heavily regulated physical infrastructures, but the emergence of cloud computing has changed this paradigm. A cloud data service is an off-site data center that is situated at a location other than the actual headquarters of a business. The amount spent on cloud IT infrastructure has increased and is expected to do so in the next years.

Figure 3. Leading countries by number of data centers as of March 2024

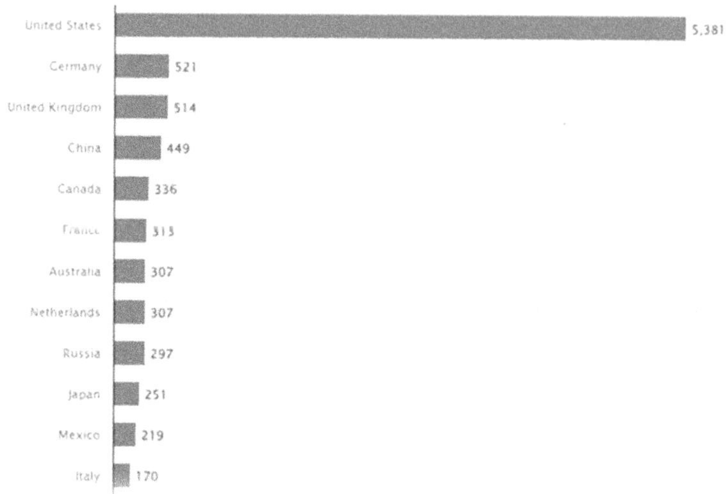

Source: Statista, 2023

Importance of Big Data for International Trade

Digital platforms are creating new trade opportunities especially for micro-, small-, and medium-sized enterprises. They might provide efficiency advantages supported by reduced transaction costs and information imbalances.

systems of ratings. Better utilization of underutilized resources, more competition, lower consumer prices, and more service provider flexibility emerge from this. systems of ratings. Better utilization of underutilized resources, more competition, lower consumer prices, and more service provider flexibility emerge from this. Both individuals and companies that buy or sell goods and services online across borders gain from international trade and cross-border e-commerce.

Information and communication technology (ICT) and digital solutions are used to automate trade operations and eliminate old ways of international commerce. It contributes to the efficacy of trade-related administrative activities and border control procedures, cutting total costs and strengthening international supply networks. Current technologies like

Blockchain systems, artificial intelligence, and big data analytics dispose of several advantages which range from improve operational efficiency, transparency, minimize trade risk to the reduction of disproportionately high expenses that small and medium-sized firms (SMEs) face while doing business overseas, hence promoting more efficiency and inclusivity in global commerce.

Trade digitalization occurs via two interrelated channels: paperless domestic trade systems and paperless international trade facilitation. In the former scenario, traditional paper-based paperwork within a single country is changed to electronic forms, streamlining procedures and lowering expenses. The latter aims to facilitate the safe and lawful cross-border interchange of trade-related data and documents in digital format between trade partner nations (UNCTAD, 2023).

Figure 4. Trade digitalization index-scores across the world

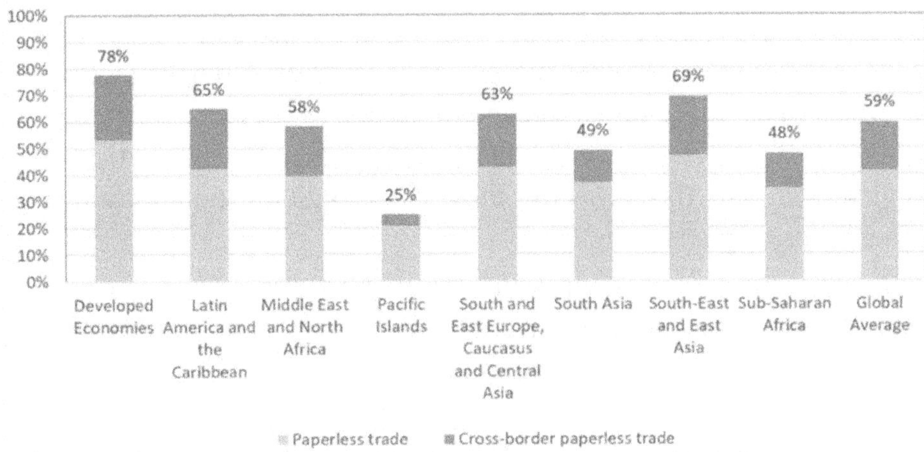

Source: Trade Digitalization in 2023

The United Nations conducted a Global Survey on Digital and sustainable trade facilitation and develop a measure of country performance called the Trade Digitalization Index (TDI), a new metric for assessing country performance, was created using data from the United Nations Global Survey on Digital and Sustainable Trade Facilitation. An overview of trends from 2021 to 2023 is provided by figure 4 with a focus on regional implementation rates.

Figure 5. Trade digitalization index-evolution across world regional between 2021-1013

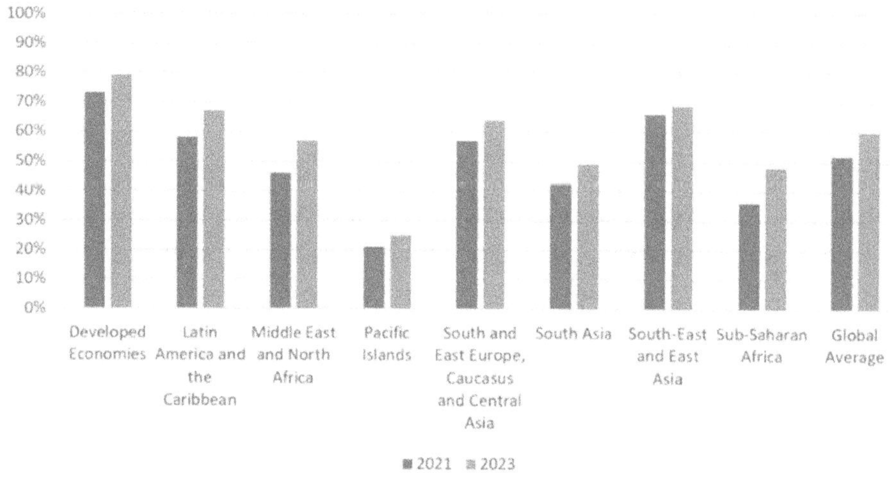

Source: Trade Digitalization in 2023

The above figure displays the progress made by different regions of the world in adopting digital technologies and processes for facilitating trade. The Trade Digitalization Index, represented on the vertical axis ranging from 0 to 100, measures the level of digitalization in trade processes across regions.

Developed Economies, shown as the first set of bars, had the highest Trade Digitalization Index in both 2021 and 2023, indicating their advanced adoption of digital trade facilitation measures.

Latin America and the Caribbean, as well as the Middle East and North Africa regions, made some progress in increasing their Trade Digitalization Index scores between 2021 and 2023, as indicated by the higher orange bars compared to the blue bars.

The Pacific Islands region had relatively low index scores, with only a slight increase from 2021 to 2023.

South and East Europe, Caucasus, and Central Asia showed moderate levels of trade digitalization, with a modest increase from 2021 to 2023. South Asia and South-East Asia had relatively low index scores in 2021 but demonstrated noticeable progress by 2023, as shown by the higher orange bars.

Sub-Saharan Africa had the lowest Trade Digitalization Index scores among the regions, indicating significant room for improvement in adopting digital trade facilitation measures.

The Global Average bars represent the overall progress made across all regions, showing a gradual increase from 2021 to 2023.

In summary, the figure highlights the varying levels of trade digitalization adoption across different world regions, with Developed Economies leading the way, while regions like Sub-Saharan Africa and the Pacific Islands lag behind in implementing digital trade facilitation processes.

Benefits of Big Data and Digital Infrastructure

The Relevance of Data in Digital Applications and Its Impact on the Economy

Digital commerce includes all economic activity pertaining to the movement of money, ideas, and information across international boundaries as well as the transfer of commodities and services (Zhang et al., 2022). Some traditional examples of digital trade are the downloading or streaming of audio-visual content, music, reading materials, software, and games, accessing online databases and cloud services, and digitized research. Digital Payment and the social development of networked standalone services (such as online consultants and remote teaching) as well as the increasing importance of aggregation platforms and related services (such as App Stores and online food delivery) are among the new and growing manifestations of digital trade today. Interviews and technology road testing by the World Bank suggest that in many jurisdictions, mobile services have now become the primary way for Micro, Small, and Medium-sized Enterprises (MSMEs) to conduct digital trade.

Big Data is the term for massive data sets that are too big for standard techniques to manage. Its goal is to find hidden patterns and move research away from a model-driven paradigm and toward a data-driven one (Taylor-Sakyi, 2016). Four characteristics define it: Volume, Velocity, Variety, and Veracity. These provide possibilities and difficulties for companies looking to use it to acquire insights and make choices.

Organizations may benefit greatly from big data; the key is understanding how to use it to your advantage and preserve a competitive edge. The complexity results from a variety of factors, including the volume of data, its quick generation, its variety of applications, and the opaqueness of the methods used to gather and handle it (Kimble & Milolidakis, 2015).

Over the last ten years, Big Data has risen across the majority of industries. Large-scale, high-volume, high-velocity, and/or high-variety information assets that need creative, economical information processing techniques to improve insight, decision-making, and process automation are referred to as big data, according to Gartner. Every minute, international trade transactions generate massive volumes of paperwork and digital data from a range of sources, such as ports, dockyards, shipping lines, borders, warehouses, distributing logistics hubs, and customs.

Across most sectors, Big Data has increased over the last 10 years. According to Gartner, big data refers to large-scale, high-volume, high-velocity, and/or high-variety information assets that need innovative, cost-effective information processing approaches to increase insight, decision-making, and process automation. Every minute, international trade transactions generate massive volumes of paperwork and digital data from a range of sources, such as ports, dockyards, shipping lines, borders, warehouses, distributing logistics hubs, and customs.

Digital Infrastructure Catalyst for Economic Growth

Digital infrastructure is the cornerstone of the digital economy, which is known also as s a digital technology-driven economy. Digital economy ensures an efficient allocation of resources (Goldfarb and Tucker, 2019). The popularization of mobile internet, and the 4G technology of mobile communication, the growth of financial technologies (fintech), new business models, artificial intelligence, blockchain and other technological advancements has accelerated the quick development of digital economy and has reduced the cost of transaction, communication and exchange between countries.

Zhoo (2022) found that Over 30% of China's total economic output comes from its digital economy. The future will see everything being connected thanks to China's rapidly developing 5G infrastructure, and science and technology infrastructure development will have made an enormous contribution to economic growth that will continue to fuel China's rapid economic expansion in the upcoming years (Ding et al., 2021).

Ma and Lin (2023) argued that digital infrastructure may overcome geographical obstacles, increase the accessibility and popularity of data and information, and reduce the cost of obtaining it. Czernich et al. (2011) claim that knowledge spillover and sharing may significantly improve technological innovation, particularly in the field of green technology. The ease with which information may be communicated in everyday life is increasing with the emergence of digital platforms. The level of uncertainty around green innovation initiatives may be decreased by regular contact between technology demanders and corporations. As a result, digital infrastructure may reduce the issue of information asymmetry, which fosters societal innovation.

Goldbeck and Lindlacher (2021) conducted a study on the Digital Infrastructure and Local Economic Growth in Sub-Saharan Africa. This research investigates if there is a causal relationship between the availability of Internet access, even at low speeds, and the overall economic development in Sub-Saharan Africa (SSA). We examine this phenomenon at the municipal level to assess if the prospective impacts seen by Hjort and Poulsen (2019) at the person level, regarding the availability of high-speed Internet in the future, also manifest themselves at a broader level. Furthermore, this enables us to investigate if the availability of the Internet has an impact that extends beyond political and economic hubs, and hence whether it may influence the regional development of nations. The research findings indicates that the presence of basic Internet access results in around a two-percentage point increase in economic development for towns in Sub-Saharan Africa (SSA) in the years following their connection, as compared to towns that were linked to the Internet at a later time but are otherwise identical. The primary driver of this outcome seems to be per capita productivity development, with migration into linked towns playing a minor role. Furthermore, the presence of the Internet is followed by a shift in regional job distribution from agricultural to industry.

Kozlov et al. (2020) focuses on examining how three Arctic regions in the Russian North-West are growing economically and industrially in relation to their digital infrastructure. Significant social and economic difficulties have recently faced these locations. Reindustrialization and technical upgrading are the only solutions to these difficulties. Contemporary industrial technologies rely on the digitization of all corporate business activities. The availability of regional digital infrastructure and information and communication technologies is a crucial aspect in the economic and industrial growth of regions.

Toader et al. (2018) investigated the impact of ICT on economic growth across EU member states during an eighteen-year period, from 2000 to 2017. The research demonstrates that ICT infrastructure adoption has a noteworthy and advantageous effect on economic growth in EU member states; the extent of the influence differs according to the technology being studied. They argued that the results exhibit a degree of concurrence with the theoretical forecasts and the findings of many relevant empirical investigations. The authors concluded that ICT infrastructure plays a major role in promoting economic growth in EU member states.

Challenges and Barriers

There are many obstacles that prevent big data analytics from being used as a driver for innovation. Some individuals worry about data, especially the ways in which it is collected and disseminated, and they also worry about the broader issue of privacy. There are more components that are relevant to the analysis. Global Pulse looked at the most prestigious ones in 2012.

One's personal space: The use of big data for development raises important ethical, legal, and technical questions, with privacy emerging as a key worry. Perhaps a better way to express it would be the individual's right to limit the publication of their personal information. More liberal definitions of privacy include the need for individuals and governments to defend their independence, the rights of their population, and the ability of companies to compete.

Maintaining an appropriate degree of privacy is essential for individuals, groups, and society at large to promote safety, diversity, inclusion, creativity, and fundamental rights.

If someone's privacy is violated, even people who are certain they have "no evidence of wrongdoing" might still be in danger.

A major issue arises when the key data sources—the users of the devices and services—are often unaware of the data they are producing or the potential for its exploitation. For example, people could rapidly choose a button to authorize data gathering without fully comprehending the implications. Likewise, it's not apparent if bloggers and Twitter users specifically agree for their data to be studied.

Given the value of privacy in a democratic society, it is critical to implement the appropriate security measures and monitor any possible privacy threats resulting from the development of new technologies. Installing suitable protections is crucial to protect individuals', businesses', and society's overall privacy in this age of extensive data gathering and processing.

Ensuring access to critical company data for development reasons while facilitating the sharing of user or consumer data may be challenging due to privacy, competition, and regulatory limitations. Organizational and technical constraints, such as inadequate data storage formats, lead to additional challenges. In order to do "privacy-preserving analysis" and guarantee data access and privacy, legal frameworks must be developed. The idea behind "data philanthropy" is that businesses need should de-identify and share their data, even if further investigation is necessary. Prior to starting, big data initiatives need to get beyond a few challenges.

According to Al Sai et al. (2019), three main challenges impedes big data adoption in an endeavor combining technology, method, and people. Information management strategies need to take human, process, and technological issues into consideration. Technology is still very young and in its infancy for many businesses. Companies need to think about other aspects that are important for Big Data projects more. If organizations are serious about investing in these projects, they need to arm themselves with a sufficient and suitable mix of tools, data management strategies, governance, technology, skills, and procedures to address the Big Data concerns. They highlighted the significance of People, Technology, Organization, Process, and Data Management as necessary elements required to ensure successful Big Data implementations.

The lack of digital skills and expertise of employees matters for the big data adoption by organizations. Extracting value from big data represents a constraint for them. Organizations are under pressure to adopt this new technology because of big data applications. A major obstacle to extracting value from big data will be the lack of expertise. Big Data adoption progressed slowly, which created a vacuum in the knowledge base needed to enable adoption-related choices and adequate preparedness. Data scientists get industry knowledge or subject expertise that they may then use to study Big Data in order to maximize profits and outcomes. Additionally, they get in-depth understanding of certain business procedures used by their company (Gao et al., 2015)

Big Data professionals are very hard to locate and costly to recruit since the field is still relatively new. Data scientists are a common term used to describe these specialists. It is essential that business professionals be involved from the outset of Big Data initiatives in order to achieve maximum success in using Big Data while concentrating on business values.

Technical challenges: managing a large volume of data is among the main obstacle of big data deployment like larger data storage system, and adequate infrastructure for storage, since Big Data projects consume a lot of data. Moreover, the enormous volume of data will be too much for the conventional database systems to handle. Big Data analytics requires new approaches, skills, and the ability to collect, store, and analyze data using big data technologies like Hadoop, Spark, and other data management systems (Chen et al., 2014). Another problem that will be included as one of the defining characteristics of Big Data is the insufficiency of current data processing and storage technologies to manage the amount of data that may be created by applying Big Data technology in business. It is challenging to use big data without a strong enough technological foundation.

Big Data requires extensive processing power as information may be in any format, including unstructured (like emails and financial transactions) and semi-structured (like structured data in standard databases). Additionally, the amount and rate of growth of data are increasing daily, which outpaces our capacity to model and analyze it at the same rate (Ali Al-Sai and Abualigah, 2017). For many firms, big data initiatives still use relatively new and inexperienced technologies. It is necessary to have a digital infrastructure able to adapt the changing velocity and scalability as main features of big data.

Organizational Difficulties

Though many organizations are still struggling to manage their transactional and operational data and are not yet ready to adopt Big Data, a small number of organizations have begun to realize the potential of Big Data as the organization world recognizes the significance of using Big Data analytics (Thomas, 2013; Gopalkrishnan et al., 2012). To enable the successful deployment of Big Data, organizational obstacles, such as those pertaining to an efficient value discovery process, direct top-level management participation, a customer-centric emphasis, and a strong business need for Big Data implementation, must be addressed (Eybers and Hattingh, 2017). It makes sense that companies trying to outperform their competitors in the market would need to enhance their data management programs in order to handle, safeguard, and broaden governance activities to deal with Big Data challenges.

Data veracity has to be acknowledged and managed. Data governance standards won't be effective if businesses can't handle the uncertainty around the quality of the data given the velocity and amount of data involved. Traditional data monitoring techniques and manual interventions won't cut it (Malik, 2013). Before using big data, one must take into account challenges pertaining to identity management, privacy, data management and protection, legal frameworks, policies, and principles, and governance.

However, in order for businesses to fully benefit from their data, a number of obstacles need to be removed. The Big Data era offers new opportunities, but in order to take advantage of these opportunities, assessing organizational readiness is a critical responsibility (Sun et al., 2016).

Strategies for Unlocking the Potential

Big Data initiatives need solving a variety of unique problems. Information management strategies must take into account employees, procedures, and technological viewpoints. In Big Data initiatives, it is particularly crucial to pay attention to non-technical aspects since the technology is still in its infancy and unfamiliar to many businesses. Big data operations need more attention to their procedures and participants (Gao et al, 2015). Global data traffic has risen by a factor of 1,000 during the last two decades, thanks to this flawless global data infrastructure supply chain, digital data may travel thousands of kilometers at astonishing speeds of up to 200,000 kilometers per second, or five full rotations of the planet in a single second. The data explosion has increased the need for data infrastructure. Countries that lack contemporary data infrastructure at the national level are unable to offer their citizens inexpensive and dependable connections. At the same time, without local broadband infrastructure, people cannot gain access to the wealth of data available, nor can data about those people be captured—so that their needs and preferences can be considered in the design and provision of public and private services. The World Development Report 2021, Data for Better Lives, pushes for greater equity in the global data system by addressing disparities in the availability of data infrastructure, both between individuals and between nations.

Data infrastructure rules, a major component of data governance, assist level the playing field in today's digital economy, providing fair access to data services for the poor in developing nations. This includes policies that enable individuals to access internet data services, as well as policies that guarantee governments have the infrastructure for effective data flow and processing.

Figure 6. Data governance layers at the national and international levels

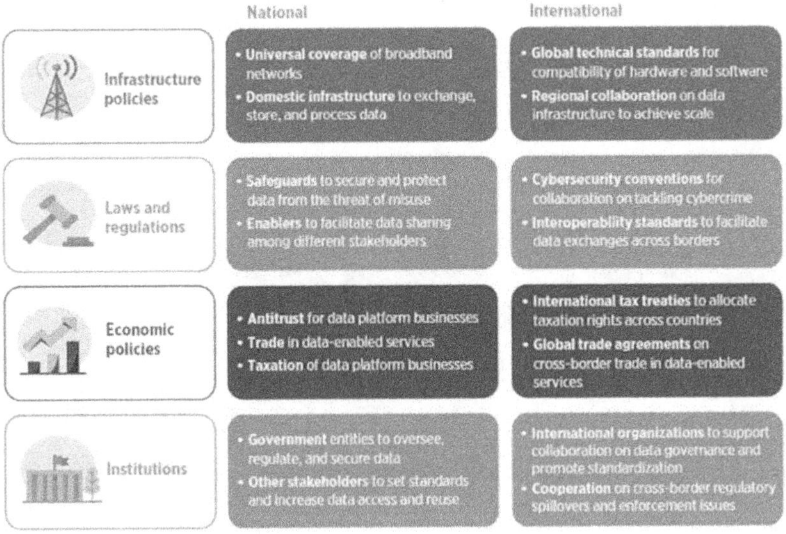

Source: World Bank Report, 2021

The existence of a strong legal framework for personal as well as non-personal data is primordial for building confidence in data exchanges. This represent one of the main elements of data governance structure, which combines rigorous cybersecurity measures to safeguard data systems and robust data protection safeguards.

Globally, legislative frameworks for personal data protection are still unevenly developed. According to the Global Data Regulation Survey, policymakers at all income levels have overlooked key aspects of data protection, including regulatory limitations on algorithmic decision making, privacy by design, and government exceptions for accessing personal data (see Figure 7).

Figure 7. Progress on personal data protection legislation differs markedly across country income groups (2020)

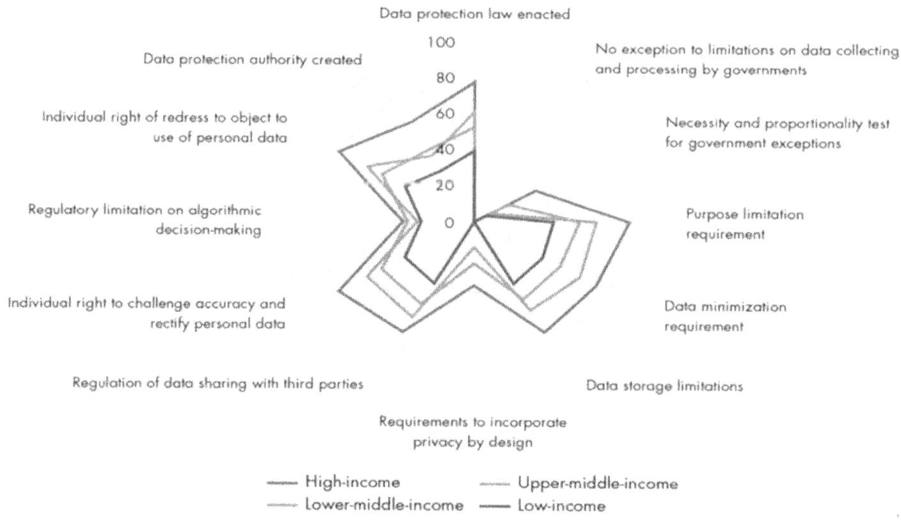

Source: World Bank Report, 2021

Organizations have had to move swiftly over the last several years to integrate new data technologies with legacy infrastructure in order to generate market-driven innovations like real-time warnings, tailored offers, and predictive maintenance.

These technological advancements, such as data lakes, customer analytics platforms, and stream processing, have greatly increased the complexity of data architectures, which frequently makes it more difficult for organizations to continue delivering new capabilities, maintaining their current infrastructures, and guaranteeing the accuracy of artificial intelligence (AI) models.

The nature of the market now precludes such slowdowns. Leaders in the industry, like Amazon and Google, are using artificial intelligence (AI) technology advancements to challenge established business models, forcing laggards to rethink parts of their own operations to stay competitive. Cloud service providers have introduced state-of-the-art products, such instantaneously deployable serverless data platforms, which provide users with more agility and a quicker time to market. In order to employ new models more rapidly, analytics users are expecting more seamless technologies, such automated model-deployment platforms. Application programming interfaces (APIs) have been widely used by enterprises to quickly integrate insights straight into front-end apps and expose data from heterogeneous systems to their data lakes. Today, flexibility and speed are even more important as businesses handle the extraordinary humanitarian catastrophe brought on by the COVID-19 epidemic and get ready for the new normal.

To get a competitive edge—or even to maintain parity—businesses will need a new approach to the planning, creation, and integration of their data stacks. This plan has to use cloud computing (beyond infrastructure as a service) and innovative concepts and elements.

Organizations must have a clear strategic strategy, and data and technology executives must make courageous decisions to prioritize adjustments that will have the most direct effect on business objectives and invest in the appropriate degree of architectural sophistication. Therefore, data-architecture designs vary greatly amongst companies.

Six shifts to create a game-changing data architecture are depicted by the following figure (How to build a data architecture, McKinsey). Six fundamental changes to firms' data-architecture blueprints that allow for faster delivery of new capabilities while substantially simplifying old architectural techniques. They affect almost all data operations, such as collecting, processing, storage, analysis, and exposure. Even while some changes may be made while keeping the basic technological stack intact, many need careful re-architecting of the current data platform and infrastructure, which includes both old and newer technologies that were previously slapped on.

Figure 8. Upgrade data architecture by making six foundational shifts

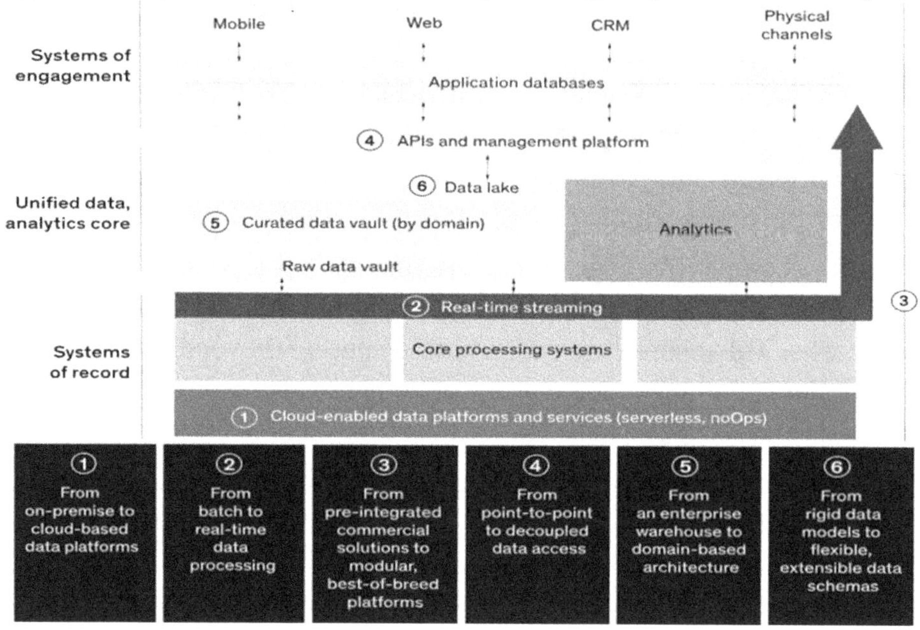

Source: McKinsey and Company, 2020

Case Studies

Efforts are underway at the UN to accelerate the identification, creation, and implementation of privacy-preserving big data apps that may revolutionize operations and assist communities worldwide in reaching the SDGs. The United Nations Privacy Policy Group (UN PPG) is an interagency group that UN Global Pulse helped form and now heads, to promote discussion and information exchange on critical matters pertaining to data privacy and protection within the United Nations system; (ii) to consolidate current initiatives pertaining to data privacy and protection; and (iii) to create a workable framework encompassing the entire United Nations system pertaining to data privacy and protection. After much deliberation, the High-Level Committee on Management (HLCM) has accepted the United Nations PPG's 2018 set of high-level principles on Personal Data Protection and Privacy.

Key success factors of the initiatives outlined in the case study include the importance of tailoring solutions to specific user needs; the effective use of technology, including support for technology adoption where required; the building of solid partnerships, often across different sectors; the leveraging of existing systems and infrastructure; the involvement of private sector stakeholders in both design and delivery phases; the phasing of interventions over time; the use of outcome-based approaches; and a flexible governing structure over projects and programs. These best practices translate into several principles that are useful to observe when designing and implementing digital initiatives that aim to facilitate international trade (Zoltners et al.2021).

The United Nations has been in the forefront of utilizing new technologies, particularly information and communication technologies (ICTs), to promote the Sustainable Development Goals (SDGs). Launched in 2009, the UN Global Pulse effort has been instrumental in testing the use of artificial intelligence (AI) and big data to provide useful insights for humanitarian relief and sustainable development (United Nations Global Pulse, 2018).

UN Global Pulse has achieved notable progress in the realm of corporate data philanthropy. UN Global Pulse has enabled the responsible sharing and use of private sector data for the public good through programs like the Data for Development challenge with mobile operator Orange and the Data for Climate Action innovation challenge with multiple private enterprises. Additionally, the UN system now has access to Twitter's data thanks to the partnership, allowing several agencies to use this resource for their initiatives.

UN Global Pulse has taken proactive steps in acknowledging the significance of privacy, protection, and ethics in the use of big data. The inter-agency UN Privacy Policy Group (UN PPG), which it co-founded and leads, has produced high-level guidelines for protecting personal data and privacy. In order to detect and address any possible ethical and human rights concerns in its innovation initiatives, UN Global Pulse also does risk, damage, and benefit evaluations (United Nations Global Pulse, 2018).

Furthermore, Uganda's experimental program, which collects voices from radio broadcasts using speech recognition technology, has the potential to make real-time information from rural regions more accessible (UN Global Pulse, 2018). Big data and artificial intelligence (AI) may tremendously benefit the SDGs, however as these technologies become more prevalent, worries about hazards and other difficulties arise.

Ezell and Koester (2023), examines how new digital technologies can support global commerce and sustainable development goals. It highlights specific technologies being used in both developed and developing countries that enable trade while having a relatively low carbon footprint (1.4% of global emissions by 2030). The study recommends changing international trade laws and WTO policies to better accommodate this new technology.

Specifically, it examines how certain new technologies may conflict with existing WTO laws and makes recommendations for changing the rules to maximize the benefits of digital technology for sustainable global commerce and development. In essence, it advocates for changes to the law to promote the use of digital technologies that might facilitate international trade while reducing its negative impacts on the environment.

Investing in a solid information and communication technology (ICT) infrastructure is crucial for realizing the full potential of digital technologies. With an expected 30 billion internet-connected devices by 2025, enabling seamless international data transmission is crucial. Data traffic has risen from 100 terabytes per day in 1992 to an incredible 150,000 gigabytes per second now, owing to services such as Google processing 100,000 searches every second throughout the world.

However, optimizing the effect of digital tools and platforms requires overcoming difficulties such as growing adoption rates, bandwidth capacity, qualified individuals, and technical skills - not just in poor countries but also in wealthy ones. The introduction of 5G networks, with their ultra-low latency and increased network capacity, enables better connection for a wide range of applications, including smart manufacturing, mobile payments, intelligent infrastructure, and digital customs paperwork.

While 5G access is now concentrated in North America, Japan, South Korea, and the European Union (with an estimated 1 billion customers by 2022), significant adoption is ongoing in China, India, South America, and the Middle East and North Africa. By 2028, there will likely be 5 billion 5G users worldwide, making up over half of all mobile users worldwide and overtaking fixed broadband use. This makes 5G the fastest-growing wireless technology to date.

In summary, realizing the revolutionary potential of digital technologies across industries and regions requires investment in strong ICT infrastructure that can handle enormous data demands and facilitate broad adoption of 5G. Figure 9 shows the mobile subscription by region and technology.

Figure 9. Mobile subscription by region and technology

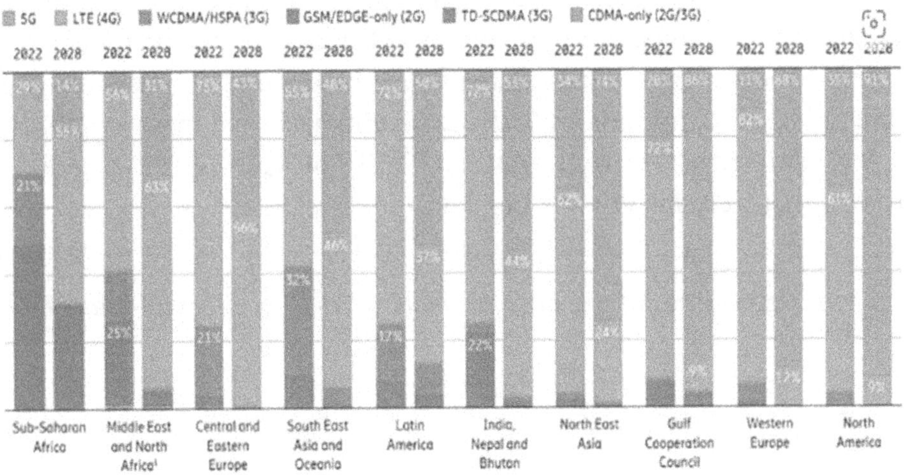

Source: Ezell and Koester, 2023

According to International Economics (2022), putting up a Big Data infrastructure is one of the main obstacles in its implementation. Big data collecting, storage, analysis, and output need, among other things, money, sufficient laws for data protection, facilities, and human capacity. Skills shortages, power supply issues, and ownership of exabyte and data farms are among the obstacles. Trade in services and data collecting from it are often hampered by missing or inadequate laws safeguarding users from data abuse. The GDPR (General Data Protection Regulation) for example restricts the kind of data that businesses may collect and raises some problems since people have the right to have their data deleted from databases even after they have given their permission to have it included.

Data transport limitations might therefore lead to inaccurate forecasts, which is against the idea of big data.

Big Data has been used by private enterprises as well to provide new services in international commerce. For example, S&P Global created Panjiva, a machine learning- and data-visualization-driven platform employing shipping data. The "U.S.A. Container Spy," utilizes the shipping line data for source factory identification, competitive analysis, and market research. North-West University spin-out TRADE Research Advisory (Pty) Ltd created the TRADE-DSM (Decision Support methodology) analytic methodology to help private companies facilitate trade. For export-ready and active companies wishing to expand their sales into foreign markets, the model finds realistic export potential (Big data in international trade, 2022). Although Big Data initiatives may be done effectively, many of them fail because technology is the main emphasis and there are no stated, well-defined objectives or results. Fig. 10 provides specifics of a few projects that were inspired by big data.

Figure 10. Examples of big data projects related to international trade

Source: International Economics, 2022

7. CONCLUSION

As businesses look increasingly to digital tools to expand opportunities, navigate challenges, and solve problems, both the public as well as political leaders have an increasing incentive to look at and address issues that go beyond moving boxes. At their heart, international transactions are exchanges of value between businesses or between businesses and customers. The more data that is available about these transactions, the more easily and securely transactions can be conducted. The costs of international trade primarily stem from the basis that international transactions are relationships between relative strangers with limited information about each other. Companies spend a significant number of resources to try and lower these information asymmetry and perceived risk. Given the potential for higher trade volumes, the more that governments can support efforts to share and protect data related to goods and service transactions the better. Data is a key trade facilitation foundation.

Key takeaways at heart, international transactions are exchanges of value between businesses or between businesses and customers. The more data that is available about these transactions, the more easily and securely transactions can be conducted. Costs of international trade primarily stem from the basis that international transactions are relationships between relative strangers with limited information about each other. Companies spend a significant number of resources to try and lower these information asymmetry and perceived risk. Given the potential for higher trade volumes, the more that governments can support efforts to share and protect data related to goods and service transactions the better. The development of big data and the ability to utilize digital infrastructure with data analytics represent some of the most powerful commercial tools available today. Efforts to harness these capabilities to support international trade must go beyond only looking at trade facilitation in terms of moving goods across borders. By better securing data related to international sales it will support the potential for more transactions, more goods and services moving across borders, and a higher quality of life around the world.

REFERENCES

Advancing Digital Transformation: Global Insights into the Digitalization of Trade Procedures | UNCTAD. (2023, Dec 29). https://unctad.org/news/advancing-digital-transformation-global-insights-digitalization-trade-procedures

Al-Sai, Z., Abdullah, R., & Husin, H. (2019). Big Data Impacts and Challenges. *RE:view*, 150–155. Advance online publication. DOI: 10.1109/JEEIT.2019.8717484

Al-Sai, Z. A., & Abualigah, L. M. (2017). Big data and E-government: A review. *2017 8th International Conference on Information Technology (ICIT)*, 580–587. DOI: 10.1109/ICITECH.2017.8080062

Belloumi, M., & Touati, K. (2022). Do FDI Inflows and ICT Affect Economic Growth? An Evidence from Arab Countries. *Sustainability (Basel)*, *14*(10), 10. Advance online publication. DOI: 10.3390/su14106293

Bukht, R., & Heeks, R. (2017). *Defining, Conceptualising and Measuring the Digital Economy* (SSRN Scholarly Paper 3431732). DOI: 10.2139/ssrn.3431732

Burri, M. (2020). *Big Data and Global Trade Law: An Introduction* (SSRN Scholarly Paper 3634430). https://papers.ssrn.com/abstract=3634430

Burri, M. (Ed.). (2021). *Big Data and Global Trade Law* (1st ed.). Cambridge University Press., DOI: 10.1017/9781108919234

Chen, M., Mao, S., & Liu, Y. (2014). Big Data: A Survey. *Mobile Networks and Applications*, *19*(2), 171–209. DOI: 10.1007/s11036-013-0489-0

Demchenko, Y., Zhao, Z., Grosso, P., Wibisono, A., & de Laat, C. (2012). Addressing Big Data challenges for Scientific Data Infrastructure. *4th IEEE International Conference on Cloud Computing Technology and Science Proceedings*, 614–617. DOI: 10.1109/CloudCom.2012.6427494

Du, X., Zhang, H., & Han, Y. (2022). How Does New Infrastructure Investment Affect Economic Growth Quality? Empirical Evidence from China. *Sustainability (Basel), 14*(6), 6. Advance online publication. DOI: 10.3390/su14063511

Edmondson, J. (2021, Dec 7). Understanding Big Data Infrastructure—A Complete Guide. *Businesstechweekly.Com.* https://www.businesstechweekly.com/operational-efficiency/data-management/big-data-infrastructure/

Ezell, S., & Koester, S. (2023). *Transforming Global Trade and Development With Digital Technologies.* Information Technology.

Gantz, J., & Reinsel, D. (n.d.). *The Digital Universe in 2020: Big Data.* Bigger Digital Shadows, and Biggest Growth in the Far East.

Gao, J., Koronios, A., & Selle, S. (n.d.). *Towards A Process View on Critical Success Factors in Big Data Analytics Projects.* Academic Press.

Gopalkrishnan, V., Steier, D., Lewis, H., & Guszcza, J. (2012). Big data, big business: Bridging the gap. *Proceedings of the ACM SIGKDD International Conference on Knowledge Discovery and Data Mining.* DOI: 10.1145/2351316.2351318

Kloza, B. (2023, Feb 27). *Impact of the Digital Divide: Economic, Social, and Educational Consequences.* Connecting the Unconnected. https://ctu.ieee.org/impact-of-the-digital-divide-economic-social-and-educational-consequences/

Koester, S. E. (2023). *Transforming Global Trade and Development With Digital Technologies.* https://itif.org/publications/2023/05/08/transforming-global-trade-and-development-with-digital-technologies/

Kozlov, A., Kankovskaya, A., & Teslya, A. (2020). Digital infrastructure as the factor of economic and industrial development: Case of Arctic regions of Russian North-West. *IOP Conference Series. Earth and Environmental Science, 539*(1), 012061. DOI: 10.1088/1755-1315/539/1/012061

Lemma, A., Mendez-Parra, M., & Naliaka, L. (n.d.). *The AfCFTA: unlocking the potential of the digital economy in Africa.* Academic Press.

Ma, R., & Lin, B. (2023). Digital infrastructure construction drives green economic transformation: Evidence from Chinese cities. *Humanities & Social Sciences Communications*, *10*(1), 1–10. DOI: 10.1057/s41599-023-01839-z

Malik, P. (2013). Governing big data: Principles and practices. *IBM J. Res. Dev.*, *57*(3–4). DOI: 10.1147/JRD.2013.2241359

Nguyen, L. A. T., & Habók, A. (2023). Tools for assessing teacher digital literacy: A review. *Journal of Computers in Education*. Advance online publication. DOI: 10.1007/s40692-022-00257-5

OECD. (2016, Sep 5). *Jobs and skills in the digital economy*. Medium. https://startupsventurecapital.com/jobs-and-skills-in-the-digital-economy-16b878ef7ee5

Oloyede, A. A., Faruk, N., Noma, N., Tebepah, E., & Nwaulune, A. K. (2023). Measuring the impact of the digital economy in developing countries: A systematic review and meta- analysis. *Heliyon*, *9*(7), e17654. DOI: 10.1016/j.heliyon.2023.e17654 PMID: 37501966

Peters, M. A. (2023). Digital trade, digital economy and the digital economy partnership agreement (DEPA). *Educational Philosophy and Theory*, *55*(7), 747–755. DOI: 10.1080/00131857.2022.2041413

Pradhan, R. P., Arvin, M. B., Nair, M., Bennett, S. E., Bahmani, S., & Hall, J. H. (2018). Endogenous dynamics between innovation, financial markets, venture capital and economic growth: Evidence from Europe. *Journal of Multinational Financial Management*, *45*, 15–34. DOI: 10.1016/j.mulfin.2018.01.002

Rohn, D., Bican, P., Brem, A., Kraus, S., & Clauß, T. (2021). Digital platform-based business models – An exploration of critical success factors. *Journal of Engineering and Technology Management*, *60*, 101625. Advance online publication. DOI: 10.1016/j.jengtecman.2021.101625

Schwertner, K. (2017). Digital transformation of business. *Trakia Journal of Sciences*, *15*(Suppl.1), 388–393. DOI: 10.15547/tjs.2017.s.01.065

Spiezia, V., Koksal-Oudot, E., & Montagnier, P. (2016). *New Skills for the Digital Economy*. DOI: 10.1787/20716826

Sun, S., Cegielski, C., Jia, A., & Hall, D. (2016). Understanding the Factors Affecting the Organizational Adoption of Big Data. *Journal of Computer Information Systems*, *58*(3), 1–11. DOI: 10.1080/08874417.2016.1222891

Taylor-Sakyi, K. (n.d.). Big Data: Understanding. *Big Data.*

Toader, E., Firtescu, B. N., Roman, A., & Anton, S. G. (2018). Impact of Information and Communication Technology Infrastructure on Economic Growth: An Empirical Assessment for the EU Countries. *Sustainability (Basel).* Advance online publication. DOI: 10.3390/su10103750

Zhou, A. (2022). Digital infrastructure and economic growth—Evidence for China. *Journal of Infrastructure. Policy and Development*, *6*(1), 1397. DOI: 10.24294/jipd.v6i1.1397

Zhou, L., & Fu, Y. (2021). The Impact of Big Data Technology on International Trade. In Huang, C., Chan, Y.-W., & Yen, N. (Eds.), *2020 International Conference on Data Processing Techniques and Applications for Cyber-Physical Systems* (pp. 889–896). Springer. DOI: 10.1007/978-981-16-1726-3_109

Zhou, L., & Fu, Y. (2021). The Impact of Big Data Technology on International Trade. In *2020 International Conference on Data Processing Techniques and Applications for Cyber-Physical Systems. Advances in Intelligent Systems and Computing, 1379.* Springer. DOI: 10.1007/978-981-16-1726-3_109

Zimmermann, H.-D. (2000). Understanding the Digital Economy: Challenges for New Business Models. SSRN *Electronic Journal.* DOI: 10.2139/ssrn.2566095

Zoltners, A. A., Sinha, P., Sahay, D., Shastri, A., & Lorimer, S. E. (2021). Practical insights for sales force digitalization success. *Journal of Personal Selling & Sales Management, 41*(2), 87–102. DOI: 10.1080/08853134.2021.1908144

Chapter 2
Analysing the Nexus of Data and International Trade:
Evaluating the Economic Impact of Big Data

R. Keerthana
Nehru Institute of Technology, India

Stemy Jaison J.
Nehru Institute of Technology, India

ABSTRACT

Big data technologies are transforming business operations and decision-making, recognized for enhancing firm competitiveness. Over 80% of firms believe big data will change the competitive landscape, seeing its adoption as vital for gaining market share. Big data analytics can revamp production standardization, operation networks, and service precision. Firms are accelerating big data initiatives to gain critical insights for competitive advantage. However, only 25% of firms report significant improvements in outcomes from big data analytics, with many lacking deep understanding and necessary conditions for generating insights. Understanding how to effectively use big data analytics to improve decision-making quality is crucial for competitive advantage.

DOI: 10.4018/979-8-3693-6592-2.ch002

INTRODUCTION

In the digital age, data is a critical asset for businesses, governments, and individuals. "Big data" refers to the vast volumes of data generated from diverse sources like social media, online transactions, and IoT devices, characterized by volume, velocity, variety, veracity, and value (Carriere-Swallow et al., 2019). This data drives data-driven decision-making, with companies like Google, Amazon, and Tesla leveraging it for real-time analytics, transforming industries and setting new innovation standards (Singala, 2019). Big data significantly impacts the economy by identifying trends, improving products, optimizing operations, and enhancing customer experiences. The economic benefits include cost savings, increased revenues, and new business models (Pradhan, 2009). However, big data presents challenges such as data privacy and security concerns, ethical issues, high infrastructure costs, and data quality management. This chapter explores the economic impact of big data, its application across sectors, the benefits and challenges of implementation, and future trends. Through case studies and statistical analyses, it provides a comprehensive overview of big data's role in transforming economies, highlighting both opportunities and obstacles.

BIG DATA IN DIFFERENT SECTORS

The impact of big data is felt across various sectors, each harnessing its potential to drive innovation, efficiency, and economic growth. This section explores the significant applications and economic contributions of big data in healthcare, finance, retail, and transportation, showcasing real-world examples and case studies to illustrate its transformative power (Serban 2017; Redd7 & Byrapu, 2023).

- ***Healthcare***

The healthcare industry is undergoing a revolution driven by big data analytics. The integration of big data in healthcare has led to substantial improvements in patient care, operational efficiency, and medical research.

Predictive Analytics for Patient Care

- Predictive analytics uses big data to forecast health trends and predict outbreaks, enabling proactive healthcare measures (Bakker, 2020).
- Hospitals utilize patient data to predict readmissions and manage chronic diseases more effectively, reducing costs and improving outcomes.

Operational Efficiency

- Big data helps optimize hospital operations, from staffing and resource allocation to reducing wait times and enhancing patient flow.
- Electronic Health Records (EHRs) provide comprehensive patient histories, improving diagnosis accuracy and treatment plans (Singala, 2019).

Case Study: Predictive Analytics in Disease Outbreaks

During the COVID-19 pandemic, big data analytics was crucial in tracking the spread of the virus, predicting hotspots, and allocating resources effectively. For example, Johns Hopkins University developed a global COVID-19 dashboard using big data to provide real-time updates and insights.

- ***Finance***

The financial sector leverages big data to enhance risk management, fraud detection, customer experiences, and regulatory compliance.

Risk Management and Fraud Detection

- Financial institutions use big data to identify and mitigate risks, monitor market trends, and predict financial crises.
- Advanced analytics detect fraudulent activities in real-time, protecting both institutions and customers.

Personalized Banking

- Big data enables banks to offer personalized financial services, improving customer satisfaction and loyalty.

- Data-driven insights help in designing tailored financial products and marketing strategies.

Case Study: Algorithmic Trading and Big Data

Investment firms employ algorithmic trading powered by big data to analyze market data and execute trades at optimal times. This has led to higher efficiency and profitability in trading operations, exemplified by companies like Renaissance Technologies.

- ***Retail***

In the retail sector, big data analytics drives personalization, optimizes supply chains, and enhances customer engagement (Swanson & Xiong, 2018).

Personalization and Targeted Marketing

- Retailers use customer data to deliver personalized shopping experiences, recommend products, and tailor marketing campaigns.
- Analyzing purchase histories and browsing patterns allows retailers to predict consumer behavior and preferences (Li & Yang, 2015).

Supply Chain Optimization

- Big data enhances inventory management, reduces waste, and ensures timely product availability.
- Predictive analytics forecasts demand, helping retailers to stock appropriately and manage supply chain disruptions.

Case Study: Amazon's Use of Big Data in Customer Insights

Amazon utilizes big data to recommend products, optimize logistics, and streamline operations. Its recommendation engine, which accounts for a significant portion of its sales, analyzes user data to suggest products customers are likely to purchase.

- *Transportation*

The transportation sector benefits from big data through optimized logistics, improved public transportation, and enhanced passenger experiences.

Logistics and Delivery Optimization

- Big data helps logistics companies optimize routes, reduce fuel consumption, and improve delivery times.
- Real-time data from GPS and sensors allows for dynamic route adjustments and better fleet management (Taylor et al., 2014).

Public Transportation

- Big data analytics improves public transportation systems by analyzing passenger flows, predicting maintenance needs, and enhancing service efficiency.
- Cities use big data to design smarter transportation networks, reducing congestion and improving urban mobility (Redd6, 2023).

Case Study: Uber's Data-Driven Approach to Ridesharing

Uber relies heavily on big data to match riders with drivers, predict demand, and optimize pricing. By analyzing real-time traffic data, rider patterns, and driver availability, Uber ensures efficient and reliable service.

The application of big data across these sectors highlights its critical role in driving economic value and innovation. Each industry leverages big data to solve unique challenges, improve efficiency, and deliver superior products and services, underscoring the transformative potential of data-driven decision-making (Swanson & Xiong, 2018).

Economic Benefits of Big Data

Big data analytics offers numerous economic advantages that drive business growth, innovation, and efficiency. This section outlines the primary economic benefits of big data, supported by statistical data and real-world examples.

- **Cost Efficiency and Waste Reduction**

  Operational Cost Savings

  - Big data helps organizations identify inefficiencies and streamline operations, leading to significant cost reductions.
  - For example, General Electric uses big data to predict maintenance needs for its machinery, reducing downtime and maintenance costs by 10-15%.

  Resource Optimization

  - By analyzing data on resource usage, companies can minimize waste and optimize the use of materials and energy.
  - In agriculture, big data analytics help farmers optimize irrigation and fertilization, reducing costs and environmental impact (Blazquez & Domenech, 2018; Li & Yang, 2015). The use of precision farming techniques can increase crop yields by up to 25% while cutting input costs by 20%.
- **Productivity Gains**

  Enhanced Decision Making

  - Big data provides actionable insights that enable better decision-making processes, leading to increased productivity.
  - A study by McKinsey found that companies using data-driven decision-making are 5% more productive and 6% more profitable than their competitors.

  Automation and Efficiency

  - Big data drives automation in various processes, from manufacturing to customer service, enhancing efficiency.

- In the automotive industry, big data analytics improve the efficiency of supply chains and production lines (Singala, 2019). Tesla, for instance, uses big data to optimize its manufacturing processes, reducing production times and costs.

- **Revenue Growth Through Innovation**

  New Business Models

  - Big data enables the creation of new business models and revenue streams, particularly in the tech and service sectors.
  - Companies like Uber and Airbnb have leveraged big data to disrupt traditional industries and create entirely new markets. Uber's data-driven approach to ridesharing has not only generated significant revenue but also revolutionized urban transportation (Reddy, 2023).

  Product and Service Innovation

  - By analyzing customer data, companies can develop new products and services tailored to market needs.
  - Netflix uses big data to analyze viewing habits and preferences, enabling it to create popular original content and recommend shows to users. This data-driven approach has been a key factor in its growth and success, leading to a 25% increase in subscriber retention rates (Hassan, 2022).

- **Competitive Advantage**

  Market Insights

  - Big data analytics provide deep insights into market trends and consumer behavior, giving companies a competitive edge.
  - Retail giants like Walmart analyze purchasing data to anticipate market trends and adjust inventory, ensuring they meet customer demand efficiently (Kumari & Malhotra, 2014).

  Personalized Customer Experiences

- Personalization driven by big data enhances customer satisfaction and loyalty, leading to increased sales and market share.
- Amazon's recommendation engine, which accounts for 35% of its sales, uses big data to personalize the shopping experience for each customer, boosting engagement and revenue.

- **Enhanced Risk Management**

  Risk Mitigation

  - Big data analytics improve risk assessment and management in various industries, from finance to manufacturing.
  - Financial institutions use big data to detect and prevent fraud, saving billions annually. For instance, JPMorgan Chase employs big data analytics to identify fraudulent transactions, reducing fraud losses by over 50%.

  Predictive Maintenance

  - In industries reliant on machinery and equipment, big data enables predictive maintenance, reducing unexpected failures and associated costs.
  - Airlines use big data to predict maintenance needs for aircraft, improving safety and reducing operational disruptions. Delta Airlines has saved millions of dollars annually by implementing predictive maintenance practices (Popovic, 2018).

By leveraging big data, organizations across different sectors can achieve significant economic benefits, including cost savings, productivity gains, revenue growth, and enhanced risk management. These benefits not only drive individual business success but also contribute to broader economic growth and innovation (Assuncao & Pelechrinis, 2019).

Challenges and Risks

Despite the substantial benefits of big data, its adoption and implementation come with several challenges and risks. Addressing these issues is crucial for organizations to fully realize the potential of big data while ensuring ethical and secure practices (Hassan & Mohamed, 2022).

- **Data Privacy and Security**

As the volume of data collected and analyzed grows, so do concerns about privacy and security. Organizations must navigate complex regulations and ensure that personal data is protected from breaches and misuse (Bakker, 2020).

- Privacy Concerns: Collecting and storing vast amounts of personal data raise significant privacy issues. Individuals' data can be misused or accessed without consent, leading to potential violations of privacy rights.
- Security Risks: Big data systems are attractive targets for cyberattacks. Ensuring robust security measures to protect sensitive information is a major challenge. Data breaches can result in substantial financial and reputational damage.
  - **Ethical Considerations**

The use of big data poses ethical dilemmas, particularly regarding the fairness and transparency of data practices. Ensuring ethical use of data is vital to maintain public trust and prevent discrimination.

-Bias and Discrimination: Algorithms and models based on biased data can perpetuate and even amplify existing inequalities. Ensuring that data and algorithms are free from bias is essential to prevent unfair treatment of individuals and groups.

- Transparency and Accountability: Organizations must be transparent about how they collect, use, and analyze data. This includes providing clear information about data practices and ensuring accountability for decisions made based on data analytics (Kumari & Malhotra, 2014).

- **High Costs of Implementation**

Implementing big data solutions requires significant investment in infrastructure, technology, and skilled personnel. The costs associated with these requirements can be a barrier, especially for smaller organizations.

- Infrastructure and Technology: Setting up and maintaining the necessary infrastructure for big data analytics involves considerable expense. This includes data storage, processing power, and advanced analytical tools.
- Talent Acquisition: The demand for data scientists, analysts, and other skilled professionals outstrips supply, driving up costs. Organizations must invest in training and hiring to build capable teams, which can be financially challenging (Hassan & Mohamed, 2022).

- **Data Quality and Management Issues**

The effectiveness of big data analytics is heavily dependent on the quality and management of data. Poor data quality and management can lead to incorrect insights and flawed decision-making (Singala, 2019).

- Data Quality: Inaccurate, incomplete, or outdated data can undermine the reliability of analytics. Ensuring high-quality data through rigorous validation and cleansing processes is crucial.
- Data Integration and Management: Integrating data from diverse sources and managing it efficiently is a complex task. Organizations often face challenges in ensuring that data is accessible, consistent, and properly governed.

Addressing these challenges and risks is essential for organizations to harness the full potential of big data responsibly and effectively. By implementing robust data governance practices, investing in security measures, and fostering ethical data use, businesses can mitigate these risks and leverage big data for sustainable economic growth (Hassan & Mohamed, 2022).

CONCLUSION

Big data has become a pivotal force in the modern economy, driving innovation, efficiency, and new business models across various sectors. From healthcare to finance, retail to transportation, the integration of big data analytics has provided organizations with unparalleled insights and opportunities for growth. The economic benefits are substantial, encompassing cost savings, productivity gains, revenue growth, and enhanced risk management. However, the journey to harnessing big data's potential is fraught with challenges. Issues related to data privacy, security, ethical considerations, high implementation costs, and data quality must be carefully navigated. Organizations must adopt robust data governance frameworks, invest in security infrastructure, and ensure ethical practices to mitigate these risks.Looking forward, the role of big data will only become more significant as technologies evolve and data generation continues to increase. Emerging trends such as the integration of artificial intelligence, the expansion of the Internet of Things (IoT), and advancements in real- time analytics will further amplify the impact of big data on the economy.For businesses and policymakers, the imperative is clear: to stay competitive and drive economic growth, they must embrace big data and address the accompanying challenges. By doing so, they can unlock the full potential of big data, fostering an era of innovation, efficiency, and sustainable development.In conclusion, while big data presents both opportunities and obstacles, its transformative power is undeniable. As organizations continue to refine their data strategies and technologies advance, the economic landscape will be increasingly shaped by data-driven insights and decisions, heralding a new era of economic prosperity.

REFERENCES

Assuncao, R., & Pelechrinis, K. (2019). Sports Analytics in the Era of Big Data: Moving Toward the Next Frontier. *Big Data*, *7*(1), 1–2.

Bajari, P. (2019). The Impact of Big Data on Firm Performance: An Empirical Investigation." AEA papers and proceedings. Vol. 109. American Economic Association.

Bakker, L. (2020). Economic evaluations of big data analytics for clinical decision-making: A scoping review. *Journal of the American Medical Informatics Association : JAMIA*, *27*(9), 1466–1475.

Bharathi, B.T. (2016). Efficient Exploration of Algorithms in Scholarly Documents Using Big Data Analytics. *International Journal of Engineering and Computer Science.* https://doi.org/10.18535/ijecs/v5i11.58

Bikakis, N., Papastefanatos, G., & Papaemmanouil, O. (2019). Big Data Exploration, Visualization and Analytics. *Big Data Research*, *18*, 100123. https://doi.org/10.1016/j.bdr.2019.100123

Blazquez, D., & Domenech, J. (2018). Big Data sources and methods for social and economic analyses. *Technological Forecasting and Social Change*, *130*, 99–113.

Carriere-Swallow, Y., & Haksar, V. (2019). The economics and implications of data: an integrated perspective. *International Monetary Fund*, 2019.

Ghasemaghaei, M., & Calic, G. (2020). Assessing the impact of big data on firm innovation performance: Big data is not always better data. *Journal of Business Research*, *108*, 147–162.

Hassan, S. M. (2022). A causal analysis on foreign trade and economic growth: The case of Somalia. (2022). *International Journal of Scientific Research and Management*, *10*(08), 3725–3731.

Hassan, S. M., & Mohamed, M. J. (2022). Comparison of Somalia and the East Africa Community in terms of economy and competition. *Daha International University Academic Journal*, *1*(1), 1–10.

Kumari, D., & Malhotra, N. (2014). Trade-led growth in India and China: A comparative analysis. *Journal of International and Global Economic Studies*, *7*(2), 68–88.

Li, Z., & Yang, D. (2015). The study on the influence of fixed asset investment and foreign trade to the economic growth of Ningbo based on VAR Model. *In 2015 International Conference on Education Technology, Management and Humanities Science* (ETMHS 2015) (pp. 341-345). Atlantis Press.

Lin Guan, J., & Hong, Y. (2012). An empirical analysis on US foreign trade and economic growth. *Aasri Procedia, 2*, 39–43.

Merendino, A. (2018). Big data, big decisions: The impact of big data on board level decision-making. *Journal of Business Research, 93*, 67–78.

Popovic, A. (2018). The impact of big data analytics on firms' high value business performance. *Information Systems Frontiers, 20*, 209–222.

Pradhan, R. P. (2009). The nexus between financial development and economic growth in India: Evidence from multivariate VAR model. *International Journal of Research and Reviews in Applied Sciences*, *1*(2), 68–79.

Reddy, Surendranadha Reddy Byrapu. (2023). Demonstrating The Payroll Reviews Based On Data Visualization For Financial Services. *Tuijin Jishu/ Journal of Propulsion Technology 44*, 4: 3886-3893.

Reddy, Surendranadha Reddy Byrapu. (2023). Digital Transformations Theoretical Investigation on the Basis of Smart Government Initiatives. *Tuijin Jishu/Journal of Propulsion Technology 44,* 4 (2023): 3894-3901.

erban, R.-A. (2017). The impact of big data, sustainability, and digitalization on company performance. *Studies in Business and Economics*, *12*(3), 181–189.

Sigala, Marianna (2019). Big data for measuring the impact of tourism economic development programs: A process and quality criteria framework for using big data. *Big Data and Innovation in Tourism, Travel, and Hospitality: Managerial Approaches, Techniques, and Applications*, 57-73.

Swanson, N. R., & Xiong, W. (2018). Big data analytics in economics: What have we learned so far, and where should we go from here? *The Canadian Journal of Economics. Revue Canadienne d'Economique, 51*(3), 695–746.

Taylor, Linnet, Ralph Schroeder, and Eric Meyer (2014). Emerging practices and perspectives on Big Data analysis in economics: Bigger and better or more of the same?. *Big Data & Society 1.2*: 2053951714536877.

Chapter 3
Analyzing the Nexus of Big Data and International Trade:
Future Trends and Emerging Technologies

K. J. Athira
Anna University, Chennai, India

R. Rahul
Nehru Institute of Technology, India

ABSTRACT

With the rapid technology augmentation, it becomes necessary to find complementary emerging computing technologies. This chapter highlights future computing technologies, emerging trends and industry buzz to identify most prominent technologies in India. In the emerging technologies, the market is perceiving the entry of local vendors covering such areas as the Internet of Things (IoT), Robotic Process Automation offerings and Machine Learning based technologies. Some technologies are of transformational nature and result in the foundation of new ecosystem; these are "Internet of Things" with its associated applications and "Machine Learning". Technologies on innovation trigger take more time for wide market acceptance. The main objective of this paper is to present a future

DOI: 10.4018/979-8-3693-6592-2.ch003

vision for a smart environment which can provide knowledge accumulation and new directions to new researchers in the related field.

INTRODUCTION

The future of technology promises groundbreaking advancements poised to revolutionize various aspects of our lives. One of the most transformative trends is the integration of artificial intelligence (AI) and machine learning, which are expected to enhance decision-making, personalize user experiences, and drive automation across industries (Nuseir & Aljumah, 2020). The proliferation of the Internet of Things (IoT) will further interconnect devices, enabling seamless communication and smarter environments. Quantum computing is on the horizon, promising unparalleled processing power to solve complex problems beyond the capabilities of classical computers. Renewable energy technologies, such as solar and wind, are set to advance, addressing environmental concerns and driving the shift towards sustainable living. Additionally, developments in biotechnology and genomics are anticipated to lead to personalized medicine, offering tailored treatments based on individual genetic profiles (Sun, 2020). The rise of 5G and subsequent communication technologies will facilitate faster, more reliable connectivity, supporting innovations in augmented and virtual reality (AR/VR), which will transform fields like education, entertainment, and remote work. As these trends converge, they will not only reshape industries but also redefine societal norms, ethical considerations, and the global economy, heralding a new era of unprecedented technological progress and opportunity.

BIG DATA AND INTERNATIONAL TRADE: AN OVERVIEW

Understanding Future Trends and Emerging Technology is crucial for staying Competitive and Driving Innovation in Today's Rapidly Evolving Landscape. Emerging technologies such as artificial intelligence, blockchain, and quantum computing drive economic growth by creating new industries, enhancing productivity, and fostering innovation. They enable companies to develop new products and services, optimize operations, and tap into new markets. Organizations that adopt and integrate emerging technologies early gain a competitive edge (Ahmad, A.Y.B., et al, 2024). They can improve their efficiency, offer superior products or services, and better meet customer needs. Staying ahead of technological trends is critical for maintaining and enhancing market position. While some technologies may displace certain jobs, they also create new employment opportunities in tech development, maintenance, and other sectors (Al Daabseh et al, 2024). Upskilling and reskilling the workforce to align with these new technologies are vital for adapting to changes in the job market. Future trends and technologies can significantly enhance the quality of life by improving healthcare through advanced medical technologies, increasing accessibility through innovations in communication, and enhancing overall living standards with smart city solutions (Cheng & Yang, 2020).

Emerging technologies like renewable energy sources, energy-efficient systems, and sustainable manufacturing processes play a crucial role in addressing environmental challenges. They help reduce carbon footprints, manage resources more effectively, and support global sustainability goals. Technologies impact social interactions, cultural practices, and community engagement. For instance, social media has transformed communication and information dissemination, while virtual reality and augmented reality are opening new avenues for cultural expression and experience. Advances in communication technologies facilitate global connectivity, allowing people and organizations to collaborate across borders. This leads to a more interconnected world where knowledge and resources can be shared more freely, fostering innovation and mutual growth (Sakhawat et al, 2024).

Emerging technologies improve security measures and safety protocols. For instance, advancements in cybersecurity protect against digital threats, while innovations in smart surveillance and disaster management technologies enhance public safety and resilience. Technologies like AI and big data analytics enable a higher degree of personalization in products and services. Businesses can offer tailored experience to customers, improving satisfaction and loyalty. The integration of technologies in education revolutionizes learning processes, making education more accessible, engaging, and effective (Maaitah, 2023).

Future Trends and Emerging Technologies

AI in Healthcare: Enhanced diagnostics, personalized medicine, and AI-driven drug discovery.
Autonomous Systems: Self-driving cars, drones, and advanced robotics.
Natural Language Processing: Improved virtual assistants, real-time language translation, and more sophisticated chatbots.
Quantum Computing: Computational Power: Solving complex problems in seconds that would take traditional computers millennia.
Cryptography: Revolutionizing data security and encryption methods.
Connectivity: Faster and more reliable internet connections, enabling the Internet of Things (IoT) on a massive scale (Ahmad et al, 2024).
Smart Cities: Enhanced infrastructure with better traffic management, energy usage, and public safety.
CRISPR and Gene Editing: Treating genetic disorders and possibly enhancing human capabilities.
Synthetic Biology: Creating new biological parts and systems, leading to innovations in medicine and biofuels (Banga, 2019).
Advanced Batteries: Long-lasting and more efficient energy storage solutions.
Solar and Wind Innovations: More efficient and cheaper renewable energy sources (Cheng & Yang, 2020).

Blockchain and Decentralized Finance (DeFi)

Cryptocurrencies: Evolving use cases beyond digital currencies, including smart contracts and decentralized applications (Ahmadian et al., 2024).
Supply Chain Management: Increased transparency and efficiency in tracking goods.
Extended Reality (XR) Virtual Reality (VR) and Augmented Reality (AR): Transforming entertainment, education, and remote work Mixed Reality (MR): Combining physical and digital worlds for enhanced interaction.

Graphene and Nanomaterials: Stronger, lighter, and more conductive materials for use in various industries.
Smart Materials: Materials that can change properties in response to external stimuli.

Space Exploration and Commercialization

Private Space Travel: Companies like SpaceX and Blue Origin making space travel more accessible.
Lunar and Martian Colonies: Plans for human settlements on the Moon and Mars (Banga, 2019).
AI-driven Security: Using AI to predict and prevent cyber threats.
Zero Trust Architecture: Enhanced security frameworks that assume no trust and continuously verify (Cheah & Wang, 2017).

Opportunities and Challenges in a Rapidly Evolving Landscape

Healthcare

Telemedicine: The rise of telemedicine and telehealth services enhances patient access to care, especially in remote areas, and reduces the burden on healthcare facilities.
Genomics and Personalized Medicine: Advances in genomics enable personalized treatment plans based on an individual's genetic makeup, leading to more effective and targeted therapies.
Artificial Intelligence (AI): AI applications in healthcare, such as diagnostic tools, predictive analytics, and robotic surgeries, improve accuracy, efficiency, and patient outcomes (Sorour & Atkins,2024).

Transportation

Autonomous Vehicles: Self-driving cars and trucks promise to revolutionize transportation by reducing accidents, improving fuel efficiency, and potentially transforming logistics and delivery services (Cheng & Yang, 2020).

Electric Vehicles (EVs): The adoption of EVs reduces greenhouse gas emissions and dependence on fossil fuels, contributing to environmental sustainability.
Urban Air Mobility: Drones and flying taxis could alleviate urban congestion and create new modes of transportation, making travel faster and more flexible (Dong & Zhao, 2020).

Finance

Blockchain and Cryptocurrencies: Blockchain technology enhances transparency, security, and efficiency in financial transactions, while cryptocurrencies offer new forms of digital assets and payment systems.
Fintech Innovations: Mobile banking, digital wallets, and peer-to-peer lending platforms provide greater financial inclusion and convenience for users worldwide.
AI and Machine Learning: These technologies optimize investment strategies, detect fraud, and provide personalized financial advice, improving overall financial management (Liu, 2019).

Work and Industry

Automation and Robotics: Automation streamlines manufacturing processes, increases productivity, and reduces costs. However, it also necessitates workforce reskilling to manage and operate advanced systems (Obeidat, 2019).
Remote Work: The shift to remote work, accelerated by the COVID-19 pandemic, continues to shape how businesses operate, impacting office real estate, employee collaboration, and work-life balance.
3D Printing: Additive manufacturing allows for rapid prototyping and custom production, transforming into industries like aerospace, automotive, and healthcare (Michael et al., 2024).

Environment and Energy

Renewable Energy: The growth of solar, wind, and other renewable energy sources reduces carbon emissions and dependency on non-renewable resources, promoting sustainable development.
Energy Storage: Advancements in battery technology and energy storage systems ensure a stable and reliable power supply, facilitating the integration of renewable energy into the grid (Obeidat, 2021).
Smart Grids: Intelligent grid systems enhance energy distribution efficiency, reduce waste, and improve the resilience of power infrastructure against disruptions.

Education

E-Learning Platforms: Online education and e-learning platforms provide access to quality education regardless of location, enabling lifelong learning and skill development.
AI in Education: AI-driven personalized learning systems adapt to individual student needs, enhancing educational outcomes and engagement.
Virtual and Augmented Reality: These technologies offer immersive learning experiences, making education more interactive and effective (Yassine et al., 2022).

Consumer Technology

Internet of Things (IoT): IoT devices, from smart homes to wearable health monitors, enhance convenience, efficiency, and data-driven decision-making in daily life.
5G Connectivity: The rollout of 5G networks promises faster internet speeds, lower latency, and the capacity to support a vast number of connected devices, driving innovation across industries.
Augmented Reality (AR) and Virtual Reality (VR): AR and VR technologies create new experiences in gaming, shopping, entertainment, and professional training (Sun, 2020).

CONCLUSION

In conclusion, the future landscape of technology is poised to be shaped by several emerging trends that promise to revolutionize various sectors. The integration of artificial intelligence and machine learning will continue to drive automation and innovation, while advancements in quantum computing could unlock new computational capabilities. The rise of 5G and beyond will enhance connectivity, paving the way for the Internet of Things (IoT) to permeate everyday life. Additionally, the growth of renewable energy technologies and advancements in biotechnology will address critical global challenges. As these technologies evolve, they will not only transform industries but also redefine the way we live and interact with the world around us. Embracing these innovations will be crucial for staying competitive and addressing the complex issues of the future.

REFERENCES

Ahmad, A., Abusaimeh, H., Rababah, A., Alqsass, M., Al-Olima, N., & Hamdan, M. (2024). Assessment of effects in advances of accounting technologies on quality financial reports in Jordanian public sector. *Uncertain Supply Chain Management*, *12*(1), 133–142. DOI: 10.5267/j.uscm.2023.10.011

Ahmad, A. Y. B., Kumari, D. K., Shukla, A., Deepak, A., Chandnani, M., Pundir, S., & Shrivastava, A. (2024). Framework for Cloud Based Document Management System with Institutional Schema of Database. *International Journal of Intelligent Systems and Applications in Engineering*, *12*(3s), 672–678.

Ahmad, A. Y. B., Tiwari, A., Nayeem, M. A., Biswal, B. K., Satapathy, D. P., Kulshreshtha, K., & Bordoloi, D. (2024). Artificial Intelligence Perspective Framework of the Smart Finance and Accounting Management Model. *International Journal of Intelligent Systems and Applications in Engineering*, *12*(4s), 586–594.

Ahmadian, M. M., Baker, D., & Paz, A. (2024). Leveraging business intelligence solutions for urban parking management. *City, Culture and Society*, *37*, 100579. DOI: 10.1016/j.ccs.2024.100579

Al Daabseh, T. K. I., Aljawarneh, N. M. S., Al Smadi, K., Alnawafleh, A., & Al-maaitah, T. A. (2024). Integration of business intelligence and marketing: Enhancing corporate reputation in the financial services sector. Journal of Infrastructure. *Policy and Development*, *8*(7), 4603. DOI: 10.24294/jipd.v8i7.4603

Al Daabseh, T. K. I., Bani-Hani, T., Aljawarneh, N. M., Alkufahy, A. M., & Al Raqqad, R. (2023). The Relationship Between Business Intelligence Capabilities and Business Outcomes of Small and Medium Sized Enterprises: The Moderating Role of Competitive Intelligence. *Journal of System and Management Sciences*, *13*(4), 535–550.

Allahham, M., & Ahmad, A. (2024). AI-induced anxiety in the assessment of factors influencing the adoption of mobile payment services in supply chain firms: A mental accounting perspective. *International Journal of Data and Network Science*, *8*(1), 505–514. DOI: 10.5267/j.ijdns.2023.9.006

Banga, R. (2019). Is India Digitally Prepared for International Trade? *Economic and Political Weekly*, *54*(5), 2.

Bani Ahmad, A. Y. A. (2024). Firm Determinants that Influences Implementation of Accounting Technologies in Business Organizations. *WSEAS Transactions on Business and Economics*, *21*, 1–11. DOI: 10.37394/23207.2024.21.1

Bao, Y. (2018). Research on the Impact of Big Data on International Economy and Trade. *Science and technique info, 16* (33): 226-227.

Cheah,, S., & Wang, S. (2017). Big data-driven business model innovation by traditional industries in the Chinese economy. *Journal of Chinese Economic and Foreign Trade Studies*, *10*(3), 229–251. DOI: 10.1108/JCEFTS-05-2017-0013

Cheng, F., & Yang, X. (2020). Challenges and Strategies of international economic and trade in the context of big data [J]. *Modern economic info, 06,* 58-60.

Cukier, K., & Mayer-Schoenberger, V. (2013). The rise of big data: How it's changing the way we think about the world. *Foreign Affairs*, *92*, 28.

Dong S.S., Zhao X.H. (2020). Analysis of the impact of big data on international economy and trade and measures. *Financial circles (Academic Edition),14*, 13-14.

Jia W.Y. (2020). Thinking on the development trend of international economy and trade under the background of big data. *Hubei agricultural mechanization, 04* 46 -46.

Li M. (2020). Analysis of the impact of big data on the international trade of enterprises in the context of economic globalization. *Times economic and trade, 06*, 19-20.

Lin, C., Ahmad, S. F., Ayassrah, A. Y. B. A., Irshad, M., Telba, A. A., Awwad, E. M., & Majid, M. I. (2023). Green production and green technology for sustainability: The mediating role of waste reduction and energy use. *Heliyon*, 22496. PMID: 38076181

Lin Z.P. (2015). Discussion on international trade financing of small and medium sized enterprises. *Mall modernization, 2,* 10.

Liu T.S. (2019). Optimization and adjustment of International Trade Industrial Structure under the new economic situation. *Brand marketing of old brands, 10,* 17-18.

Maaitah, T. (2023). The role of business intelligence tools in the decision-making process and performance. *Journal of intelligence studies in business, 13*(1), 43-52.

Maaitah, T. (2023). The Role of Entrepreneurship on the Economic Growth and Development.

Masa'd, F. M., Al-maaitah, T. A., Al-maaitah, D. A., Qawasmeh, E. F., & Qatawneh, N. A. (2024). Harnessing artificial intelligence for human resources management: Tools, advantages, and risks in the energy sector. In *E3S Web of Conferences*, 541, p. 02004). EDP Sciences. DOI: 10.1051/e3sconf/202454102004

McLean, E. R. (2003). The DeLone and McLean model of information systems success: A ten-year update. *Journal of Management Information Systems*, *19*(4), 9–30. DOI: 10.1080/07421222.2003.11045748

Michael, C. I., Ipede, O. J., Adejumo, A. D., Adenekan, I. O., Adebayo, D., Ojo, A. S., & Ayodele, P. A. (2024). Data-driven decision making in IT: Leveraging AI and data science for business intelligence. *World Journal of Advanced Research and Reviews*, *23*(1), 472–480. DOI: 10.30574/wjarr.2024.23.1.2010

Nuseir, M., & Aljumah, A. (2020). The role of digital marketing in business performance with the moderating effect of environment factors among smes of uae. International Journal of Innovation. *Creativity and Change*, *11*(3), 310–324.

Obeidat, A. (2019). IT adaption with knowledge conversion process (SECI)? *Management Science Letters*, *9*(13), 2241–2252. DOI: 10.5267/j.msl.2019.7.029

Obeidat, A. M. (2021). E-Marketing and Its Impact on The Competitive Advantage. *Ilkogretim Online, 20*(5).

Sakhawat, A. R., Fatima, A., Abbas, S., Ahmad, M., & Khan, M. A. (2024). Emerging Technologies for Enhancing Robust Cybersecurity Measures for Business Intelligence in Healthcare 5.0. Strengthening Industrial Cybersecurity to Protect Business Intelligence, 270-293.

Sorour, A., & Atkins, A. S. (2024). Big data challenge for monitoring quality in higher education institutions using business intelligence dashboards. *Journal of Electronic Science and Technology*, 100233.

Sun B. (2020). Challenges and Countermeasures of international trade under the background of big data. China business theory, (01), 73-74

Yassine, F. L. Y. A., Maaitah, T. A., Maaitah, D. A., & Al-Gasawneh, J. A. (2022). Impact of COVID-19 on the university education system in Jordan. *Journal of Southwest Jiaotong University*, *57*(1), 649–663. DOI: 10.35741/issn.0258-2724.57.1.58

Chapter 4
Are Shocks in Import Temporary? Permanent? Evidence From Fourier ADF Unit Root Test

Ibrahim Ozayturk
https://orcid.org/0000-0001-5292-6313
Nigde Omer Halisdemir University, Turkey

ABSTRACT

In recent years, experts have focused on oil, agricultural, and commodity import changes. The G7 nations have used various economic tactics to adjust import levels according to oil, agricultural, and commodity price swings throughout the previous four decades. Several variables directly affect national economic policies. First, most G7 nations import oil. Second, global warming and population expansion generate unanticipated price changes for agricultural products. Finally, iron, copper, and aluminum costs, which affect many everyday items, are always changing. This study examines whether industrialized G7 oil, agricultural, and commodity import shocks are permanent or temporary. The sudden swings in oil, agricultural, and commodity imports are examined using 1980–2020 annual data. Enders and Lee (2012) recommended using the Fourier ADF (FADF) structural break unit root test to assess the series' stationarity. If the series remains stationary, import shocks will last. Based on the outcomes, a conclusion and policy proposal will be prepared.

DOI: 10.4018/979-8-3693-6592-2.ch004

1. INTRODUCTION

Fluctuations in imports can have a direct or indirect impact on national economies. Due to the widespread adoption of open economic structures and direct economic ties between countries, most nations are susceptible to the macroeconomic fluctuations occurring in other countries, which can have either beneficial or negative impacts. This condition compels governments to make judgments based on the economic swings of other countries. Imports, which are an extremely important macroeconomic determinant, may have a significant impact on the decisions made by policymakers, particularly when there are sudden fluctuations in import levels. The G7 countries, including the United States of America (USA), Canada, Germany, Italy, France, Japan, and the United Kingdom (UK) may need to modify their economic policies in response to abrupt fluctuations in their bilateral commerce and imports from other nations. These abrupt changes can occasionally be long-lasting and fleeting. This research will address the policy proposals that the G7 countries should follow in response to both permanent and temporary shocks.

The primary focus of this investigation is determined by abrupt fluctuations in imports. The aim of this study is to assess if abrupt disruptions in the oil, agricultural goods, and commodity imports sectors have a lasting or transitory impact. Regarding this aspect, the study distinguishes itself from other studies and addresses the lack of information in the existing literature. Policy suggestions will be presented to the appropriate nation group based on the current state of the shocks. The data utilized consisted of annual import figures for oil, agricultural products, and commodities from G7 countries spanning the years 1980 to 2020. To determine whether the shocks are permanent or transient, we employ the Fourier structural break unit root test developed by Enders & Lee (2012) based on the available data. According to the test results, if the series has a unit root, the shocks will have a long-lasting impact. Alternatively, the shocks have a transient impact.

The study concludes by providing policy suggestions to help scholars undertaking research on the nations in question. Furthermore, considering the evidence that shocks impact the economic policies of nations, the length of this impact is contingent upon the intensity of the shocks. Abrupt fluctuations in oil prices can either raise or lower the import expenses of countries. Agricultural product prices have a direct influence on food prices, while commodity prices can be influenced by the political agendas of nations. Consequently, the study aims to determine whether the impact of shocks on imports is enduring or transitory. The study's analysis results have led to the formulation of policy suggestions.

The study has five sections. The introduction segment serves as the initial portion, providing an overview of the study. The literature review, which supports the research and includes the work of other scholars in the field, constitutes the second component of the study. The third component of the study will cover the methodology used for the analysis. The next step is the application portion, where we will acquire and assess the analysis's outcomes. The study will culminate with the fifth segment, which will present the results and provide policy suggestions.

2. LITERATURE REVIEW

The literature frequently discusses the hysteresis of macroeconomic variables, such as import, export, economic growth, unemployment, shocks to the economy, etc. It is uncommon to find studies in the literature examining the shocks in oil imports, agricultural product imports, and commodity imports. This component of the study will incorporate the literature on hysterical research. A literature review is necessary to gain a deeper knowledge of the study, and Table 1 provides the relevant literature review for the study.

Table 1. Literature review

Author/Year	Country/ Period	Tittle of Publication	Method	Result
Murray & Ginman (1976)	Canada Q3:1950-Q4:1964	An Empirical Examination of the Traditional Aggregate Import Demand Model	Time Series - OLS	The primary discovery of this work is that the relative price specification employed in the traditional import demand model is inadequate for properly forecasting the characteristics of aggregate import demand. Hence, it is imperative to include the import price, the domestic price index of traded commodities, and the domestic price index of non-traded items in the models.
Johnson (1987)	-	Currency Depreciation and Imports	-	Currency depreciation in developing countries need not lead to a contraction of a real imports. It can, as part of a broader policy package, facilities an expansion of imports.
Sinha (1997)	Thailand 1953-1990	Determinants of Import Demand in Thailand	Ordinary Least Square (OLS)	Writer used the import price of good for the model. Import demand has a higher degree of responsiveness to fluctuations in the price of imported items.

continued on following page

Table 1. Continued

Author/Year	Country/ Period	Tittle of Publication	Method	Result
Pawlos (2004)	Ethiopia 1960/61-1999/2000	The Relationship Between Import and GDP Growth in Ethiopia: An Empirical Analysis	Johansen's Cointegration Approach	Writers try to find the effect of Gross Domestic Product (GDP) growth on import, and the contribution of imported intermediate and capital goods to economic growth. The findings from the analysis of the impact of imported intermediate and capital goods on economic growth suggest that, over an extended period, the use of imported intermediate products has a positive and substantial effect on the growth of real GDP.
Michelis & Zestos (2004)	Six EU Countries (Belgium, France, Germany, Greece, Italy and the Netherlands) 1950-1990	Exports, Imports and GDP Growth: Causal Relations in Six European Union Countries	A Vector Error Correction Model (VECM)	Writers have discovered compelling evidence of a two-way causal relationship between GDP and both exports and imports in all nations, except for the Netherlands, where the evidence is only moderately strong.
Altinay (2007)	Türkiye 1980-2005	Short-run and long-run elasticities of import demand for crude oil in Turkey	The Autoregressive Distributed Lag (ARDL) Bounds Test	The limits test findings indicate the presence of a long-term cointegration connection between crude oil imports and the explanatory variables, namely nominal price and income. However, this link does not exist in the model that incorporates the real price in home currency.

continued on following page

Table 1. Continued

Author/Year	Country/ Period	Tittle of Publication	Method	Result
Donnefeld & Haug (2007)	The USA	Currency invoicing of US imports	GARCH	As the exchange rate becomes more volatile, a greater proportion of imports are billed in the currency of the importer.
Arize & Malindretos (2012)	India, Japan, Korea, Singapore and Thailand 1973:2 – 2005:4	Foreign Exchange Reserves in Asia and Its Impact on Import Demand	Fully modified OLS, dynamic OLS and ARDL	Foreign exchange reserves are significant for import demand, both in the long term and in the short term.
Sweidan (2013)	Jordan 1976-2009	The Effect of Exchange Rate on Exports and Imports: The Case of Jordan	Ordinary Least Square (OLS)	Jordan's competitiveness has a consistent pattern of decline. The impact of Jordan's exchange rate on exports and imports is effective only in the short term.
Gilani (2015)	Pakistan 1980-2010	The Impact of Agricultural Imports and Exports on Agricultural Productivity	Granger Causality	Imports and exports have a one-way relationship, while agricultural imports refer specifically to completed products.
Adewuyi (2016)	Nigeria 1984-2013	Determinants of import demand for non-renewable energy (petroleum) products: Empirical evidence from Nigeria	The Autoregressive Distributed Lag (ARDL) Bounds Test	Writer used the domestic energy production to define the import demand and domestic energy production is the drivers of import demand in the long-run.

continued on following page

Table 1. Continued

Author/Year	Country/ Period	Tittle of Publication	Method	Result
Oluyemi & Isaac (2017)	Nigeria 1996-2015	The Effect of Exchange Rate on Imports and Exports in Nigeria from January 1996 to June 2015	The Vector Autoregression (VAR)	Imports exerted a beneficial influence on exchange rates, whereas exports had an adverse influence.
Paital, Dutta & Dash (2019)	India 1987-2016	Crude Oil Import Elasticity of Demand in India: An Empirical Analysis 1987-2016	The Autoregressive Distributed Lag (ARDL) Cointegration Test	Crude oil demand in India has a higher degree of sensitivity to changes in income rather than changes in price. One possible factor might be the Government of India's complete control over the retail pricing of petroleum products during the period of our investigation.
Baranauskaite & Jureviciene (2021)	Lithuania	Import Risks of Agricultural Products in Foreign Trade	Multicriteria Decision Support Methods - SAW, TOPSIS and Geometric Means	By conducting a comprehensive analysis of scientific literature, researchers have discovered eight distinct kinds of dangers associated with the importation of agricultural goods. This list of hazards includes risks related to supply, demand, production, management, operations, infrastructure, logistics, political, policy, and regulation, as well as financial.

Previous studies mostly examine the impact of currency and GDP on import. The results show that the import and other macroeconomic variable have various relationships. The currency, for instant, and the import have negative relationship. The GDP have a positive relationship with import. Agricultural product import depends on mostly weather conditions. Therefore, agricultural import shock has a dependence for other factors. The results of this study exhibit parallelism with the studies in the literature, as demonstrated in the subsequent sections.

3. DATA AND METHODOLOGY

This study attempted to determine whether the shocks in oil imports, agricultural product imports, and commodity imports of the G7 countries considered industrialized, are permanent or transient. Using yearly data for the period 1980–2022. Based on a literature study, it has been shown that shocks applied to macroeconomic variables might result in either temporary or long-lasting effects. The FADF unit root test will be employed to ascertain if the shock's effect on the macroeconomic variable is of a transient nature or of a persistent nature. The next section provides specific instructions on how to apply a unit root test.

While several factors influence the volume of imports made by countries, a handful of key criteria play a crucial role in determining imports (Goldstein and Khan, 1985; Gafar, 1988; King, 1993; Vacu & Odhiambo, 2020). The nation's GDP and real effective exchange rate can incorporate these variables. Weather conditions may significantly affect agricultural goods. The price of oil, like the price of agricultural products, can have a significant impact, similar to the price of agricultural products. Additionally, export, inflation, populations etc. could use to estimate import function (Narayan & Smyth, 2005; Bayrattutan & Bıdırdı, 2010). Thus, the model could use in the form of$M = f(GDP, CURR, IP, W)$. IP denotes the import price of products and W denotes the weather for agricultural products. Additionally, Table 2 provides information on the origin of the research data.

Table 2. A brief synopsis of criteria

Indicator	Codes	Value or Percentage	Sources
Oil Import	OIL	Thousand of Barrels	U.S. Energy Information Administration - USEA
Agricultural Product Import	AGRI	% of merchandise imports	World Bank - WB
Commodity Product Import	COM	% of merchandise imports	World Bank - WB

The descriptive statistics of the data is on Table 3.

Table 3. Descriptive statistics

	AGRI	OIL	COM
Mean	*2.543.657*	*2.487.952*	*4.041.840*
Median	*1.915.055*	*1.665.680*	*3.538.275*
Maximum	*8.855.951*	*10126.00*	*1.028.506*
Minimum	*0.791460*	*2.510.000*	*1.698.192*
Std. Dev.	*1.742.599*	*2.308.122*	*1.703.845*
Probability	*0.000000*	*0.000000*	*0.000000*
Observations	*287*	*287*	*287*

3.1. Ender and Lee (2012) Fourier Augmented Dickey-Fuller Unit Root Test (FADF)

In their research publication, Enders & Lee (2012) give a thorough description of the Fourier DF-type unit root test. The study used a similar methodology; the use of an ADF-type test was the primary difference. This test successfully handles the presence of serial correlation as well as the decrease in statistical power when the series' starting value is large. Even though Enders and Lee only provided critical values for the DF version, we used a similar method to determine the Fourier ADF critical values using Monte Carlo simulations.

The ADF test for a time-varying function is shown below:

$$y_t = \alpha(t) + \delta y_{t-1} + \gamma t + \varepsilon_t \quad (1)$$

Here, $\alpha(t)$ represents a deterministic function, and ε_t represents a stationary disturbance with a variance of σ_ε^2.

The unit root null hypothesis (or δ =1), is put to the test. It becomes problematic to use any linear unit root test if the form of $\alpha(t)$ is unknown. Consequently, the Fourier expansion might be considered an alternative to the unidentified functional form of $\alpha(t)$:

$$(t) = \alpha_0 + \sum_{k=1}^{n} \alpha_k \sin\left(\frac{2\pi \mathrm{kt}}{\mathrm{T}}\right) + \sum_{k=1}^{n} \beta_k \cos\left(\frac{2\pi \mathrm{kt}}{\mathrm{T}}\right), n \leq \frac{T}{2} \tag{2}$$

n is the total number of frequencies considered in the approximation, whereas k represents the total number of observations.

According to Gallant (1981), the presence of a structural break or a temporal trend in a data series necessitates the existence of at least one Fourier frequency in the process that generates the data. Due to its global nature, the Fourier approximation is not suitable for incorporating several frequencies inside a regression framework. Hence, it is crucial to select the appropriate number of frequencies in Equation (2).

Assuming the utilization of a solitary frequency k, and the subsequent regression:

$$\Delta y_t = \rho y_{t-1} + c_1 + c_2 t + c_3 \sin\left(\frac{2\pi \mathrm{kt}}{\mathrm{T}}\right) + c_4 \cos\left(\frac{2\pi \mathrm{kt}}{\mathrm{T}}\right) + e_t \tag{3}$$

The t-statistic T(ADF) tests the null hypothesis δ =0. Enders and Lee (2012), assert that the frequency k and sample size T alone determine the critical values for the null hypothesis of a unit root, without any influence from the coefficients of the Fourier terms or other deterministic factors. Therefore, Enders and Lee's (2012), method is followed by conducting simulations and tabulating the critical values.

Followed various procedures. Firstly, calculate equation (3) for all frequencies, specifically for all integer values of k between 1 and 5. Therefore, select the optimal value of k from the regression analysis that has the lowest sum of squared residuals (SSR). Next, assess the presence of structural fractures using a conventional F-test, with the null hypothesis being c_3=c_4=0. The analysis's Fourier test, which incorporates several frequencies into the Fourier function, is consistent with Enders and Lee's (2012) study approach. Conduct the Monte Carlo simulations with 10,000 replications at a 5% significance level (Ender & Lee, 2012: 196-97).

4. EMPIRICAL FINDING

This study investigates the hysteresis impact of abrupt changes in oil imports, agricultural products, and commodities in G7 countries. The Fourier ADF structural unit root test, which was recommended by Enders and Lee (2012), is used to analyze the data. The initial phase of the three-stage Fourier ADF structural unit root test involves determining the best frequency value and the suitable lag length. Table 4 displays the test result for the lag length that is suitable, which is computed using the sum of the residual squares derived from the Fourier ADF equation. This calculation is used to find the ideal frequency value and the Akaike Information Criterion (AIC). Table 4 shows that the smallest value for the sum of the residual squares occurs when k = 1. The lag length that minimizes the AIC information criteria and is determined to be 12 is considered the optimal lag length.

Table 4. Optimal frequency and appropriate delay length for agricultural product import

Frequency (k)	**MinKKT**
1	***18.55892***
2	*18.54680*
3	*18.52589*
4	*18.49557*
5	*18.45629*
L	*12*
AIC	*-0.894276*

Note: The k optimum frequency, MinKKT represents the sum of the Minimum Residual squares, and L the appropriate delay length. Akaike information criterion (AIC).

The results of the unit root test are shown in Table 5. Based on the findings of the unit root test, the estimated statistical value (5.90) is higher than the critical values of the test in absolute terms, indicating that the H_0 hypothesis is rejected. This scenario demonstrates that the series are stationary, meaning they do not possess a unit root. This discovery demonstrates that the phenomenon of agricultural product import hysteresis is not valid for G7 countries.

Table 5. FADF Structural Unit Root test result

Variable	Statistic	Decision
AGRI	*-5.908710*	***H_0: Rejected***
Critical Values		
1%	*5%*	*10%*
-4.37	*-3.78*	*-3.47*

In the study, the statistical significance of the trigonometric terms is not assessed for agricultural product import hysteresis. The Wald test is employed for this purpose, utilizing the F statistic values. Table 6 displays the Wald test results. Therefore, as the computed F statistics value (2.05) lower than the critical value (6.25) from the table, the null hypothesis (H_0) is rejected, indicating that the trigonometric terms are not important. Hence, it may be concluded that the Fourier ADF unit root test is not suitable and need to use ADF unit root test for panel.

Table 6. Wald test result

		F Statistic
Fourier ADF		*2.053512*
Critical Values		
1%	*5%*	*10%*
10.02	*7.41*	*6.25*

The stationarity of the agricultural product variable, in which trigonometric terms have no substantial impact, was assessed using the ADF unit root test of ADF - Fisher (2002). Table 7 presents the results of the fixed model ADF-Fisher unit root test.

Table 7. ADF Unit Root test result

		ADF - Fisher Chi-square
AGRI		*44.4064*** (0.000)*

Note: ***, and ** indicate the significance levels of %1, and %5 correspondingly. The value included in the parentheses represents the p-value.

The ADF-Fisher unit root test findings in Table 7 indicate that the null hypothesis, which suggests the presence of a unit root, was rejected for agricultural product imports. Therefore, it was determined that the agricultural product import variable was stationary. As a result, it was seen that shocks had a temporary effect on the agricultural product import variable.

As shown in Table 8, the sum of the residual squares is minimized when k is equal to 5. The best lag duration is determined to be 11, as it minimizes the AIC information criterion.

Table 8. Optimal frequency and appropriate delay length for oil product import

Frequency (k)	MinKKT
1	*11523872*
2	*11528922*
3	*11535216*
4	*11539034*
5	***11534896***
L	*11*
AIC	*13.14005*

Note: The k optimum frequency, MinKKT represents the sum of the Minimum Residual squares, and L the appropriate delay length. Akaike information criterion (AIC).

Table 9 presents the results of the unit root test. According to the results of the unit root test, the calculated statistical value (2.34) is smaller than the critical values of the test in absolute terms. This suggests that we cannot reject the H_0 hypothesis. This situation illustrates that the series are non-stationary, indicating the presence of a unit root. This finding confirms the validity of the concept of oil product import hysteresis in G7 nations.

Table 9. FADF Structural Unit Root test result

Variable	**Statistic**	**Decision**
OIL	*-2.342934*	**H0: Not Rejected**
Critical Values		
1%	5%	10%
-4.37	*-3.78*	*-3.47*

The study evaluates the statistical significance of the trigonometric terms in relation to oil product import hysteresis. The Wald test is used for this purpose, using the F statistic values. The results of the Wald test are presented in Table 10. Thus, since the calculated F statistics value (2.83) is lower than the crucial value (6.25) obtained from the table, we reject the null hypothesis (Ho), which suggests that the trigonometric components are not significant. Therefore, it may be inferred that the Fourier ADF unit root test is not appropriate and the ADF unit root test for panel data should be used instead.

Table 10. Wald test result

		F Statistic
Fourier ADF		*2.838332*
Critical Values		
1%	*5%*	*10%*
10.02	*7.41*	*6.25*

The stationarity of the oil product variable was evaluated using the ADF unit root test of ADF - Fisher (2002), which determined that the trigonometric terms had no significant effect. The findings of the fixed model ADF-Fisher unit root test are presented in Table 11.

Table 11. ADF Unit Root test

		ADF - Fisher Chi-square
OIL		*13.2537 (0.5067)*

The ADF - Fisher unit root test findings in Table 11 indicate that the null hypothesis, which states the absence of a unit root, is rejected. Thus, it was concluded that the variable representing the import of oil products was not in a stable state. Consequently, the variable of oil product imports showed a lasting impact from shocks and shocks are permanent.

According to Table 12, the sum of the residual squares is minimized when the value of k is 1. The lag duration that minimizes the AIC information criterion and is determined to be 8 is called the ideal lag length.

Table 12. Optimal frequency and appropriate delay length for commodity products import

Frequency (k)	MinKKT
1	**71.42136**
2	71.47998
3	71.58153
4	71.73200
5	71.93928
L	8
AIC	1.262014

Note: The k optimum frequency, MinKKT represents the sum of the Minimum Residual squares, and L the appropriate delay length. Akaike information criterion (AIC).

Table 13 displays the outcomes of the unit root test. Based on the findings of the unit root test, the estimated statistical value (2.52) is less than the critical values of the test in absolute terms, indicating that the H_0 hypothesis cannot be rejected. This scenario demonstrates that the series are non-stationary, meaning they possess a unit root. This discovery demonstrates that the phenomenon of commodity product import hysteresis is valid for G7 countries.

Table 13. FADF Structural Unit Root test result

Variable	**Statistic**	**Decision**
COM	*-2.523504*	**H0:Not Rejected**
Critical Values		
1%	5%	10%
-4.37	*-3.78*	*-3.47*

In the last step of the study, the statistical significance of the trigonometric terms is assessed. The Wald test is employed for this purpose, utilizing the F statistic values. Table 14 displays the Wald test results. Therefore, as the computed F statistics value (7.42) exceeds the crucial value (7.41) from the table, the null hypothesis (H_0) is rejected, indicating that the trigonometric terms are valid Hence, it may be concluded that the Fourier ADF unit root test is suitable.

Table 14. Wald test result

		F Statistic
Fourier ADF		*7.428656***
Critical Values		
1%	5%	10%
10.02	*7.41*	*6.25*

Note: ***, and ** represent the significance levels of %1, and %5 respectively.

Based on the results of the study, it was determined that the import hysteresis hypothesis was applicable to the G7 economy during the specified time period. Thus, the disturbance in the G7 economy resulted in an enduring departure from the mean in commodity products imports, which continued to rise long after the shock's impact subsided.

5. CONCLUSIONS AND POLICY RECOMMENDATIONS

The study examines if the fluctuations in the import of oil, agricultural, and commodity items for G7 countries are of a lasting or transient nature. The study utilizes yearly data from 1980 to 2020 and applies the Fourier ADF unit root test recommended by Enders and Lee (2012) for analysis. This analysis distinguishes itself from other studies in the literature by including a broad time span and investigating the importation of three specific product categories. Furthermore, it fills the existing gap in the literature.

The study examines the import of three distinct product groupings individually. The initial analysis of agricultural product imports reveals the existence of a unit root. This instance demonstrates the enduring nature of shocks in agricultural product imports. Furthermore, enduring disruptions change the future state of the economy, and unanticipated fluctuations have a long-term impact on it. To address these long-standing circumstances, the relevant national group must implement preventive measures. Consumers and farmers must get assistance to mitigate the impact of abrupt price fluctuations resulting from the importation of agricultural products on the local market. Furthermore, given that shocks are enduring, it is imperative that these supports not be of a transient kind. Support may manifest in many ways. Fiscal actions such as tax reductions and transfer payments can provide permanent support to producers that experience losses owing to a fall in import volume. An analogous scenario is observed in the importation of petroleum products. Petroleum, an irreplaceable commodity, has the highest level of external reliance among all G7 countries, with the exception of the United States. Thus, it is unavoidable that shocks will impact local markets. States should formulate fiscal and monetary policies to mitigate the impacts of these shocks. Furthermore, the utilization of renewable energy can effectively diminish the consumption of petroleum goods. This measure also serves to mitigate environmental contamination.

The commodity is another product that undergoes analysis to see whether shocks in imports are permanent or transient. The analytical results indicate that import shocks in the commodities product group are more transient than those in the other two product groups. Fluctuations in commodity imports have a temporary impact on G7 countries' economic structures or domestic markets. In this scenario, the pertinent states may choose to implement temporary measures rather than permanent ones in response to unexpected disruptions, in contrast to the other two product categories. These actions may involve implementing temporary adjustments to import tariffs, either by raising or lowering them, or by providing assistance for the manufacturing of alternative goods. Furthermore, the metrics can assess actions, including direct purchases of products from foreign markets by the public. Furthermore, an example of credits that can be granted to the customers can be provided.

REFERENCES

Adewuyi, A. O. (2016). Determinants of Import Demand for Non-Renewable Energy (Petroleum) Products: Empirical Evidence from Nigeria. *Energy Policy*, *95*, 73–93. DOI: 10.1016/j.enpol.2016.04.035

Altinay, G. (2007). Short-Run and Long-Run Elasticities of Import Demand For Crude Oil in Turkey. *Energy Policy*, *35*(11), 5829–5835.

Arize, A. C., & Malindretos, J. (2012). Foreign Exchange Reserves in Asia and Its Impact on Import Demand. *International Journal of Economics and Finance*, *4*(3), 21–32.

Baranauskaitė, L., & Jurevičienė, D. (2021). Import Risks of Agricultural Products in Foreign Trade. *Economies*, *9*(3), 102.

Bayraktutan, Y., & Bıdırdı, H. (2010). Türkiye Ithalatının Temel Belirleyicileri. *Ege Academic Review*, *10*(1), 351–369.

Donnenfeld, S., & Haug, A. A. (2008). Currency Invoicing of US Imports. *International Journal of Finance & Economics*, *13*(2), 184–198.

Enders, W., & Lee, J. (2012). The Flexible Fourier Form and Dickey–Fuller Type Unit Root Tests. *Economics Letters*, *117*(1), 196–199. DOI: 10.1016/j.econlet.2012.04.081

Gafar, J. S. (1988). The Determinants of Import Demand in Trinidad and Tobago: 1967–84. *Applied Economics*, *20*(3), 303–313. DOI: 10.1080/00036848800000044

Gilani, S. W. (2015). The Impact of Agricultural Imports and Exports on Agricultural Productivity. *Journal of Economics and Sustainable Development*, *6*(11).

Goldstein, M., & Khan, M. S. (1985). Income and Price Effects in Foreign Trade, R.W. Jones and P.B. Kenen (ed.) *Handbook of International Economics, 2*. New York: Elsevier Science Publications, 1041-1105.

Johnson, O. (1987). Currency Depreciation and Imports. *Finance & Development*, *24*(2), 18.

King, A. (1993). The functional form of import demand: The case of UK motor vehicle imports, 1980-90. *Journal of Economic Studies (Glasgow, Scotland), 20*(3), 36–50. DOI: 10.1108/01443589310040396

Michelis, L., & Zestos, G. K. (2004). Exports, Imports and GDP Growth: Causal Relations in Six European Union Countries. *Journal of Economic Asymmetries, 1*(2), 71–85. DOI: 10.1016/j.jeca.2004.02.004

Murray, T., & Ginman, P. J. (1976). An Empirical Examination of the Traditional Aggregate Import Demand Model. *The Review of Economics and Statistics, 58*(1), 75–80. DOI: 10.2307/1936011

Narayan, S., & Narayan, P. K. (2005). An Empirical Analysis of Fiji's Import Demand Function. *Journal of Economic Studies (Glasgow, Scotland), 32*(2), 158–168.

Oluyemi, O., & Isaac, E. D. (2017). The Effect of Exchange Rate on Imports and Exports in Nigeria from January 1996 to June 2015. *International Journal of Economics and Business Management, 3*(2), 66–77.

Paital, R. R., Dutta, S., & Dash, A. K. (2019). Crude Oil Import Elasticity of Demand in India: An Empirical Analysis 1987–2016. *Applied Econometrics and International Development, 19*(2), 125–136.

Pawlos, S. (2004). The Relationship between Import and GDP Growth in Ethiopia: An Empirical Analysis. http://www. eeaecon. org/EEA/conferences/papers/Sewasew.

Sinha, D. (1997). Determinants of Import Demand in Thailand. *International Economic Journal, 11*(4), 73–873.

Sweidan, O. D. (2013). The Effect of Exchange Rate on Exports and Imports: The Case of Jordan. *Guoji Maoyi Wenti, 27*(2), 156–172.

Vacu, N. P., & Odhiambo, N. M. (2020). The Determinants of Import Demand: A Review of International Literature. Acta Universitatis Danubius. *Economica, 16*(5), 101–117.

KEY TERMS AND DEFINITIONS

Bilateral Trade: Bilateral trade is the exchange of goods between two nations promoting trade and investment.

Currency: A currency system that is widely used in a certain nation.

Domestic Industry: All domestic producers of similar commodities, or those whose combined production accounts for a significant share of the overall domestic output of such items, are considered to be part of the "Domestic Industry.

Export: Send (goods or services) overseas for commercial purposes.

Import: Bring (goods or services) into a nation from elsewhere in order to sell them.

Gross Domestic Product: The traditional way of measuring the value added produced in a nation over a given time period via the creation of goods and services is called the gross domestic product, or GDP.

Hysteresis: Hysteresis in economics refers to an event in the economy that persists into the future, even after the factors that led to that event have been removed.

Trade Imbalance: Trade imbalances arise when certain nations maintain consistent surpluses in their trade accounts (i.e., exports exceed imports), while other nations encounter ongoing and frequently substantial external deficits.

Chapter 5
Big Data and International Trade: What It Is and Why It Matters

Emre Kadir Özekenci
Cag University, Turkey

ABSTRACT

Technological advancements in recent decades have significantly transformed the global economy, leading to remarkable growth, enhanced productivity, and increased innovation. This shift has been marked by the widespread use of information and communication technologies (ICT), the emergence of the internet, and the incorporation of cutting-edge technologies like big data, artificial intelligence (AI) and blockchain. These developments have brought about a revolution in multiple industries, including manufacturing, finance, logistics, healthcare, and education, promoting a more interconnected and streamlined global economic environment. Businesses have been able to leverage big data to analyze large volumes of data and extract valuable insights on market trends, consumer behavior, and operational efficiency. Accordingly, this chapter provides an overview of Big Data and its applications in international trade. It is important to understand the implications of big data on global trade in order to effectively navigate the ever-changing realm of international trade.

DOI: 10.4018/979-8-3693-6592-2.ch005

INTRODUCTION

Technological advancements are driving the accumulation, processing, sharing, and utilization of data in digital formats at lower costs and on a larger scale. While data management is not a recent development, the capability to store vast quantities of data in diverse formats and analyze it swiftly is relatively novel. The growing volume and increased analysis of data have caused to the emergence of big data. Big data can be defined as the aggregation of extensive datasets of diverse types, generated rapidly from a multitude of sources (e.g., the Internet of Things, sensors, social media, and financial market data collection). These datasets are processed, often in real-time, utilizing information technology tools such as robust processors, software, and algorithms (EBA, 2020). As every aspect of modern technological life is generating more and more data, big data has become one of the hottest topics in recent years. Additionally, the expansion of scientific endeavors has prompted widespread engagement in the extraction and utilization of vast quantities of data across various domains including business, consumer behavior, financial transactions, healthcare, and other research fields. The potential of data-driven decision-making is increasingly acknowledged, fostering growing interest in the notion of big data (Smaya, 2022).

Over the last two decades, a significant amount of data has been generated in almost every area. Data is a pivotal element for decision-makers, offering insights into economic, social, and political landscapes. However, traditional approaches to gathering data, such as surveys, censuses, and administrative records, have become insufficient in fulfilling the need for precise and timely data, particularly during crises like the Covid-19 pandemic (Alrousan, 2023). Besides, a large amount of data is generated daily regarding economic and social activities due to the increasing use of electronic devices and networks, as well as digitalizing production processes (Davies, 2016). According to recent report published by Statista (2023) while the total amount of data generated and consumed was 2 zettabytes (or 2 trillion gigabytes) in 2010, it was reached 64.2 zettabytes in 2020. The volume of data created, captured, copied and stored is expected to reach more than 180 zettabytes by 2025. Due to the Covid 19 pandemic, the amount of data worldwide was increased significantly since as many of the world population was stayed at home. Fortune Business Insights (2024) pointed out that the worldwide market for Big Data Analytics was worth $307.51 billion in 2023, and is expected to increase from $348.21 billion in 2024 to $924.39 billion by 2032.

With the rapid expansion and accessibility of data in recent years, an important phenomenon has emerged within the global trade community. The method of data gathering and sharing is gaining greater significance than ever before. Easy accessibility to data has emerged as a pivotal aspect for enhancing understanding and transparency within the global supply chain, thereby enabling better management and facilitation of the flow of goods. As the rate and complexity of global trade continue to rise, both Customs authorities and traders encounter unprecedented challenges, necessitating the utilization of innovative technologies to leverage big data for enhanced insights. Real-time data is essential for effectively harnessing big data to recognize opportunities, discern trends, identify errors, and generate insights. The refinement and harmonization of data are integral components that complement each other in the streamlining and standardization process, ensuring the utmost levels of compliance and security within the realm of global trade. Establishing agreed-upon formats and standards for data exchange will bolster trade efficiency and promote transparency between authorities and traders (Keyes, 2016). The opportunities for data exploitation will grow as the modern world becomes increasingly digitized and volumes of data are increasing. Accordingly, this paper provides an overview of Big Data and its applications in international trade. The remainder of the paper is structured as follows: Section two provides an overview of Big Data. Section three discusses the applications of Big Data in international trade. Section four delves into the discussion and conclusion. Furthermore, the editing and proofreading, including addressing grammatical errors and enhancing the clarity of the manuscript, were conducted with the assistance of ChatGPT. Nonetheless, the final iteration of the study was scrutinized by the author to ensure adherence to ethical standards.

AN OVERVIEW OF BIG DATA

Big data is one of the most discussed and hottest concepts among the emerging technologies in today's business world. Big data has been defined in multiple ways by numerous researchers, however there is no consensus on a definition of big data. Every concept requires a clear definition before it can be fully understood in all its aspects. Definitional conflicts regarding core concepts are a common problem in emerging disciplines. In fact, the level of consensus within a scientific community when defining a concept can be seen as an indicator of the discipline's advancement (Ronda-Pupo & Guerras-Martin, 2012). In parallel, various organizations and academicians have described big data based on different themes such as information, technologies, methods and impacts. Big data can be described as datasets that size is larger than the capabilities of traditional database software tools to capture, store, manage and analyze (Manyika et al., 2011). The term "big data" refers to a greater volume of data, novel types of data and analysis, or the emerging requirements for more real-time information analysis (Schroeck et al., 2012). Big Data is an information asset that is characterized by a larger volume, velocity, and variety, necessitating specialized technology and analytical techniques for its transformation into value (De Mauro et al., 2016). According to Rahul et al. (2023) big data refers to the accumulation and combination of substantial amounts of data in various formats that are difficult in terms of storage, comprehension, and processing for an application. Tiao (2024) emphasized that big data is data with greater variety, arrives at larger volumes and with higher velocity. By considering the definitions above mentioned, it can be said that big data has been characterized by the three main dimensions, namely variety, volumes and velocity (3V's). However, the dimensions regarding the big data have been updated day by day since data is created by everyone and for everything (Panimalar et al., 2017). Figure 1 illustrates the different dimensions associated with big data.

Figure 1. Various Dimensions on Big Data (Panimalar et al., 2017)

As Uprichard (2013) stated many v-words have been utilized to describe big data including veracity, validity, value, venue, variability, vulgar, violating, venomous, virtuosity and visionary. Additionally, p-words such as productive, personal, political, predictive, privacy, playful, have also been suggested for describing big data (Lupton, 2015). Over the last decades, a wide variety and large amounts of data have been created by numerous organizations and such data that need to be analyzed. According to Kitchin and McArdle (2016), big data differs significantly from traditional types of small data in a number of aspects that extend beyond the data's essential qualities (such as methodologies, sampling, quality of data, repurposing, and management). The reduction of costs related to the handling and storage of data has resulted in a growth in Big Data information encompassing numerous areas of social and business life. Both private and public institutions collect data. Moreover, corporations are looking for ways to use the advantages of big data to enhance their ability to make decisions, gain a competitive advantage, or increase business performance. Nowadays, a new approach has been offered to analyze the large amount of data (Big Data), called Big Data Analytics. Big Data Analytics (BDA) also known as Big Data Management, covers the application of advanced analytical methods for analyzing massive quantities of data for useful information that may help in decision-making processes (Batko & Ślęzak, 2022; Pizło et al., 2023). BDA is widely used to solve complex problem in various areas, such as cloud computing (Berisha et al., 2022), supply chain management

(Bag et al., 2020; Rashid et al., 2024), healthcare (Khanra et al., 2020), finance (Kumar et al., 2022) and manufacturing (Sahoo, 2022). Figure 2 demonstrates the different applications areas of Big Data.

Figure 2. Related Topics on Big Data (De Mauro et al., 2016)

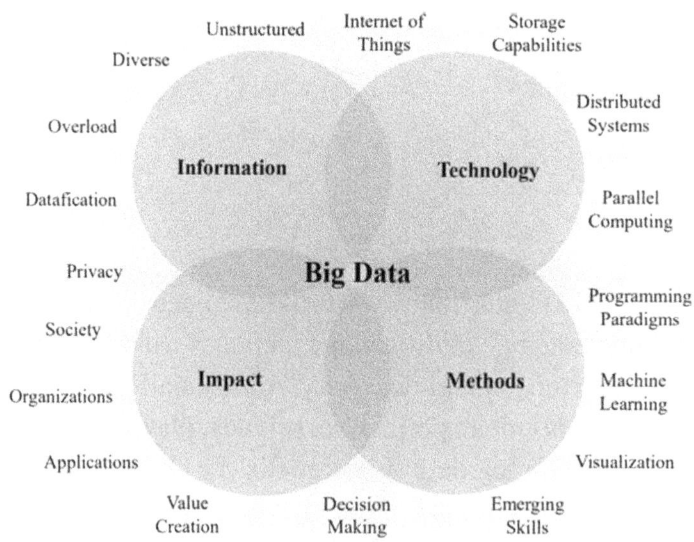

McKinsey emphasized that the effective use of big data has the potential to transform economies, delivering a new wave of productivity growth and consumer surplus. Leveraging valuable knowledge beyond Big Data is a core competitive strategy for businesses. With the help of Big Data, businesses can obtain several advantages, such as enhanced operational efficiency, informed strategic decision-making, elevated customer service standards, innovation in product development, and expansion into new customer segments and markets (Manyika et al., 2011). While Big Data provides a great number of opportunities, it also poses several risks and challenges (Naeem et al., 2022). For instance, Mishra and Sharma (2015) highlighted that data complexity, computational complexity and system complexity are major challenges of Big Data. Garoufallou and Gaitanou (2021) pointed out that legal, policy, privacy, data ownership, infrastructural issues, data complexity, insufficient data quality and lack of data standardization are main obstacles of Big Data. Additionally, managing data from a variety of sources, concern about the security, privacy and confidentiality, advanced analytical methods and quality of data are considered as key challenges of Big Data (Goyal & Malviya, 2023). In today's global economy, effective solutions to these challenges can allow businesses to get full advantage of the potential of Big Data and generate sustainable growth. In the following section, the impact of Big Data in international trade is examined.

BIG DATA APPLICATIONS IN INTERNATIONAL TRADE

Data transmission across international boundaries has emerged as a fundamental component of various economic activities. Facilitated by the expansive reach of the Internet, these transmissions are commonly acknowledged for their role in enhancing productivity and fostering growth. They promote trade, innovation, and entrepreneurship while also offering new avenues for social interaction and knowledge dissemination, thereby enriching societal dynamics. The unrestricted exchange of information across borders is bolstering a growing number of economic endeavors. These activities frequently entail measures aimed at enhancing the efficiency of production processes, such as the geographical clustering of standard business operations within multinational corporations, the integration of global production processes through the Internet of Things (IoT), coordination of international supply chains, as well as the utilization of Big Data analytics and Cloud computing (Spiezia & Tscheke, 2020). International trade includes various and complex characteristics. The international trade brings together a number of roles, such as producers, customs, logistics and end customers, which are linked to the needs of each country in order to establish an international market. Thus, international trade is very fragmented and chaotic. However, the lack of application of advanced technology such as big data, blockchain, IoT, artificial intelligence is a major reason for the low efficiency in international trade (Lian, 2022, p.2).

In the past, data across different industries and departments were typically isolated and siloed, lacking communication and integration with other relevant departments. In the realm of international trade implementation, product market demand was often assessed based solely on individual experience, frequently resulting in inaccurate judgments and unscientific predictions. However, through the utilization of big data information technology, pertinent departments now have the capability to access, view, and share information resources conveniently, accurately, and intuitively across various platforms. Previously, international trade primarily focused on the exchange of goods and services, with minimal emphasis on information exchange. Information often existed as a supplementary aspect of goods and services and did not fully realize its potential in guiding enterprise operations. However, with the advent of the big data era, this paradigm has fundamentally shifted. The international trade industry has transitioned towards guiding business development based on the value of information. The circulation rate of data has significantly increased, leading to reduced costs associated with enterprise management and storage technology. Additionally, big data has expanded the channels through which relevant departments can access data. Data, once confined to individual blocks, is now dispersed across various ports, facilitating faster acquisition for enterprises. Consequently, businesses can provide accurate responses, lower the cost of information maintenance, and enhance the operational efficiency of each department. The integration of the logistics industry with big data has optimized and streamlined the steps involved in international trade. In the past, countries often only needed to export semi-finished products before implementing the value-added process once the goods were sold to other countries. Traditionally, demand forecasting for regional trade relied heavily on the authorities' experience, which often felt distant from the everyday lives of ordinary people and lacked direct impact on their realities. However, in the era of big data, businesses can influence relevant policies and guidelines, and engage with the public through open and diversified channels to address public needs (Yu, 2021, p. 142-143). Some applications of big data in international trade activities are presented in Figure 3.

Figure 3. Applications of Big Data in International Trade (International Economics, 2022)

As seen above, big data plays a significant role in enhancing the effectiveness of customs, logistics, and various other aspects of international trade. Besides, big data and predictive analytics can further enhance efficiency by enabling companies to optimize logistics, improve the accuracy of demand forecasting, and strategically time product launches. With the potential for real-time optimization and more accurate long-term predictions, value chains will become increasingly resilient. Moreover, advanced data analytics and computing will simplify the process of supply chains, allowing for the identification of potential vulnerabilities and the evaluation of modifications, resulting in more reliable trade operations (Kohen, 2015). The utilization of big data to analyze shipping data and customs operations has empowered authorities to forecast trade flows and pinpoint potential bottlenecks. Machine learning algorithms process real-time data from ports worldwide, offering insights into global goods movement. This information subsequently guides infrastructure development and policy adjustments. Furthermore, in trade negotiations, big data serves as a critical element for evidence-based decision-making. Real-time analytics offer negotiators insights into the potential effects of proposed trade tariffs or regulations before they are implemented. This capability allows for the simulation of various scenarios, enabling countries to negotiate from a well-informed position. For instance, the United States International Trade Commission (USITC) employs increasingly data-driven economic models to evaluate the impact of trade agreements. By analyzing data on trade flows, tariff schedules, and regulatory standards, negotiators gain a clearer understanding of potential outcomes, leading to more advantages. Additionally, in the realm of regulatory compliance, the application of big data has become increasingly advanced. Algorithms now cross-reference import-export data across various jurisdictions to detect discrepancies that might indicate fraud or smuggling. For example, the European Union's Customs Risk Management system (CRMS) utilizes big data to evaluate the risks associated with goods crossing borders, thereby enhancing compliance with trade regulations. In terms of compliance and enforcement, big data tools such as the Automated Commercial Environment (ACE) system, used by U.S. Customs and Border Protection, enable the tracking of goods across borders and help ensure that trade partners adhere to their commitments. Also, big data has become crucial for identifying and addressing market access issues. The World Trade Organization (WTO) leverages trade data to monitor the implementation of agreements and to detect potential barriers to trade. For instance, analyzing customs data can help identify non-tariff measures that may impact trade flows (Ogbonna, 2023). Certainly, numerous additional applications leveraging big data are employed in international trade to improve diverse areas such as supply chain management, trade facilitation, customs operations, and regulatory compliance. Some examples are as follows:

- **TradeLens:** TradeLens is a platform developed by IBM and Maersk in 2016, aimed at digitizing and modernizing international trade operations. The TradeLens platform utilizes some advanced technologies such as Blockchain and Big Data, to provide secure and transparent digital records of transactions and documents as goods move through the supply chain. TradeLens leverages big data analytics to extract insights from the vast amounts of data generated by global trade activities. By analyzing this data, TradeLens aims to provide stakeholders with valuable insights into supply chain performance, such as real-time tracking of shipments, predictive analytics for demand forecasting, and identification of potential obstacles or inefficiencies in the supply chain (Jovanovic et al. 2022; TradeLens, 2024).

- **The World Integrated Trade Solution (WITS):** The WITS **is** an integrated trade data and analysis platform developed by the WB and other partner institutions. It has emerged as a valuable resource for millions of yearly users looking to analyze and understand international trade data. It also provides users tools to analyze the data for better understanding of complex trade data, regulations, tariffs, and market trends. Additionally, WITS includes features such as data visualization tools, tariff analysis modules, and trade competitiveness indicators, making it a valuable resource for understanding global trade dynamics and supporting evidence-based decision-making in trade policy and business strategy (Kaushik, 2024).
- **Trade Analysis Information System (TRAINS):** The United Nations Conference on Trade and Development (UNCTAD), Trade Analysis and Information System (TRAINS) is a comprehensive information system that integrates data on trade, customs tariffs, and non-tariff measures. It includes tariff data based on the Harmonized System (HS) for over 170 countries and multiple years. TRAINS serves as both a data repository and an analytical tool tailored for policymakers and businesses involved in international trade. Additionally, it is a valuable resource for facilitating multilateral or bilateral trade negotiations and conducting research on global merchandise trade. The tariff and trade data provided by TRAINS are disseminated through the WITS application (UNCTAD, 2024).
- **Port Community Systems (PCS):** The PCS are digital collaborative platforms facilitating the smooth exchange of information among various stakeholders within a port, encompassing customs agencies, port authorities, shipping and logistics firms, and freight forwarders. By digitizing processes, PCS platforms reduce the paperwork and administrative burdens inherent in port logistics, resulting in faster decision-making and enhanced operational efficien-

cy. The advantages extend to bolstering competitiveness, fortifying supply chains, cutting costs, and curbing greenhouse gas emissions (Sahu et al., 2023).

DISCUSSION AND CONCLUSION

The digital revolution is currently causing a significant transformation in global economies and livelihoods. Just like previous technological advancements, such as the invention of the combustion engine and electrification, digital technologies are changing societies and economies. The digital economy plays a crucial role in promoting economic growth and enhancing productivity, while also facilitating inclusive development. This growth is evident through the widespread adoption of digital technologies by consumers, businesses, and governments, although the pace of adoption varies across different sectors and countries. Embracing and utilizing digital technologies, such as Big Data, IoT, Blockchain not only enhances the efficiency of capital and labor but also enables active participation in global value chains (Dahlman et al., 2016).

Over the last few decades, Big Data is one of the most discussed and hottest technology in international trade activities. The integration of Big Data in global trade has undergone a substantial evolution in the management of trade operations, logistics, and regulatory adherence. The utilization of Big Data technology offers numerous benefits, such as enhancing the effectiveness of customs processes, streamlining logistics, and enhancing the transparency of trade practices. By harnessing data analytics, customs officials can predict trade trends and identify potential challenges. For instance, machine learning algorithms are used to analyze live data from different ports globally, providing insights into the flow of goods worldwide. This information helps in planning infrastructure projects and policy adjustments. Consequently, customs processes are streamlined, delays are reduced, and compliance with trade regulations is encouraged. Manyika (2011) and Chen et al. (2012) stressed out that the optimization of logistics activities using Big Data and predictive analytics has substantial consequences for global trade. These tools empower businesses to predict demand with greater precision, streamline supply chain, and enhance the timing of product releases. As a result, value chains become more resilient and efficient, with reduced costs and improved service delivery.

Moreover, the utilization of Big Data facilitates the adoption of evidence-based decision-making in trade negotiations. By employing real-time analytics, negotiators gain valuable insights into the potential consequences of proposed trade tariffs or regulations even before they are implemented. This capability was clearly demonstrated during the renegotiation of North American Free Trade Area (NAFTA) into the United States-Mexico-Canada Agreement (USMCA), as negotiators effectively leveraged Big Data to comprehend the potential impacts of changes and foster agreement on critical matters. The inclusion of digital trade provisions in the USMCA underscores the significance of data localization and cross-border data flows, guaranteeing the unrestricted transfer of data across borders. This is particularly vital for businesses that heavily rely on cloud computing and e-commerce (Palacios & Norton, 2024).

Additionally, Big Data is increasingly important for regulatory compliance. Algorithms are able to analyze import-export data from different regions to uncover any irregularities that may indicate fraudulent behavior or smuggling. For example, the European Union's Customs Risk Management System (CRMS) utilizes Big Data to evaluate the risks associated with the movement of goods across borders, thereby improving compliance with trade regulations. Similarly, in the United States, the Automated Commercial Environment (ACE) system used by Customs and Border Protection helps track goods across borders and ensures adherence to trade commitments (European Commission, 2024; CBP, 2024). Furthermore, the utilization of Big Data in recognizing and addressing market access issues is remarkable. The World Trade Organization (WTO) uses trade data for overseeing agreement implementation and detecting possible trade barriers. Examination of customs data aids in identifying non-tariff measures that could impact trade patterns, laying the groundwork for policy modifications to enhance market access (WTO, 2019).

To summarize, the incorporation of Big Data in global trade represents a fundamental change in the management and enhancement of trade operations. The applications of Big Data are diverse, such as it improves the effectiveness of customs procedures, streamline logistics, facilitate data-driven trade discussions, ensure adherence to regulations, and tackle market entry challenges. Such advancements contribute to more robust and effective global supply chains, reducing operational expenses, and enhancing service. Hence, it is important to understand the implications of big data on global trade in order to effectively navigate the ever-changing realm of international trade. This requires the integration of various disciplines such as economics, business, technology, law, and policy to formulate strategies and frameworks that optimize the advantages of big data while minimizing its risks and difficulties. Additionally, it is vital to foster collaboration and knowledge exchange among stakeholders to establish trust, encourage innovation, and advocate for inclusive and sustainable trade practices in the digital era. Correspondingly, future studies should prioritize the investigation of the applications of Big Data in different aspect of global trade. Moreover, the development of novel analytical frameworks that integrate Big Data with other emerging technologies, like blockchain, IoT, artificial intelligence, has the potential to offer profound insights and foster additional advancements in this field. With the continuous evolution of global trade, the significance of Big Data is bound to intensify, playing a pivotal role in shaping the forthcoming prospects of international trade.

REFERENCES

Alrousan, A. (2023). From Big Data to Big Insights: The Power and Efficiency of Big Data and Data Science in Statistical Work. https://sdgs.un.org/documents/ahmad-policy-using-big-data-official-statistical-centers-support-decision-makers-52426.

Bag, S., Wood, L. C., Xu, L., Dhamija, P., & Kayikci, Y. (2020). Big data analytics as an operational excellence approach to enhance sustainable supply chain performance. *Resources, Conservation and Recycling*, *153*, 104559.

Batko, K., & Ślęzak, A. (2022). The use of Big Data Analytics in healthcare. *Journal of Big Data*, *9*(1), 3. PMID: 35013701

Berisha, B., Mëziu, E., & Shabani, I. (2022). Big data analytics in Cloud computing: An overview. *Journal of Cloud Computing (Heidelberg, Germany)*, *11*(1), 24. PMID: 35966392

CBP. (2024). ACE and Automated Systems. U.S. Customs and Border Protection. https://www.cbp.gov/trade/automated.

Chen, H., Chiang, R. H., & Storey, V. C. (2012). Business intelligence and analytics: From big data to big impact. *Management Information Systems Quarterly*, 1165–1188.

Dahlman, C., Mealy, S., & Wermelinger, M. (2016). Harnessing the digital economy for developing countries. OECD Development Centre Working Papers, No. 334. https://www.oecd-ilibrary.org/development/harnessing-the-digital-economy-for-developing-countries_4adffb24-en.

Davies, R. (2016). Big Data and Data Analytics: The Potential for Innovation and Growth. *European Parliamentary Research Service*. https://www.europarl.europa.eu/RegData/etudes/BRIE/2016/589801/EPRS_BRI(2016)589801

De Mauro, A., Greco, M., & Grimaldi, M. (2016). A formal definition of Big Data based on its essential features. *Library Review*, *65*(3), 122–135.

EBA. (2020). EBA Report on Big Data and Advanced Analytics. https://www.eba.europa.eu/publications-and-media/press-releases/eba-report-identifies-key-challenges-roll-out-big-data-and.

European Commission. (2024). EU Customs Risk Management Systems. https://taxation-customs.ec.europa.eu/customs-4_en.

Fortune Business Insights. (2024). Big Data Analytics Market. https://www.fortunebusinessinsights.com/big-data-analytics-market-106179.

Garoufallou, E., & Gaitanou, P. (2021). Big data: Opportunities and challenges in libraries, a systematic literature review. *College & Research Libraries*, *82*(3), 410.

Goyal, P., & Malviya, R. (2023). Challenges and opportunities of big data analytics in healthcare. *Health Care Science*, *2*(5), 328–338. PMID: 38938583

International Economics. (2022). Big Data in International Trade: What is Working & What Have We Learnt so Far? https://tradeeconomics.com/big-data-in-international-trade-what-is-working-what-have-we-learnt-so-far/#_ftn1.

Jovanovic, M., Kostić, N., Sebastian, I. M., & Sedej, T. (2022). Managing a blockchain-based platform ecosystem for industry-wide adoption: The case of TradeLens. *Technological Forecasting and Social Change*, *184*, 121981.

Kaushik, S. (2024). How the World Integrated Trade Solution (WITS) is helping understand global commerce.https://blogs.worldbank.org/en/opendata/how-world-integrated-trade-solution-wits-helping-understand-global-commerce.

Keyes, L. (2016). Data Analytics: How data analytics can simplify and facilitate trade with the European Union. https://www.erasmusfiscalstudies.nl/upload/Keyes (15.05.2024)

Khanra, S., Dhir, A., Islam, A. N., & Mäntymäki, M. (2020). Big data analytics in healthcare: A systematic literature review. *Enterprise Information Systems*, *14*(7), 878–912. DOI: 10.1080/17517575.2020.1812005

Kitchin, R., & McArdle, G. (2016). What makes Big Data, Big Data? Exploring the ontological characteristics of 26 datasets. *Big Data & Society*, *3*(1).

Kohen, A. (2015). How big data will transform global trade. https://www.weforum.org/agenda/2015/04/how-big-data-will-transform-global-trade/.

Kumar, S., Sharma, D., Rao, S., Lim, W. M., & Mangla, S. K. (2022). Past, present, and future of sustainable finance: Insights from big data analytics through machine learning of scholarly research. *Annals of Operations Research*, 1–44. PMID: 35002001

Lian, G. (2022). Blockchain-based secure and trusted distributed international trade big data management system. *Mobile Information Systems*.

Lupton, D. (2015). The thirteen Ps of big data. *This Sociological Life*. https://simplysociology.wordpress.com/2015/05/11/the-thirteen-ps-of-big-data/.

Manyika, J., Chui, M., Brown, B., Bughin, J., Dobbs, R., Roxburgh, C., & Hung Byers, A. (2011). Big data: The next frontier for innovation, competition, and productivity. https://www.mckinsey.com/capabilities/mckinsey-digital/our-insights/big-data-the-next-frontier-for-innovation.

Mishra, R., & Sharma, R. (2015). Big Data: Opportunities and Challenges. *International Journal of Computer Science and Mobile Computing*, *4*(6), 27–35.

Naeem, M., Jamal, T., Diaz-Martinez, J., Butt, S. A., Montesano, N., Tariq, M. I., De-La-Hoz-Valdiris, E. (2022). Trends and future perspective challenges in big data. In *Advances in Intelligent Data Analysis and Applications:Proceeding of the Sixth Euro-China Conference on Intelligent Data Analysis and Applications,Arad, Romania* (pp. 309-325). Springer Singapore. DOI: 10.1007/978-981-16-5036-9_30

Ogbonna, C. (2023). Big Data and International Trade: Navigating A Data-Driven Landscape.https://nationaleconomy.com/?s=Big+Data+And+International+Trade%3A+Navigating+A+Data-Driven+Landscape.

Palacios, A., & Norton, C. (2024). Trade in a digital interoperability era. https://www.brookings.edu/articles/trade-in-a-digital-interoperability-era/.

Panimalar, A., Shree, V., & Kathrine, V. (2017). The 17 V's of big data. *International Research Journal of Engineering and Technology*, *4*(9), 329–333.

Pizło, W., Kulykovets, O., Prokopowicz, D., Mazurkiewicz-Pizło, A., Kałowski, A., Paprocka, M. W., & Skarzyńska, E. (2023). The importance of Big Data Analytics technology in business management. *Cybersecurity and Law*, *10*(2), 270–282.

Rahul, K., Banyal, R. K., & Arora, N. (2023). A systematic review on big data applications and scope for industrial processing and healthcare sectors. *Journal of Big Data*, *10*(1), 133.

Rashid, A., Baloch, N., Rasheed, R., & Ngah, A. H. (2024). Big data analytics-artificial intelligence and sustainable performance through green supply chain practices in manufacturing firms of a developing country. *Journal of Science and Technology Policy Management*.

Ronda-Pupo, G. A., & Guerras-Martin, L. Á. (2012). Dynamics of the evolution of the strategy concept 1962–2008: A co-word analysis. *Strategic Management Journal*, *33*(2), 162–188.

Sahoo, S. (2022). Big data analytics in manufacturing: A bibliometric analysis of research in the field of business management. *International Journal of Production Research*, *60*(22), 6793–6821.

Sahu, S. P., Saragiotis, P., Hartmann, O., Saslavsky, D., Ollivier, P., & Gupta, N. (2023). Port Community Systems: Driving Trade in the 21st Century. https://www.worldbank.org/en/topic/trade/publication/port-community-systems-driving-trade-in-the-21st-century.

Schroeck, M., Shockley, R., Smart, J., & Tufano, P. (2012). Analytics: the real-world use of big data: How innovative enterprises extract value from uncertain data, Executive Report IBM.

Smaya, H. (2022). The influence of big data analytics in the industry. *OAlib*, *9*(2), 1–12. DOI: 10.4236/oalib.1108383

Spiezia, V., & Tscheke, J. (2020). International agreements on cross-border data flows and international trade: A statistical analysis. OECD Science, Technology and Industry Working Papers.

Statista. (2023). Amount of data created, consumed, and stored 2010-2020, with forecasts to 2025. https://www.statista.com/statistics/871513/worldwide-data-created/.

Tiao, S. (2024). Big Data Defined. https://www.oracle.com/big-data/what-is-big-data/.

TradeLens. (2024). Discover how TradeLens solutions can work for you. https://www.tradelens.com/.

UNCTAD. (2024). Data, Statistics and Trends in International Trade. https://unctad.org/topic/trade-analysis/data-statistics-and-trends.

Uprichard, E. (2013). Focus: Big data, little questions? *Discover Society*, (1). https://archive.discoversociety.org/2013/10/01/focus-big-data-little-questions/.

WTO. (2019). World Trade Report 2019: The Future of Services Trade. World Trade Organization. https://www.wto.org/english/res_e/booksp_e/00_wtr19_e.pdf.

Yu, Y. (2021). Opportunities and Challenges of International Trade under the Background of Big Data. *In2021 International Conference on Education Technology and E-Business Management,Hangzhou, China,* (pp. 142-145). Chartered Society of Physiotherapy (CSP): The UK.

KEY TERMS AND DEFINITIONS

Big Data: Big Data pertains to exceptionally large and intricate datasets that exceed the capacity of conventional data processing tools to manage effectively.

Customs: Customs pertains to the governmental bodies tasked with overseeing the importation and exportation of merchandise across a nation's borders.

Data Analytics: Data analytics encompasses the examination of unprocessed data to identify trends, patterns, correlations, and insights.

Digital Trade: Digital trade encompasses the transaction of goods and services through digital platforms, which include e-commerce, online services, and digital products.

International Trade: International trade involves the transfer of goods, services, and capital between countries.

Logistics: Logistics encompasses the activities involved in the planning, execution, and management of the effective transportation and storage of products, services, and information from the point of origin to the point of consumption.

Smart Contracts: Smart contracts are automated agreements that execute themselves, with the conditions of the contract encoded directly within the programming.

Trade Flows: Trade flows denote the exchange of goods and services across national borders.

Chapter 6
Cultivating Resilience:
The Intersection of Trade Finance and Risk Management

K. Tamilarasi
https://orcid.org/0009-0006-9284-9053
Nehru Institute of Technology, India

P. Krishnakumar
Nehru College of Management, India

ABSTRACT

In the dynamic landscape of global commerce, the nexus of trade finance and risk management emerges as a critical domain for businesses seeking resilience and sustainability. This chapter delves into the multifaceted interplay between trade finance practices and risk management strategies, elucidating their symbiotic relationship in navigating the complexities of international trade. At its core, trade finance serves as the lifeblood of commerce, facilitating transactions across borders by mitigating financial risks inherent in cross-border trade. However, in an era fraught with geopolitical uncertainties, economic volatility, and disruptive technological advancements, the landscape of risk has evolved exponentially. Furthermore, the chapter delves into emerging trends and innovations reshaping the trade finance and risk management landscape, including the digitization of trade finance processes, the rise of blockchain technology,

DOI: 10.4018/979-8-3693-6592-2.ch006

and the advent of predictive analytics.

INTRODUCTION

In the dynamic landscape of global commerce, the nexus of trade finance and risk management emerges as a critical domain for businesses seeking resilience and sustainability. This chapter delves into the multifaceted interplay between trade finance practices and risk management strategies, elucidating their symbiotic relationship in navigating the complexities of international trade. At its core, trade finance serves as the lifeblood of commerce, facilitating transactions across borders by mitigating financial risks inherent in cross-border trade (Engle & van Senten, 2022). However, in an era fraught with geopolitical uncertainties, economic volatility, and disruptive technological advancements, the landscape of risk has evolved exponentially. Consequently, effective risk management has become indispensable for businesses to safeguard their interests and adapt to the ever-changing market dynamics. Furthermore, the chapter delves into emerging trends and innovations reshaping the trade finance and risk management landscape, including the digitization of trade finance processes, the rise of blockchain technology, and the advent of predictive analytics. It highlights the transformative potential of these advancements in enhancing operational efficiency, transparency, and risk mitigation capabilities for businesses engaged in global trade. Through real-world case studies and practical insights, this chapter equips readers with the knowledge and tools necessary to navigate the intersection of trade finance and risk management effectively. By fostering a holistic understanding of the interconnectedness between financial transactions and risk exposure, businesses can proactively mitigate threats, seize opportunities, and cultivate resilience in an increasingly volatile global marketplace.

OVERVIEW OF TRADE FINANCE AND RISK MANAGEMENT

In the ever-evolving global economy, the field of trade finance and risk management stands as a cornerstone of international commerce. Trade finance involves the financial products and instruments that facilitate international trade and commerce. Risk management, on the other hand, involves identifying, assessing, and prioritizing risks followed by coordinated and economical application of resources to minimize, monitor, and control the probability or impact of unfortunate events. Together, these domains ensure the smooth functioning of global trade, mitigating risks that can disrupt the intricate web of international transactions (Haywood, 2022).

The modern landscape of trade finance is complex, shaped by geopolitical shifts, economic fluctuations, technological advancements, and regulatory changes (Min & Borch, 2022). As businesses expand their operations across borders, they encounter a myriad of challenges, from currency fluctuations and credit risks to political instability and logistical hurdles. Effective trade finance and risk management strategies are essential for navigating these uncertainties, ensuring that companies can operate efficiently and profitably in the global marketplace (Tall et al, 2021).

At its core, trade finance provides liquidity and mitigates risks associated with international trade. Financial instruments such as letters of credit, trade credit insurance, and factoring enable exporters and importers to manage their cash flow and protect against default. Banks and financial institutions play a pivotal role in facilitating these transactions, offering expertise and resources to support businesses in their international endeavours (Min & Borch, 2022).

However, the global nature of trade finance also exposes businesses to a wide range of risks. Currency exchange rates can fluctuate rapidly, affecting the profitability of transactions. Political events can disrupt supply chains and alter market conditions. Economic crises can lead to credit shortages and increased default rates. To navigate these challenges, businesses must develop robust risk management frameworks that allow them to anticipate, assess, and respond to potential threats (Baines & Hager, 2022).

In recent years, technological advancements have transformed the trade finance landscape. Digital platforms and blockchain technology are streamlining processes, increasing transparency, and reducing the risk of fraud. These innovations are not only making trade finance more efficient but also opening up new opportunities for businesses to access financial services and expand their operations (Baldissera & Annalisa, 2023).

Regulatory frameworks also play a crucial role in shaping trade finance practices. Governments and international bodies establish rules and standards to ensure the stability and integrity of financial systems. Compliance with these regulations is essential for businesses to operate legally and avoid penalties. Understanding the regulatory environment is a key aspect of effective risk management in trade finance.

As it delve deeper into the world of trade finance and risk management, this book aims to provide a comprehensive guide to understanding and navigating the complexities of this field. Each chapter will explore different aspects of trade finance, from the foundational principles to advanced risk management strategies. We will examine the role of various financial instruments, the impact of global events, and the latest technological advancements. Through case studies and practical examples, we will illustrate how businesses can build resilience and thrive in the face of uncertainty (Akomea-Frimpong, Isaac, et al, 2022).

Whether you are a business owner, financial professional, or student, this book will equip you with the knowledge and tools to navigate the ever-changing landscape of trade finance. By understanding the intricacies of this field and adopting best practices in risk management, you can ensure that your business is well-positioned to succeed in the global marketplace (Qiao & Zhao, 2023).

The Foundations of Trade Finance

Trade finance is the backbone of international commerce, enabling businesses to engage in cross-border trade with confidence and efficiency. This chapter lays the groundwork for understanding trade finance, exploring its fundamental concepts, instruments, and significance in facilitating global trade (Studzinski & Pasteur, 2020).

The Importance of Trade Finance

Trade finance is essential for the smooth operation of international trade, providing the necessary financial tools and services that mitigate the inherent risks and challenges of cross-border transactions. It helps businesses manage cash flow, reduce payment risk, and ensure that trade operations proceed without disruption.

Role in Global Trade

Trade finance supports global trade by addressing key issues such as:

Payment Risk: Ensuring that exporters receive payment and importers receive goods as agreed.
Cash Flow Management: Providing working capital solutions that allow businesses to operate smoothly and fulfill orders.
Risk Mitigation: Offering instruments that protect against non-payment, currency fluctuations, and political instability.

Key Concepts in Trade Finance

Understanding the core concepts of trade finance is crucial for comprehending its role and functionality. Here, we explore the primary components and principles that underpin trade finance (Baines & Hager, 2022).

Letter of Credit (LC)

A letter of credit is a promise by a bank to pay the exporter on behalf of the importer, provided that the exporter meets the conditions outlined in the LC. This instrument mitigates payment risk by ensuring that the seller receives payment if they fulfil their contractual obligations (Min & Borch, 2022).

Types of LCs: There are various types of letters of credit, including revocable, irrevocable, confirmed, and unconfirmed LCs, each with different levels of security and conditions.

Bill of Exchange

A bill of exchange is a written, unconditional order by one party to another to pay a specified sum of money on demand or at a predetermined future date. It is commonly used in international trade to facilitate payment.

Usage: Bills of exchange are used to guarantee payment and can be transferred between parties, providing flexibility and liquidity.

Trade Credit

Trade credit is an arrangement where a buyer is allowed to purchase goods or services and pay for them at a later date. It helps businesses manage cash flow and maintain liquidity.

Terms: Trade credit terms vary, with typical periods ranging from 30 to 90 days, depending on the agreement between the trading parties (Haywood, 2022).

Export and Import Financing

Export and import financing involves various financial products designed to support businesses in fulfilling international trade transactions. These include pre-shipment and post-shipment financing, which provide working capital at different stages of the trade process.

Pre-shipment Financing: Provides funds to exporters to produce and ship goods.
Post-shipment Financing: Ensures liquidity for exporters while awaiting payment from importers.

Trade Finance Instruments

Trade finance instruments are the tools and mechanisms that facilitate international trade by providing payment assurance and risk mitigation. Here, we discuss the primary instruments used in trade finance.

Letters of Credit (LCs)

Letters of credit are widely used in international trade to mitigate payment risk. They offer a secure payment method by involving banks as intermediaries, ensuring that the exporter gets paid once the terms of the LC are fulfilled.

Process: The importer's bank issues the LC, guaranteeing payment to the exporter upon receipt of specified documents (e.g., bill of lading, invoice, packing list).

Documentary Collections

Documentary collections involve the exporter entrusting the collection of payment to their bank, which sends documents to the importer's bank with instructions to release them to the importer upon payment (West et al, 2021).

Types: There are two main types of documentary collections: Documents Against Payment (D/P) and Documents Against Acceptance (D/A).

Trade Credit Insurance

Trade credit insurance protects exporters against the risk of non-payment by covering losses due to buyer insolvency, protracted default, and political risks. This instrument enhances the security of international transactions and can improve access to financing.

Factoring and Forfaiting

Factoring involves selling accounts receivable to a third party (factor) at a discount in exchange for immediate cash. Forfaiting is a similar process but involves selling longer-term receivables.

Benefits: Both factoring and forfaiting provide businesses with immediate liquidity, reduce credit risk, and improve cash flow.

Regulatory and Compliance Considerations

Engaging in international trade finance requires adherence to various regulatory and compliance standards. Understanding these requirements is crucial for ensuring smooth and lawful trade operations.

Anti-Money Laundering (AML) and Know Your Customer (KYC)

Financial institutions involved in trade finance must comply with AML and KYC regulations to prevent money laundering and terrorist financing. This involves verifying the identities of trading partners and monitoring transactions for suspicious activities (Carr, 2020).

International Trade Regulations

Businesses must navigate a complex web of international trade regulations, including tariffs, import/export restrictions, and trade sanctions. Compliance with these regulations is essential to avoid legal issues and penalties.

Basel III

Basel III is a set of international banking regulations developed by the Basel Committee on Banking Supervision to strengthen the regulation, supervision, and risk management of banks. It affects trade finance by imposing capital requirements and liquidity standards.

Trade finance is a fundamental component of global commerce, providing the tools and mechanisms necessary to facilitate and secure international trade. By understanding the foundational concepts and instruments of trade finance, businesses can better navigate the complexities of cross-border transactions and mitigate associated risks. This foundational knowledge sets the stage for exploring more advanced topics in trade finance and risk management, helping businesses build resilience and thrive in the global market (Engle & van Senten, 2022).

Risk Management in International Trade

International trade offers significant opportunities for growth and expansion, but it also involves a multitude of risks that can impact businesses adversely. Effective risk management is essential for navigating these challenges and ensuring sustainable success in global markets.

Understanding Risks in International Trade

International trade exposes businesses to a variety of risks that can disrupt operations, affect profitability, and hinder growth. These risks can be broadly categorized into financial, operational, and strategic risks.

Financial Risks

Credit Risk: The risk that a buyer will default on payment obligations. This is particularly critical when trading with new or unverified partners.

Currency Risk: The risk that fluctuations in exchange rates will adversely affect the value of transactions. Currency volatility can significantly impact profit margins.
Liquidity Risk: The risk of a business facing cash flow problems due to delays in payment or unforeseen expenses, which can affect the ability to meet financial obligations (Al-Banna et al., 2023).

Operational Risks

Logistics and Supply Chain Risk: The risk of disruptions in the supply chain, such as delays in shipping, customs clearance issues, or transportation strikes, which can delay deliveries and increase costs.
Compliance and Legal Risk: The risk of non-compliance with international trade regulations, including tariffs, import/export restrictions, and trade sanctions, which can result in legal penalties and operational delays.
Cybersecurity Risk: The risk of cyberattacks that can compromise sensitive data, disrupt operations, and damage a company's reputation (Studzinski & Pasteur, 2020).

Strategic Risks

Political Risk: The risk of political instability or changes in government policies in the trading partner's country that can affect trade operations. This includes expropriation, currency controls, and trade embargoes.
Market Risk: The risk of adverse market conditions, such as changes in consumer demand, competition, or economic downturns, impacting sales and profitability.
Environmental Risk: The risk of natural disasters, climate change, and environmental regulations affecting supply chains and production capabilities.

Strategies for Managing Risks

Effective risk management involves identifying potential risks, assessing their impact, and implementing strategies to mitigate them. The key strategies for managing risks in international trade:

Financial Risk Management

1. **Credit Risk Management:**
    - **Due Diligence:** Conduct thorough background checks and credit assessments of potential trading partners to evaluate their financial stability and payment history.
    - **Letters of Credit (LCs):** Use LCs to secure payment by ensuring that the buyer's bank guarantees payment to the seller upon fulfillment of specific conditions.
    - **Trade Credit Insurance:** Purchase trade credit insurance to protect against the risk of non-payment by foreign buyers due to insolvency, protracted default, or political risks.
2. **Currency Risk Management:**
    - **Hedging:** Use financial instruments such as forward contracts, options, and swaps to hedge against currency fluctuations and lock in favorable exchange rates.
    - **Invoicing in Stable Currencies:** Negotiate contracts to invoice in stable currencies, such as the US dollar or euro, to reduce exposure to volatile currencies.
    - **Currency Clauses:** Include currency adjustment clauses in contracts to allow for price adjustments in case of significant exchange rate movements.
3. **Liquidity Risk Management:**
    - **Factoring and Forfaiting:** Use factoring and forfaiting to sell receivables and obtain immediate cash, improving cash flow and reducing credit risk.
    - **Export Financing:** Secure pre-shipment and post-shipment financing to ensure adequate working capital for fulfilling orders and managing cash flow.

Operational Risk Management

1. **Supply Chain Risk Management:**
    - o **Diversification:** Diversify suppliers and logistics providers to reduce dependence on a single source and mitigate the impact of disruptions.
    - o **Contingency Planning:** Develop contingency plans for potential disruptions, including alternative routes, backup suppliers, and inventory management strategies.
    - o **Technology Integration:** Use supply chain management software and technology to enhance visibility, track shipments in real-time, and optimize logistics processes.
2. **Compliance and Legal Risk Management:**
    - o **Stay Informed:** Keep abreast of international trade regulations, tariffs, and sanctions to ensure compliance and avoid legal penalties.
    - o **Legal Expertise:** Engage legal experts specializing in international trade to navigate complex regulatory environments and draft compliant contracts.
    - o **Customs Brokers:** Utilize customs brokers to handle customs clearance processes, ensuring compliance with import/export regulations and reducing the risk of delays.
3. **Cybersecurity Risk Management:**
    - o **Robust Security Measures:** Implement robust cybersecurity measures, including firewalls, encryption, and intrusion detection systems, to protect sensitive data and systems.
    - o **Employee Training:** Train employees on cybersecurity best practices to prevent phishing attacks, data breaches, and other cyber threats.
    - o **Incident Response Plan:** Develop an incident response plan to quickly address and mitigate the impact of cyberattacks and data breaches.

Strategic Risk Management

1. **Political Risk Management:**

- **Political Risk Insurance:** Purchase political risk insurance to protect against losses due to political instability, expropriation, and currency controls in the trading partner's country.
- **Market Research:** Conduct thorough market research to assess the political and economic stability of potential trading partners and markets.
- **Diversification:** Diversify markets and trading partners to spread political risk and reduce reliance on any single country or region.

2. **Market Risk Management:**
    - **Market Analysis:** Continuously analyze market trends, consumer behavior, and competitive landscape to anticipate changes and adjust strategies accordingly.
    - **Product Diversification:** Diversify product offerings to mitigate the impact of changing consumer preferences and market conditions.
    - **Strategic Partnerships:** Form strategic partnerships and alliances to enhance market presence, share risks, and capitalize on new opportunities.
3. **Environmental Risk Management:**
    - **Sustainability Practices:** Implement sustainable practices in operations and supply chains to comply with environmental regulations and reduce the impact of natural disasters.
    - **Insurance Coverage:** Secure comprehensive insurance coverage for natural disasters and environmental risks to protect assets and operations.
    - **Climate Risk Assessment:** Conduct climate risk assessments to understand potential environmental impacts on supply chains and operations, and develop mitigation strategies.

Managing risks in international trade is crucial for building a resilient business capable of thriving in a complex and dynamic global environment. By understanding the various risks involved and implementing effective risk management strategies, businesses can mitigate potential disruptions, safeguard their operations, and capitalize on opportunities in international markets.

Financial Instruments in Trade Finance

Financial instruments are essential tools in trade finance, providing the necessary support to facilitate international transactions and mitigate associated risks. These instruments help ensure that exporters receive payment and importers receive goods, thereby enabling smooth and secure trade operations. This section explores the primary financial instruments used in trade finance, detailing their functions, benefits, and application in international trade (Bowen, 2009).

Letters of Credit (LCs)

A letter of credit is a critical instrument in trade finance that guarantees payment from the buyer's bank to the seller, provided that the seller meets specific conditions outlined in the LC. This instrument reduces the risk of non-payment for exporters and assures importers that payment will only be made if the terms of the contract are fulfilled (Blessing & Amaresh, 2009).

Types of Letters of Credit

Revocable Letter of Credit: Can be altered or cancelled by the issuing bank without prior notice to the beneficiary (seller). This type is less common due to its higher risk for the exporter.

Irrevocable Letter of Credit: Cannot be changed or cancelled without the consent of all parties involved. This provides greater security for both exporters and importers.

Confirmed Letter of Credit: A second bank (usually in the exporter's country) adds its guarantee to the LC, providing additional assurance to the exporter that they will receive payment.

Unconfirmed Letter of Credit: Only the issuing bank is responsible for payment, which may pose higher risk for the exporter if the issuing bank's creditworthiness is uncertain.

Process of Letters of Credit

Issuance: The importer requests their bank to issue an LC in favor of the exporter.
Advising: The issuing bank sends the LC to the exporter's bank, which advises the exporter of the LC.
Shipment: The exporter ships the goods and provides the required documents to their bank.
Presentation: The exporter's bank forwards the documents to the issuing bank.
Payment: The issuing bank reviews the documents and, if they meet the LC conditions, releases payment to the exporter.

Bills of Exchange

A bill of exchange is a written, unconditional order by one party to another to pay a specified sum of money on demand or at a future date. It serves as a negotiable instrument that facilitates international trade by providing a secure payment method.

Characteristics of Bills of Exchange

Drawer: The party that issues the bill (usually the exporter).
Drawee: The party required to pay (usually the importer).
Payee: The party to whom the payment is made (usually the exporter or a designated third party).

Types of Bills of Exchange

Sight Bill: Payable on demand or upon presentation to the drawee.
Term Bill: Payable at a future date specified in the bill.

Benefits of Bills of Exchange

Flexibility: Can be transferred or endorsed to other parties, providing liquidity.

Security: Provides a legal framework for enforcing payment.
Negotiability: Can be discounted or sold to a bank for immediate cash.

Trade Credit Insurance

Trade credit insurance protects exporters against the risk of non-payment by foreign buyers due to commercial or political reasons. It enhances the security of international transactions and can improve access to financing by reducing the perceived risk for lenders.

Coverage and Benefits

Commercial Risks: Covers buyer insolvency, protracted default, and failure to pay within the agreed timeframe.
Political Risks: Covers risks such as war, expropriation, currency inconvertibility, and government actions that prevent payment.

Application Process

Policy Application: The exporter applies for a trade credit insurance policy, specifying the buyers and transactions to be covered.
Risk Assessment: The insurer evaluates the creditworthiness of the buyers and the political risks of the importer's country.
Policy Issuance: The insurer issues a policy outlining the coverage terms, conditions, and premium costs.
Claim Filing: In case of a loss, the exporter files a claim with the insurer, providing necessary documentation to support the claim.

Factoring and Forfaiting

Factoring and forfaiting are financial services that provide immediate cash flow to exporters by selling their receivables to a third party at a discount. These instruments help manage credit risk and improve liquidity.

Factoring

Factoring involves selling short-term receivables to a factor, who assumes the risk of collecting the payments.

Recourse Factoring: The exporter remains liable if the buyer defaults.
Non-Recourse Factoring: The factor assumes the full risk of non-payment.

Forfaiting

Forfaiting involves selling medium to long-term receivables, usually from capital goods or high-value transactions, to a forfeiter.

Non-Recourse: The forfeiter assumes the full risk, providing the exporter with immediate cash and freeing them from credit risk.

Benefits

Improved Cash Flow: Immediate access to funds tied up in receivables.
Risk Mitigation: Transfer of credit risk to the factor or forfaiter.
Focus on Core Business: Reduced administrative burden of managing receivables and collections.

Documentary Collections

Documentary collections involve the exporter entrusting the collection of payment to their bank, which sends the documents to the importer's bank with instructions to release them upon payment or acceptance of a draft.

Types of Documentary Collections

Documents Against Payment (D/P): The importer receives the documents only after paying the amount due.

Documents Against Acceptance (D/A): The importer receives the documents after accepting a bill of exchange, agreeing to pay at a future date.

Process of Documentary Collections

Exporter's Bank: The exporter ships the goods and submits the shipping documents to their bank.
Transmittal: The exporter's bank sends the documents to the importer's bank with instructions.
Importer's Bank: The importer's bank notifies the importer and releases the documents upon payment or acceptance.
Payment Collection: The importer's bank transfers the payment to the exporter's bank, which then credits the exporter.

Financial instruments in trade finance are vital for facilitating international trade by providing payment assurance, risk mitigation, and liquidity. Understanding and effectively utilizing these instruments can significantly enhance the security and efficiency of cross-border transactions.

Strategies for Mitigating Financial Risk

Financial risk is a critical concern in international trade, encompassing a variety of challenges such as credit risk, currency risk, and liquidity risk. Effective risk mitigation strategies are essential for safeguarding business operations and ensuring long-term success in global markets. This chapter explores various strategies for managing and mitigating financial risk in international trade, providing practical insights and tools to enhance financial stability (Qiao & Zhao, 2023).

Identifying Financial Risks

Understanding the specific financial risks involved in international trade is the first step in developing effective mitigation strategies. The primary financial risks include:

Credit Risk: The risk that a trading partner will default on their payment obligations.
Currency Risk: The risk that exchange rate fluctuations will negatively impact the value of international transactions.
Liquidity Risk: The risk of insufficient cash flow to meet financial obligations.

Strategies for Mitigating Credit Risk

Credit risk is one of the most significant financial risks in international trade. It arises when a buyer fails to pay for goods or services, leading to potential financial losses for the seller. Here are key strategies to mitigate credit risk:

Conduct Thorough Due Diligence

Before entering into a trade agreement, conduct comprehensive due diligence on potential trading partners. This includes:

Credit Assessments: Evaluate the creditworthiness of the buyer by reviewing their financial statements, credit history, and payment behavior.
Background Checks: Investigate the buyer's business reputation, legal standing, and market position (Baines & Hager, 2022).

Utilize Trade Credit Insurance

Trade credit insurance provides protection against non-payment by covering losses due to buyer insolvency, protracted default, and political risks. Benefits include:

Risk Transfer: Shifts the risk of non-payment to the insurer.
Enhanced Financing: Insured receivables can improve access to financing by reducing lender risk.

Employ Letters of Credit (LCs)

Letters of credit are widely used to secure payment in international trade. Key benefits include:

Guaranteed Payment: The issuing bank guarantees payment to the exporter upon fulfilment of the LC terms.
Reduced Risk: Mitigates the risk of non-payment and disputes.

Establish Clear Payment Terms

Clearly defined payment terms help manage credit risk by setting expectations and deadlines. Consider:

Advance Payment: Request partial or full payment before shipping goods.
Progress Payments: Use milestone-based payments for long-term contracts.
Shorter Credit Terms: Reduce the credit period to minimize exposure.

Strategies for Mitigating Currency Risk

Currency risk, or exchange rate risk, arises from fluctuations in exchange rates that can affect the value of international transactions. Strategies to mitigate currency risk include:

Hedging with Financial Instruments

Hedging involves using financial instruments to offset potential losses from currency fluctuations. Common hedging tools include:

Forward Contracts: Agreements to buy or sell a currency at a fixed exchange rate on a future date, locking in the exchange rate and reducing uncertainty.

Options: Contracts that give the buyer the right, but not the obligation, to exchange currency at a predetermined rate, providing flexibility and protection against adverse movements.
Currency Swaps: Agreements to exchange cash flows in different currencies, helping manage exposure to exchange rate fluctuations.

Invoicing in Stable Currencies

Negotiating contracts to invoice in stable currencies, such as the US dollar or euro, can reduce exposure to volatile currencies. Benefits include:

Reduced Risk: Minimizes the impact of exchange rate volatility.
Simplified Accounting: Easier financial planning and accounting in stable currencies.

Currency Clauses in Contracts

Including currency adjustment clauses in trade contracts allows for price adjustments in case of significant exchange rate movements. Consider:

Exchange Rate Triggers: Define specific exchange rate thresholds that trigger price adjustments.
Periodic Reviews: Schedule regular reviews of exchange rates to adjust pricing as needed.

Strategies for Mitigating Liquidity Risk

Liquidity risk involves the potential for cash flow shortages that can impact a business's ability to meet its financial obligations. Strategies to mitigate liquidity risk include:

Factoring and Forfaiting

Factoring and forfaiting provide immediate cash flow by selling receivables to a third party at a discount. Benefits include:

Immediate Cash: Access to funds tied up in receivables, improving liquidity.
Risk Transfer: Transfer of credit risk to the factor or forfaiter.

Export Financing

Export financing provides working capital to exporters at different stages of the trade process. Key options include:

Pre-Shipment Financing: Funds to produce and ship goods before receiving payment.
Post-Shipment Financing: Ensures liquidity after goods are shipped but before payment is received.

Maintain Cash Reserves

Maintaining adequate cash reserves helps manage unexpected cash flow shortages. Strategies include:

Contingency Funds: Set aside funds specifically for emergencies and unforeseen expenses.
Liquidity Ratios: Monitor liquidity ratios, such as the current ratio and quick ratio, to ensure financial health.

Optimize Working Capital Management

Effective working capital management ensures that a business can meet its short-term obligations. Consider:

Inventory Management: Optimize inventory levels to reduce excess stock and free up cash.
Accounts Receivable Management: Implement efficient invoicing and collections processes to accelerate cash inflows.
Accounts Payable Management: Negotiate favorable payment terms with suppliers to improve cash flow.

Technology and Financial Risk Management

Technology plays a crucial role in managing financial risks by providing tools for better analysis, monitoring, and decision-making. Consider leveraging:

Financial Management Software

Financial management software helps businesses monitor cash flow, manage receivables and payables, and forecast financial needs. Benefits include:

Real-Time Data: Access to real-time financial data for informed decision-making.
Automation: Automated processes for invoicing, collections, and payments, reducing errors and improving efficiency.

Big Data and Analytics

Big data and analytics provide insights into market trends, customer behavior, and potential risks. Applications include:

Risk Assessment: Analyzing large datasets to identify patterns and predict risks.
Market Analysis: Monitoring market conditions and exchange rate trends to inform hedging strategies.

Blockchain Technology

Blockchain technology enhances transparency and security in trade finance by providing a decentralized ledger of transactions. Benefits include:

Tamper-Proof Records: Immutable records of transactions reduce the risk of fraud.

Enhanced Trust: Increased trust between trading partners through transparent and secure documentation.

Mitigating financial risk in international trade requires a comprehensive approach that combines thorough risk assessment, strategic planning, and the use of appropriate financial instruments and technologies. By implementing the strategies outlined in this chapter, businesses can safeguard against financial uncertainties, enhance stability, and ensure sustainable growth in the global marketplace. Effective risk management is not only about protecting assets but also about seizing opportunities and maintaining a competitive edge in international trade.

Real-world examples provide valuable insights into how companies manage risks in international trade. This section presents several case studies that highlight different aspects of risk management, showcasing strategies and lessons learned from actual business scenarios. These case studies cover a range of industries and regions, illustrating the diverse challenges and solutions in managing financial, operational, and strategic risks (Jerez & Morrissey, 2023).

Case Study 1: Managing Credit Risk in the Textile Industry

Background

A mid-sized textile exporter based in India, TexGlobal, frequently shipped goods to various retailers in Europe and North America. The company faced significant credit risk due to the possibility of non-payment by its international buyers.

Challenge

TexGlobal encountered a major issue when one of its largest buyers, a retailer in the UK, declared bankruptcy, leaving an outstanding invoice of $500,000 unpaid. This incident threatened TexGlobal's cash flow and financial stability.

Strategy

To mitigate such risks in the future, TexGlobal implemented several credit risk management strategies:

Trade Credit Insurance:

- o TexGlobal purchased trade credit insurance to cover potential losses from non-payment. The insurance policy protected up to 90% of the invoice value against commercial risks like bankruptcy and protracted default.

Letters of Credit (LCs):

- o The company started using irrevocable letters of credit for new buyers and large orders. This ensured that payment was guaranteed by the buyer's bank upon meeting specific shipment conditions.

Enhanced Due Diligence:

- o TexGlobal strengthened its due diligence process by conducting thorough credit assessments of new buyers, including financial health checks and background investigations.

Outcome

By implementing these strategies, TexGlobal significantly reduced its exposure to credit risk. The trade credit insurance provided financial security, while the use of LCs and improved due diligence processes ensured better payment assurance. As a result, TexGlobal was able to maintain its cash flow and continue its operations without major disruptions.

Developing a Risk Management Culture

A robust risk management culture is essential for businesses operating in the dynamic landscape of international trade. This culture integrates risk awareness, proactive management, and continuous improvement into the organizational fabric, ensuring that risks are effectively identified, assessed, and mitigated. Developing such a culture requires commitment from all levels of the organization, from the boardroom to frontline employees. This chapter explores the steps and strategies necessary to cultivate a strong risk management culture, providing practical insights for businesses aiming to enhance their resilience.

Understanding Risk Management Culture

Risk management culture refers to the collective mindset and behaviors within an organization that prioritize the identification, assessment, and mitigation of risks. It encompasses the values, beliefs, knowledge, and practices that guide how employees at all levels approach risk-related decisions and activities (Tall et al., 2021).

Key Elements of a Risk Management Culture

1. **Leadership Commitment:**
   - o Leadership plays a crucial role in setting the tone for risk management. Senior executives and the board of directors must demonstrate a commitment to risk management by integrating it into strategic planning and decision-making processes.
2. **Employee Engagement:**
   - o Engaging employees at all levels is essential for building a risk-aware culture. Employees should understand the importance of risk management and be encouraged to identify and report risks proactively.
3. **Communication and Transparency:**
   - o Open communication channels and transparency are vital for effective risk management. Employees should feel comfortable

discussing risks without fear of retribution, and risk-related information should be shared openly across the organization.

4. **Continuous Learning and Improvement:**
   - o A risk management culture thrives on continuous learning and improvement. Organizations should regularly review and update their risk management practices based on new information and changing circumstances.

Steps to Develop a Risk Management Culture

Step 1: Establish a Clear Risk Management Framework

A well-defined risk management framework provides the foundation for a strong risk management culture. This framework should outline the organization's risk management objectives, policies, procedures, and roles and responsibilities.

Components of a Risk Management Framework

- **Risk Management Policy:**
  - o A formal document that articulates the organization's commitment to risk management, including its objectives, scope, and guiding principles.
- **Risk Appetite and Tolerance:**
  - o Clear definitions of the levels and types of risk the organization is willing to accept in pursuit of its objectives.
- **Risk Assessment and Reporting Processes:**
  - o Standardized processes for identifying, assessing, monitoring, and reporting risks across the organization.

Step 2: Demonstrate Leadership Commitment

Leadership commitment is critical to embedding a risk management culture. Leaders should actively promote and participate in risk management activities, demonstrating that risk management is a priority for the organization.

Actions for Leaders

- **Role Modeling:**
  - o Leaders should exemplify risk-aware behavior and decision-making, setting a positive example for employees.
- **Resource Allocation:**
  - o Allocate sufficient resources, including time, budget, and personnel, to support risk management initiatives.
- **Regular Communication:**
  - o Communicate the importance of risk management regularly through meetings, memos, and other communication channels.

Step 3: Engage and Educate Employees

Employee engagement and education are essential for fostering a risk-aware culture. Employees should be equipped with the knowledge and skills necessary to identify and manage risks effectively.

Strategies for Employee Engagement

- **Training Programs:**
  - o Develop and deliver risk management training programs that cover risk identification, assessment, and mitigation techniques.
- **Workshops and Seminars:**
  - o Organize workshops and seminars to discuss specific risks relevant to different departments and functions.
- **Risk Champions:**
  - o Appoint risk champions within each department to promote risk management practices and serve as points of contact for risk-related issues.

Step 4: Foster Open Communication and Transparency

Creating an environment of open communication and transparency is vital for effective risk management. Employees should feel safe to report risks and discuss risk-related concerns without fear of negative consequences.

Practices to Encourage Open Communication

- **Anonymous Reporting:**
  - o Implement anonymous reporting mechanisms, such as hotlines or digital platforms, to allow employees to report risks confidentially.
- **Regular Risk Meetings:**
  - o Hold regular meetings to discuss risk-related issues, share information, and develop collective solutions.
- **Feedback Loops:**
  - o Establish feedback loops to ensure that risk reports and concerns are addressed promptly and effectively.

Step 5: Integrate Risk Management into Decision-Making

Integrating risk management into decision-making processes ensures that risks are considered in strategic and operational decisions. This integration helps align risk management with the organization's overall objectives.

Techniques for Integration

- **Risk Assessments in Planning:**
  - o Include risk assessments as part of the strategic planning and project management processes to evaluate potential risks and their impacts.
- **Decision-Making Tools:**
  - o Use decision-making tools, such as risk matrices and scenario analysis, to assess and compare the risks associated with different options.
- **Cross-Functional Teams:**
  - o Form cross-functional teams to address complex risks that span multiple departments or functions, ensuring a holistic approach to risk management.

Step 6: Promote Continuous Improvement

Continuous improvement is a hallmark of a strong risk management culture. Organizations should regularly review and refine their risk management practices to adapt to new challenges and opportunities.

Methods for Continuous Improvement

- **Regular Audits and Reviews:**
  - o Conduct regular audits and reviews of risk management processes to identify areas for improvement and ensure compliance with best practices.
- **Lessons Learned:**
  - o Analyze past incidents and near-misses to extract lessons learned and apply them to prevent future occurrences.
- **Benchmarking:**
  - o Benchmark the organization's risk management practices against industry standards and peers to identify gaps and opportunities for enhancement.

Developing a robust risk management culture is a continuous process that requires commitment, engagement, and collaboration across the organization. By establishing a clear risk management framework, demonstrating leadership commitment, engaging and educating employees, fostering open communication, integrating risk management into decision-making, and promoting continuous improvement, organizations can build a resilient culture that effectively manages risks and supports long-term success in international trade. Cultivating this culture not only enhances risk management capabilities but also strengthens the overall organizational performance and competitiveness in the global market.

Developing a Risk Management Culture

In today's dynamic business environment, fostering a robust risk management culture is imperative for organizations aiming to navigate uncertainties effectively and achieve long-term success. A risk management culture encompasses the values, beliefs, and behaviors within an organization that prioritize the identification, assessment, and mitigation of risks at all levels. Cultivating such a culture requires commitment, engagement, and collaboration across the organization, from senior leadership to frontline employees (Haywood, 2022).

Understanding Risk Management Culture

A risk management culture goes beyond merely complying with policies and procedures; it involves ingraining risk awareness into the organizational mindset and DNA. Key elements of a risk management culture include:

- **Leadership Commitment:** Senior leaders must champion risk management initiatives, demonstrating a commitment to prioritizing risk awareness and proactive mitigation efforts.
- **Employee Empowerment:** All employees should be empowered to identify and report risks, fostering a culture where risk management is everyone's responsibility.
- **Open Communication:** Encouraging open dialogue and transparency about risks creates an environment where concerns can be addressed promptly and effectively.
- **Continuous Improvement:** Emphasizing continuous learning and improvement ensures that risk management practices evolve in response to changing circumstances and emerging threats.

Steps to Cultivate a Risk Management Culture

1. Establish Clear Expectations

Define clear expectations regarding risk management responsibilities and behaviors across the organization. Develop a formal risk management policy that articulates the organization's commitment to identifying, assessing, and mitigating risks.

2. Provide Training and Education

Equip employees with the knowledge and skills necessary to understand and manage risks effectively. Offer comprehensive training programs covering risk awareness, risk assessment techniques, and the use of risk management tools and processes.

3. Foster Open Communication

Create channels for open communication and feedback regarding risks at all levels of the organization. Encourage employees to report risks and raise concerns without fear of reprisal, fostering a culture of transparency and accountability.

4. Lead by Example

Senior leaders should lead by example, demonstrating a proactive approach to risk management in their decision-making and actions. Incorporate risk considerations into strategic planning discussions and visibly support risk management initiatives.

5. Recognize and Reward Risk Awareness

Acknowledge and reward individuals and teams that demonstrate exemplary risk awareness and proactive risk management efforts. Recognizing and celebrating success reinforces the importance of risk management within the organization.

6. Integrate Risk Management into Processes

Embed risk management into key business processes and decision-making frameworks. Incorporate risk assessments into project planning, performance evaluations, and strategic initiatives to ensure risks are considered at every stage.

7. Promote Continuous Learning

Encourage a culture of continuous learning and improvement by providing opportunities for ongoing training, development, and knowledge sharing related to risk management. Regularly review and update risk management practices in response to lessons learned and emerging trends.

Benefits of a Strong Risk Management Culture

A strong risk management culture offers numerous benefits to organizations, including:

- **Enhanced Resilience:** Organizations are better prepared to anticipate and respond to risks, minimizing their impact on operations and performance.
- **Improved Decision Making:** Risk-aware decision-making leads to more informed and strategic choices that align with organizational objectives and priorities.
- **Increased Stakeholder Confidence:** Stakeholders, including investors, customers, and regulators, have greater confidence in organizations with robust risk management practices.
- **Opportunity Identification:** A proactive approach to risk management enables organizations to identify and capitalize on opportunities for innovation and growth.

Cultivating a risk management culture is not a one-time effort but an ongoing journey that requires dedication, collaboration, and adaptability. By establishing clear expectations, providing training and education, fostering open communication, leading by example, integrating risk management into processes, promoting continuous learning, and recognizing the benefits of a strong risk management culture, organizations can build resilience, enhance decision-making, and achieve sustainable success in today's dynamic business landscape.

Technology and Innovation in Trade Finance

In the rapidly evolving landscape of international trade, technology and innovation play a pivotal role in reshaping traditional trade finance practices and driving efficiency, transparency, and accessibility. From digitizing trade processes to leveraging emerging technologies such as blockchain and artificial intelligence (AI), organizations are embracing innovative solutions to overcome challenges and unlock new opportunities in trade finance.

Digitization of Trade Processes

The digitization of trade processes is revolutionizing the way transactions are conducted, documented, and financed. Key aspects of digitization include:

- **Electronic Documentation:** Moving away from paper-based documentation to electronic formats, reducing administrative burdens and streamlining document exchange.
- **Digital Platforms:** Utilizing online platforms and portals for trade finance activities such as letter of credit issuance, invoice financing, and supply chain management, enabling faster and more efficient transactions.
- **E-signatures and Authentication:** Adopting electronic signatures and advanced authentication methods to verify the authenticity and integrity of trade documents, enhancing security and reducing fraud risks.

Blockchain Technology

Blockchain technology holds immense potential to transform trade finance by providing a secure, decentralized ledger of transactions. Key applications of blockchain in trade finance include:

- **Smart Contracts:** Automating trade finance agreements through self-executing smart contracts, which automatically trigger transactions based on predefined conditions, reducing the need for intermediaries and streamlining processes.

- **Supply Chain Traceability:** Enhancing supply chain transparency and traceability by recording transactional data on a blockchain, enabling stakeholders to track the movement of goods and verify their authenticity.
- **Trade Finance Platforms:** Developing blockchain-based platforms for trade finance, where all parties involved in a transaction can access a shared ledger, improving visibility and reducing disputes.

Artificial Intelligence (AI) and Machine Learning

AI and machine learning technologies are increasingly being leveraged to optimize trade finance processes and decision-making. Key applications of AI in trade finance include:

- **Risk Assessment:** Using AI algorithms to analyze vast amounts of data and assess creditworthiness, enabling more accurate risk assessments and informed lending decisions.
- **Fraud Detection:** Employing machine learning algorithms to detect patterns indicative of fraudulent activities, enhancing fraud prevention measures and reducing financial losses.
- **Trade Finance Analytics:** Harnessing AI-driven analytics to derive insights from trade finance data, such as transaction histories and market trends, enabling organizations to identify opportunities for optimization and growth.

Emerging Trends and Innovations

In addition to digitization, blockchain, and AI, several other emerging trends and innovations are shaping the future of trade finance:

- **Internet of Things (IoT):** Integrating IoT devices into supply chains to capture real-time data on the movement and condition of goods, enhancing visibility and efficiency.

- **Big Data Analytics:** Leveraging big data analytics to analyze large datasets from diverse sources, such as trade flows, economic indicators, and geopolitical developments, to inform trade finance decisions and strategies.
- **Regulatory Technology (RegTech):** Utilizing RegTech solutions to streamline regulatory compliance processes, such as anti-money laundering (AML) and know your customer (KYC) requirements, reducing compliance costs and enhancing efficiency.

CONCLUSION

Technology and innovation are driving a paradigm shift in trade finance, offering unprecedented opportunities for organizations to streamline processes, mitigate risks, and unlock new sources of value. By embracing digitization, blockchain, AI, and other emerging technologies, businesses can enhance efficiency, transparency, and accessibility in trade finance, paving the way for a more inclusive and resilient global trade ecosystem. As organizations continue to adapt and innovate in response to evolving market dynamics, technology will undoubtedly remain a key enabler of success in trade finance now and in the future.

REFERENCES

Akomea-Frimpong, I., Adeabah, D., Ofosu, D., & Tenakwah, E. J. (2022). 'A Review of Studies on Green Finance of Banks, Research Gaps and Future Directions'. *Journal of Sustainable Finance & Investment*, *12*(4), 1241–1264. https://doi.org/DOI:10.1080/20430795.2020.1870202

Al-Banna, A., Rana, Z. A., Yaqot, M., & Menezes, B. (2023). Interconnectedness between Supply Chain Resilience, Industry 4.0, and Investment. *Logistics (Basel)*, *7*(3), 50.

Baines, J., & Hager, S. B. (2022). Commodity traders in a storm: Financialization, corporate power and ecological crisis. *Review of International Political Economy*, *29*(4), 1053–1084.

Baldissera, A. (2023). 'Sustainability Reporting in Banks: History of Studies and a Conceptual Framework for Thinking about the Future by Learning from the Past'. *Corporate Social Responsibility and Environmental Management*, *30*(5), 2385–2405. Advance online publication. DOI: 10.1002/csr.2491

Becker, P. (2023). *Sustainability science: Managing risk and resilience for sustainable development*. Elsevier.

Blessing, L. T. M., & Chakrabarti, A. (2009). *DRM, a Design Research Methodology*. Springer.

Bowen, G. A. (2009, August). 'Document Analysis as a Qualitative Research Method'. *Qualitative Research Journal*, *9*(2), 27–40. DOI: 10.3316/QRJ0902027

Broman, G., & Robèrt, K.-H. (2017). 'A Framework for Strategic Sustainable Development'. *Journal of Cleaner Production*, *140*(January), 17–31. DOI: 10.1016/j.jclepro.2015.10.121

Bryman, A. (2016). *Social Research Methods* (5th ed.). Oxford University Press.

Carr, E. R. (2020). Resilient livelihoods in an era of global transformation. *Global Environmental Change*, *64*, 102155.

Engle, C. R., & van Senten, J. (2022). Resilience of communities and sustainable aquaculture: Governance and regulatory effects. *Fishes*, *7*(5), 268.

Haywood, L. K. (2022). Putting risk management into the corporate sustainability context. *Social Responsibility Journal*, *18*(8), 1485–1504.

Hoffman, J. (2022). *Speculative Futures: Design Approaches to Navigate Change, Foster Resilience, and Co-Create the Citie s We Need.* North Atlantic Books.

Hynes, W., Trump, B. D., Love, P., Kirman, A., Galaitsi, S. E., Ramos, G., & Linkov, I. (2020). Resilient financial systems can soften the next global financial crisis. *Challenge*, *63*(6), 311–318.

Jerez Columbié, Y., & Morrissey, J. (2023). Subaltern learnings: Climate resilience and human security in the Caribbean. *Territory, Politics, Governance*, *11*(1), 19–38. DOI: 10.1080/21622671.2020.1837662

Min, B. H., & Borch, C. (2022). Systemic failures and organizational risk management in algorithmic trading: Normal accidents and high reliability in financial markets. *Social Studies of Science*, *52*(2), 277–302. DOI: 10.1177/03063127211048515 PMID: 34612758

Mullan, M., & Ranger, N. (2022). Climate-resilient finance and investment: Framing paper.

Qiao, R., & Zhao, L. (2023). Highlight risk management in supply chain finance: Effects of supply chain risk management capabilities on financing performance of small-medium enterprises. *Supply Chain Management*, *28*(5), 843–858.

Studzinski, N. G., & Pasteur, L. (2020). *Comprehensive pandemic risk management: A systems approach.* Visiting International Research Fellow Policy Institute, King's College.

Tall, A., Lynagh, S., Blanco Vecchi, C., Bardouille, P., Montoya Pino, F., Shabahat, E., & Kerr, L. (2021). *Enabling Private Investment in Climate Adaptation and Resilience: Current Status.* Barriers to Investment and Blueprint for Action. DOI: 10.1596/35203

West, C. D., Stokeld, E., Campiglio, E., Croft, S., Detges, A., Duranovic, A., & Reyer, C. P. (2021). Europe's cross-border trade, human security and financial connections: A climate risk perspective. *Climate Risk Management, 34*, 100382. DOI: 10.1016/j.crm.2021.100382

Yumagulova, L., & Vertinsky, I. (2021). Managing trade-offs between specific and general resilience: Insights from Canada's Metro Vancouver region. *Cities (London, England), 119*, 103319. DOI: 10.1016/j.cities.2021.103319

Zanotti, L., Ma, Z., Johnson, J. L., Johnson, D. R., Yu, D. J., Burnham, M., & Carothers, C. (2020). Sustainability, resilience, adaptation, and transformation: Tensions and plural approaches. *Ecology and Society, 25*(3), art4. DOI: 10.5751/ES-11642-250304

Chapter 7
Data Visualization and Decision Support Tools for Trade Analysis

S. Nanduja
Nehru Institute of Technology, India

B. Thirumoorthi
Nehru Institute of Technology, India

D. Gayathri
Nehru Institute of Technology, India

E. Manoj
Nehru Institute of Technology, India

ABSTRACT

This abstract presents a thorough method for improving trade analysis by combining data visualization strategies with decision support technologies. This chapter's first section addresses the value of trade analysis in the modern, globalized economy. It emphasizes how crucial data-driven insights are for supply chain optimization, spotting developing markets, and boosting competitiveness. It also highlights the necessity of creative approaches to effectively manage the enormous volume of trade data. Then it explores data visualization's function in trade analysis. Charts, graphs,

DOI: 10.4018/979-8-3693-6592-2.ch007

and maps are examples of visual representations that provide easy ways to study large, complex datasets and spot patterns that might not be seen in raw data. Users can dynamically filter, dive down, and examine trade data from several viewpoints by utilizing interactive visualization tools, which facilitates more informed decision-making. At the core of effective trade analysis lies the ability to process and interpret vast amounts of data.

INTRODUCTION

Businesses and governments need to be able to efficiently assess large amounts of data to make well-informed decisions in the quickly changing world of global trade. In this scenario, a data visualization and decision assistance tool for trade analysis is a crucial tool. It offers a thorough platform for gathering, preparing, evaluating, and displaying trade data, empowering participants to make data-driven decisions that can improve their competitive edge, streamline their supply chains, and react early to shifts in the market (Knaflic, 2015).

The nature of trade data is intrinsically complicated, encompassing a multitude of measures including volume of imports and exports, trade balances, commodity prices, and market patterns among diverse nations and regions. Simplifying this complexity is the main goal of a data visualization and decision support tool (Meloncon & Warner, 2017). Through interactive visualizations, users may immediately understand underlying patterns, correlations, and trends that would otherwise be hidden in standard tabular data formats, turning raw data into clear and actionable insights.

Sturdy data collection procedures are the first step towards building an efficient trade analysis process. It combines information from several trustworthy sources, such as trade publications, financial markets, and official databases like UN Comtrade and the World Bank. The tool can employ APIs to retrieve real-time trade information in addition to static data to guarantee that users have the most recent insights at their fingertips (Rashidi, Maria et al, 2018).

After the data is gathered, it goes through a thorough processing stage. This includes resolving missing numbers, standardizing the data for consistency, and cleaning to remove discrepancies. The process of converting unstructured data into a structured format makes analysis and visualization simpler. Following processing, the data is kept in databases to facilitate effective retrieval and querying, enabling historical analysis and real-time monitoring. The tool's user interface is made with easy-to-use navigation and interactive features that improve the user experience in mind (Budiharto, W. 2021). Thanks to customization possibilities, users can create customized visualizations, modify their views, and filter data to suit their requirements. Furthermore, the ability to export visualizations and data makes it easier to create reports and presentations, which supports more extensive decision-making and communication processes (Ghazali et al., 2022).

To sum up, in the current trading environment, data visualization and decision support tool for trade research is a priceless asset. Utilizing sophisticated data processing, analytical methods, and user-friendly visualizations, gives users the ability to make wise judgments, anticipate market developments, and confidently negotiate the challenges of international trade (Leung et al., 2017). A technology like this gives companies trying to streamline their supply chains and governments trying to improve trade regulations the knowledge and insight they need to succeed in a changing global economy.

Figure 1. Data visualization and trade analysis

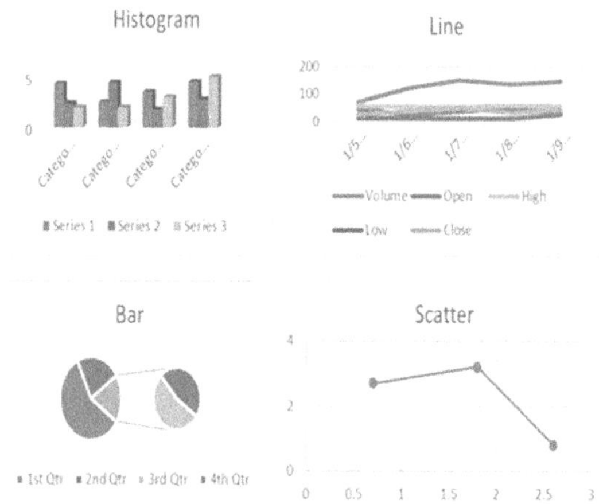

APPEARANCE

Recognizing Patterns and Trends

Price Movements: Charting past commodity, stock, or currency prices can be used to see upward or downward patterns.

Volume Analysis: Trading volumes over time can be displayed on charts, indicating spikes or troughs in activity that could be indicators of mood in the market.

Evaluation via Comparison

Market Comparison: Bar charts, scatter plots, and heat maps can be used to compare several markets, sectors, or assets side by side to identify correlations and relative performance.

Time-Series Analysis: Line graphs are useful for comparing the performance of several assets over a given amount of time.

Taking Charge of Risks

Volatility Visualization: Traders can better comprehend the risk involved in a given deal by referring to graphs that illustrate volatility, such as volatility indices or Bollinger Bands.

Loss/Profit Distribution: To help with risk assessment, box plots or histograms can display the distribution of returns (Meloncon & Warner, 2017).

Recognizing Possibilities

Technical Indicators: Traders can identify possible buy or sell signals with the use of visual tools like as moving averages, MACD, and RSI.

Market Sentiment: Sentiment analysis graphics from news and social media, like word clouds or sentiment trend lines, can show the mood of the market.

Performance Tracking Portfolio Performance:

A trading portfolio's performance and diversity can be monitored using pie charts, area charts, and other visual aids.

Benchmarking: Individual asset performance can be compared using visualizations to indices or benchmarks.

Emphasizing Distinctions

Outlier Detection: Box plots and scatter plots can be used to identify outliers or odd trends that might require more research.

Pattern Recognition: Formations that portend future price movements can be found using candlestick charts and other pattern recognition software (Ward et al., 2015).

Simplifying Complex Data Summary Statistics:

Quick insights can be obtained from dashboards that highlight important statistics (such the Sharpe ratio and average return).

Interactive Dashboards: Providing users with the ability to manipulate and filter data, as well as zoom in and out, can enhance the usability and accessibility of complicated datasets (Knaflic, 2015).

Figure 2. Steps for using data visualization tools for trade analysis

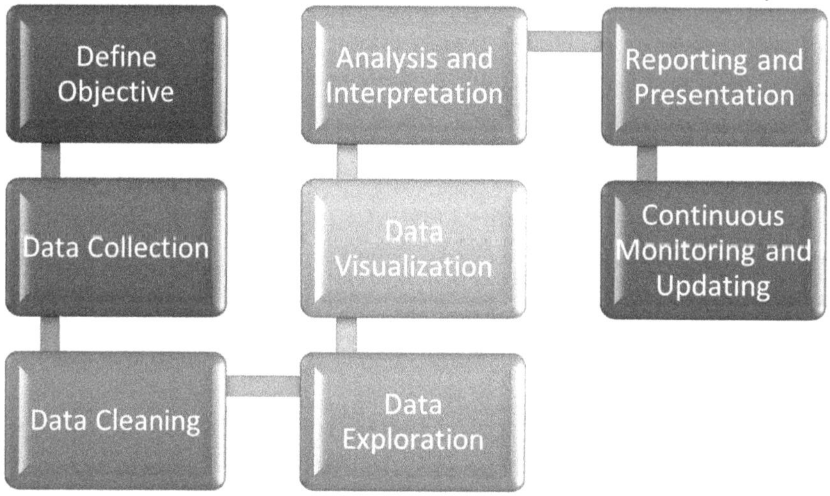

Define Objective:

Objective Setting: Determine the precise queries or objectives of the trade study, such as finding lucrative transactions, examining market patterns, or assessing risk.

Data Collection:

Data Sources: Compile information from pertinent sources, such as market data, trade data from the past, economic indicators, and other financial data.

Data Integration: If required, merge data from several sources.

Data Cleaning:

Managing Missing Values: Take care of incomplete or missing data.

Data transformation: It is transforming data into an analysis-ready format by adding new variables, aggregating it, or standardizing it.

Data Exploration:

Initial Analysis: To comprehend the fundamental properties of the data, apply summary statistics and exploratory data analysis (EDA) methods.

Determine Trends: Examine the data for trends, patterns, and anomalies.

Data Visualization:

Choose Appropriate Visuals: Select the right type of visualization (e.g., line charts, bar charts, scatter plots, heatmaps) based on the analysis objectives.

Create Visualizations: Use the selected tool to create visualizations. They are,

Figure 3. Tools

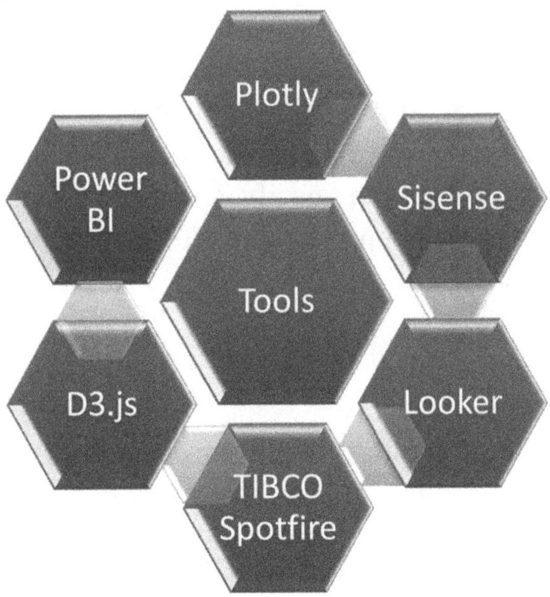

Plotly:

An open-source graphing package called Plotly creates online graphs that are interactive and suitable for publications. It's commonly used to create Python, R, and JavaScript interactive charts, dashboards, and visualizations. Additionally, Plotly provides Plotly Dash, a paid platform for creating analytical web applications (Ceballos et al., 2016).

Sisense:

Sisense is a business intelligence tool that lets users combine, examine, and display data from many sources. Large data volumes can be handled by it, and it offers tools for making interactive dashboards and reports. Sisense is well-known for its in-chip technology, which expedites analytics and data processing (Budiharto, 2021).

Looker:

Google Cloud now includes Looker, a business intelligence and data visualization application. It is intended to make it simple for businesses to investigate, evaluate, and disseminate real-time business analytics. Teams working with data can specify relationships in their data and produce strong, repeatable computations with Looker's special modeling language, LookML.

Tibco Spotfire:

Predictive analytics, business intelligence, and data visualization are all provided by the analytics platform TIBCO Spotfire. It enables users to build interactive dashboards and visualizations as well as conduct thorough data analysis. Spotfire's capacity to manage complicated data and offer profound insights makes it useful across a range of sectors.

D3.js:

A JavaScript framework called D3.js (Data-Driven Documents) is used to create dynamic, interactive data visualizations in web browsers. It makes data come to life with HTML, SVG, and CSS. Because of D3.js's great flexibility and capability, programmers may design intricate data representations and unique visualizations.

POWER BI:

Microsoft created Power BI, a corporate analytics application that lets users share insights, display data, and make decisions based on that data. It includes dynamic dashboards, interacts with multiple data sources, and has strong reporting features for efficiently analyzing and presenting data (Triantaphyllou, 2013).

ANALYSIS AND INTERPRETATION

Analyze Visuals: Gain understanding by interpreting the visuals. Validate predictions or hypotheses based on the visual data using hypothesis testing.
Reporting and Presentation: Build Dashboards: Gather visualizations and arrange them into dashboards for a thorough overview.
Share Insights: Using interactive dashboards, reports, or presentations, give the results to stakeholders.
Continuous Monitoring and Updating: Real-time Data: To maintain current visuals, set up real-time data sources as needed.
Iterative Improvement: As new data becomes available or business needs change, continuously improve analyses and representations.

How will Data Visualization Utilize the Decision-Making

Simplifies Data Interpretation: Compared to text or raw figures, visualizations such as charts, graphs, and maps convey data in a format that is easier to understand. Decision-makers can quickly and easily understand important information because of this simplification (Leung et al., 2017).

Finds Patterns and Trends: Visual tools draw attention to data that spreadsheets could miss, such as outliers, correlations, and trends. This facilitates the long-term pattern recognition that is essential to strategic planning.

Facilitates Comparison: Using visual aids makes it easier to compare various data sets or performance measures. The comparison of variables side by side is made simple by scatter plots, pie charts, and bar charts.

Improves Communication: For stakeholders with different degrees of data literacy, visualizations offer a universal language that may efficiently communicate complicated ideas. This enhances dialogue.

CONCLUSION

To sum up, decision support tools for data visualization are essential for trade analysis since they provide a clear understanding of intricate information. These technologies enable stakeholders to make well-informed decisions, recognize patterns, and optimize tactics for improved trade performance by converting raw data into actionable information. Users may confidently and precisely traverse the ever-changing global trade scene thanks to their detailed infographics. These tools are vital resources in the data-driven world of today, helping to create sustainable growth in trade operations and facilitate effective decision-making.

REFERENCES

Bezerianos, A. F. Chevalier, P. Dragicevic, N. Elmqvist, and J. D. Fekete (2010). Graphdice: A system for exploring multivariate social networks," in Proceedings of the 12th Eurographics / IEEE VGTC Conference on Visualization, ser. EuroVis10. Chichester, GBR: The Eurographs Association & John Wiley & Sons, Ltd., 2010, p. 863872. DOI: 10.1111/j.1467-8659.2009.01687.x

Ceballos, B. M. Lamata, and D. Pelta (2016) A comparative analysis of multi-criteria decision-making methods," in Prog Artif Intell, p. 315322DOI: 10.1111/j.1467-8659.2009.01687.x

Booshehrian, M., Möller, T., Peterman, R. M., & Munzner, T. (2014). Vismon: M. Sedlmair, C. Heinzl, S. Bruckner, H. Piringer, and T. Möller, "Visual parameter space analysis: A conceptual framework,". *IEEE Transactions on Visualization and Computer Graphics, TVCG, 20*(12), 2161–2170. PMID: 26356930

Boukhelifa, N., Cancino, W., Bezerianos, A., & Lutton, E. "Evolutionary visual exploration: evaluation with expert users," in Computer Graphics Forum, 32(3) pt1. Wiley Online Library, pp. 31-40.

Cash, D., Clark, W., Alcock, F., Dickson, N., Selin, N., Guston, D., Jäger, J., & Mitchell, R. (2003). Knowledge Systems for Sustainable Development. *Proceedings of the National Academy of Sciences of the United States of America, 100*(14), 8086–8091. DOI: 10.1073/pnas.1231332100 PMID: 12777623

Chen, C. (2006). Detecting and Visualising Emerging Trends and Transient Patterns in Scientific Literature. *Journal of the Association for Information Science and Technology, 57*, 359–377.

Elmqvist, N., Dragicevic, P., & Fekete, J. (2008). Rolling the dice: Multidimensional visual exploration using scatterplot matrix navigation. *IEEE Transactions on Visualization and Computer Graphics, TVCG, 14*(6), 1539–1148. PMID: 18989007

Erl, T., Khattak, W., & Buhler, P. (2016). *Big data fundamentals: Concepts, drivers and techniques*. Prentice Hall.

Booshehrian, M., Moller, T., Pterman, R., & Munzner, T. (2012). Facilitating analysis of trade-offs, uncertainty, and sensitivity in fisheries management decision making." in *Computer Graphics Forum, 31*(3) pt3. Wiley Online Library, pp. 1235-1244.

French, S., Carter, E., & Niculae, C. (2007). Decision support in nuclear and radiological emergency situations: Are we too focused on models and technology? *International Journal of Risk Assessment and Management*.

French, S., & Turoff, M. (2007). Decision Support Systems. *Communications of the ACM*, *50*(3), 39–40. DOI: 10.1145/1226736.1226762

Friendly, M., & Denis, D. J. (2001). Milestones in the history of thematic cartography, statistical graphics, and data visualization.https://www.datavis.ca/milestones/

Ghazali, A. F., Alias, S., & Amran, Z. A. (2020). Decision Support Systems in a Smart City: A Review, International Conference on Industry 4.0: A Global Revolution in Business and Productivity, SEGi University Kota Damansara.

Ghazali, A. F., Mokhtar, N. A., Suhaimi, A., & Yusoff, R. M. (2021). Visual Decision Support System Model for Managing Unemployment by Hybrid Education. *Emerging Advances in Integrated Technology*, *2*(2), 16–22.

Ghazali, A. F., Noor, N. M. M., Mohemad, R., & Saman, M. Y. M. (2016). Development of a Decision Support System with Risk: Supporting Police and Government in Crime Prevention. *Research Journal of Applied Sciences*, *11*(6), 340–344.

Ghazali, A. F., & Suhaimi, A. (2020). Visual Decision Support System for Food Security, *ASEAN Workshop on Information Science and Technology (AWIST 2020)*.

Ghazali, A. F., Suhaimi, A., Yusoff, R. M., & Mokhtar, N. A. (2022). Mobile-based Visual Decision Support System for Hybrid Learning in Post-COVID-19 Pandemic, Proceedings of the 2nd International Conference on Design Industries & Creative Culture, Design Decoded 2021, 24th, European Union Digital Library.

Gratzl, S., Lex, A., Gehlenborg, N., Pfister, H., & Streit, M. (2013). Lineup: Visual analysis of multi-attribute rankings," IEEE Transactions on Visualization and Computer Graphics. *TVCG, 19*(12), 2277–2286.

S. Pajer, M. Streit, T. Torsney-Weir, F. Spechtenhauser, T. Möller, and H. Piringer (2016). Weightlifter: Visual weight space exploration for multi- criteria decision making," IEEE Transactions on Visualization and Computer Graphics, *TVCG, 23*(1), pp. 611-620, 2016.

Knaflic, C. N. (2015). *Storytelling with data: A data visualization guide for business professionals*. Wiley.

Kuhlman, T., & John, F. (2010). What is Sustainability? *Sustainability (Basel), 2*(11), 3436–3448. Advance online publication. DOI: 10.3390/su2113436

Leung, X. Y., Sun, J., & Bai, B. (2017). Bibliometric of Social Media Research: A Co-citation and Co-word Analysis. *International Journal of Hospitality Management, 66*, 35–45. DOI: 10.1016/j.ijhm.2017.06.012

Meloncon, L., & Warner, E. (2017). Data visualizations: A literature review and opportunities for technical and professional communication. Professional Communication Conference (ProComm), IEEE International, Madison, WI, USA. DOI: 10.1109/IPCC.2017.8013960

Mohemad, R., Hamdan, A. R., Othman, Z. A., & Noor, N. M. M. (2010). Decision support systems (DSS) in construction tendering processes, *International Journal of Computer Science Issues.*

Noor, N. M. M., Ghazali, A. F., Mohd, M. Y. B., & Nor, M. N. M. (2014). Framework of Risk-based Decision Support System in Crime Investigation, *International Conference Decision Support System Technology*, 447-458.

Perianes-Rodriguez, A., Waltman, L., & van Eck, N. J. (2016). Constructing Bibliometric Networks: A Comparison Between Full and Fractional Counting. *Journal of Informetrics, 10*(4), 1178–1195. DOI: 10.1016/j.joi.2016.10.006

Rashidi, M., Ghodrat, M., Samali, B., & Mohammadi, M. (2018). *Decision Support Systems*. Advance online publication. DOI: 10.5772/intechopen.79390

Jain, Rajni. (2016). Decision Support Systems: an Overview.DOI: 10.5772/intechopen.79390

Seuring, S., & Müller, M. (2008). From a Literature Review to a Conceptual Framework for Sustainable Supply Chain Management. *Journal of Cleaner Production*, *16*, 1699–1710.

Shneiderman, B. (1996). The eyes have it: A task by data type taxonomy for information visualizations. *Proceedings of IEEE Symposium on Visual Languages Boulder*, Colorado.

Triantaphyllou (2013). Multi-criteria decision making methods: A comparative study," Springer Science & Business Media, *44*.

Budiharto, W. (2021). Data science approach to stock prices forecasting in Indonesia during Covid-19 using Long Short-Term Memory (LSTM). *Journal of Big Data*, *8*, 47.

Ward, M. O., Grinstein, G., & Keim, D. (2015). Interactive data visualization: Foundations, techniques, and applications. https://ebookcentral.proquest.com/lib/uql/detail.action?docID=1786691

Wikipedia. (2017). Information visualization. https://en.wikipedia.org/wiki/Information_visualization

Wikipedia. (2017). Scientific visualization. https://en.wikipedia.org/wiki/Scientific_visualization

Chapter 8
Effect of Behavioral Biases on Investment Decisions Using Big Data to Avoid Bias

Kesu Singh
Chandigarh University, India

Satinder Pal Singh
Chandigarh University, India

Nitin Pathak
https://orcid.org/0000-0002-8062-0554
Chandigarh University, India

ABSTRACT

Based on the presumption that individuals make fair predictions about the future and make rational decisions, the subject of finance has developed during the past few decades. Different behavioral biases have a significant impact on investors' decision-making processes. The study's major goal is to identify the cognitive and emotional biases that influence investor decisions and to ascertain whether there is a connection between behavioral biases and investment choices. The major goal of the study is to identify and rank the behavioral aspects that affect investors' decision-making

DOI: 10.4018/979-8-3693-6592-2.ch008

processes. The study also explores how using big data can prevent bias in decision making. Through a survey, information was gathered from 396 people in Northern India, which was then examined. The results of this study suggest that emotional and cognitive biases might affect investing decisions. Both constructs have significant effects and is important for the development of attitudes towards investment decisions as well as for investment intentions.

INTRODUCTION

According to the definition of finance, it is the study of how humans distribute scarce resources and how they are managed, acquired, and invested over time. Because it is anticipated that they would accurately interpret the newly available information that makes the financial markets efficient, the essential tenet of classical finance theories is the rationality of market participants. One of the most significant contributions to the subject of finance is the Efficient Market Hypothesis, which was first proposed by Markowitz in 1952 and further refined by Fama in 1971.

Researchers have long been interested in how people make decisions. Early writings on the subject e.g. (Adam & Shauki, 2014).; (Chittedi, 2014) had taken an economic stance. The utility hypothesis, which advocated that people make decisions by taking the predicted results of such decisions into account, was one of the widely accepted theories at the time. In this regard, a logical decision-maker will use all the information at their disposal, analyze the possibilities, and choose the ideal action to take (Schiffman & Kanuk, 2007). Prior research argued in favor of the rational decision-making of the individual. However, these ideas are no longer seen as being plausible because it is uncommon for people to have access to sufficient knowledge, incentive, or time to make such a perfectly sensible decision (Simon, 1997). Humans do not "naturally" make decisions in the way that a logical person should, according to behavioural economics. Rather, it is a widely acknowledged truth that people frequently make poor decisions (Tomer, 2016). People are frequently characterized as looking for adequate options rather than the best ones when making decisions (Tversky & Kahneman, 1974).

Understanding investors' cognitive, social, and emotional biases and how these biases affect market pricing, returns, and resource allocation are the main goals of behavioural finance theories. As a result, behavioural finance is a modern science that employs psychological theories to comprehend investor and financial market behaviour.

According to (Dargham, 2009), behavioural finance has posed a challenge to traditional finance since it focuses on how investors respond to information that is freely available to them, which in turn helps to comprehend the investors' behaviour and actual market practices. As a result, behavioural finance educates investors about their cognitive biases and empowers them to make wiser financial choices under challenging circumstances. According to (Shefrin, 2002), practitioners learning behavioural finance should be able to see their own mistakes as well as those of others and make an effort to avoid them in their subsequent investment decisions.

Behavioral bias-influenced decisions frequently result in poorer-than-ideal investment returns (Shukla et al., 2020). When making investing decisions, investors are vulnerable to psychological anomalies known as behavioural biases, which can result in illogical choices and a failure to meet investment objectives (Kapoor & Prosad, 2017). identified behavioural biases as the cause of investors' illogical behaviour and defined them as instruments to comprehend the deviations from the economic fundamentals of rationality while making an investment choice behavior in investment decisions hindering the grown perspective.

It is proven that even in the present era, it is important to comprehend how these biases affect investors' psychological states. By conquering and avoiding the ensuing mistake of judgment, individual investors might enhance their performance by concentrating on these biases (Shabarisha, 2015; Sahi, 2012). Due to internal biases, there has been a noticeable rise in the number of investors who are more focused on a small number of investment options and frequently overlook everything else. Given their rising numbers, it is crucial to comprehend these investors' motivations since they are creating unanticipated momentum in the stock market (Wood & Zaichkowsky, 2004).

The researchers had several queries based on the viewpoints that were previously presented. Which behavioural biases affect the decisions made when making investments? Do the financial markets still exhibit these biases that have been identified throughout the years? Do these biases still affect, or are they still important, retail investors' judgments on what to invest in the financial markets? By analyzing and analyzing their present significance in the financial markets and the extent to which they influence the investment decisions of retail investors in the target demographic, the research seeks to provide an answer to this question. Does the link between these investing biases and investment decisions become tempered by the selected sector of the market? The purpose of the research is to determine if retail investors' preferences—that is, their preferred investment sector in the context of the current study—have an impact on how much behavioural biases influence investing decisions. As previously mentioned, demographic and regional variables impact how much these biases affect decision-making. One such element considered in this study is the favorite investment sector of the retail participants in the research. Studies focusing on the impact of behavioural biases on investing decisions are few. By investigating the impact of behavioural bias on investment decisions made in the insurance and pharmaceutical sectors, this study aims to close the gap. Keeping all of these topics in mind, the study's researchers aimed to identify behavioural and internal biases and their impact on return investors' investing choices. Therefore, the study's goal was to determine how various behavioural biases affected investors' investing decisions.

Humans are born with behavioural biases, which can influence financial decisions. The following are a few typical behavioural biases that may influence investing decisions:

Bias in confirmation: This is the propensity to look for evidence to support our preexisting opinions and disregard evidence to the contrary. For instance, an investor may ignore unfavorable news or analysis in favor of information that supports their choice to purchase a specific stock.

The propensity to base our judgments unduly on the first piece of information we are given is known as anchoring bias. An investor can, for example, base their selections only on the historical performance of a certain stock, disregarding shifts in the market or other variables.

The inclination to fear losses more than we appreciate gains is known as loss aversion. An investor can be reluctant to purchase a well-performing stock, for instance, out of concern that its value would decrease.

The propensity to fabricate tales to justify actions or situations is known as narrative bias. An investor could fabricate a story about a stock's success, for example, ignoring factual information.

Psychological Strategies for Addressing Behavioural Biases in Investing

The psychological aspects that affect our decisions must be understood to address behavioural biases in investing. The following techniques can assist investors in overcoming their behavioural biases:

Take a long-term view: Rather than concentrating on ephemeral market swings, investors should consider long-term objectives. Investors can avoid rash judgments based on transient market patterns by adopting a long-term view.
Establish definite goals: Before investing, investors should clarify their risk tolerance and investment goals. This can assist them in maintaining goal focus and preventing emotional decision-making.
Spread out your holdings: Investors can lower their risk of suffering losses as a result of a single stock's underperformance by spreading their holdings. Additionally, it can assist investors avoid the anchoring bias by minimizing their reliance on the performance of a particular asset.
Employ data-driven decision-making: When choosing investments, investors must rely on impartial data and research. Taking into account all of the facts at hand can assist them in avoiding confirmation bias and narrative bias.
Engage in mindfulness: Deep breathing exercises and other mindfulness techniques can make investors more conscious of their thoughts and feelings. This can assist them in maintaining focus on long-term objectives and avoiding rash judgments based on emotions.

Impact of Behavioural Biases on Investing

Investment decisions can be significantly impacted by behavioural biases. Confirmation bias can lead an investor, for example, to ignore all the bad news or research and instead purchase a stock that has been performing well. If the stock performs poorly, this might result in large losses. Similar to this, an investor susceptible to anchoring bias would buy a stock based only on its historical performance, disregarding shifts in the market. In addition, if the stock's performance deteriorates, losses may result.

Behavioral biases have a big influence on investing decisions and frequently provide investors worse than worse-than-ideal results. These psychologically based biases have the potential to impair judgment and skew the way that decisions are made. As per Barber and Odean (2000), investors may become overconfident in their ability to forecast market movements due to overconfidence bias, which in turn can result in excessive trading and increased transaction costs. Similarly, loss aversion bias makes investors put minimizing profits ahead of preventing losses, which makes them reluctant to sell underperforming investments—even in situations where doing so could make sense (Kahneman & Tversky, 1979). Confirmation bias is another factor that may affect investing decisions. Investors often ignore contradicting facts in favor of information that supports their preexisting ideas, which results in a lack of portfolio diversity and higher risk (Odean, 1998).

These biases have practical significance for investors and have been well-researched and documented in academic studies. Investors can lessen the influence of these biases on decision-making processes by being aware of and cognizant of them. Behavioral biases may be countered and more logical and effective investing results can result from strategies including searching out varied opinions, keeping a diversified portfolio, and following a disciplined investment strategy (Statman, 2017).

Behavioural Finance and Behavioural Biases

The study of psychological effects on investors and financial markets is known as behavioural finance. The theory that describes the psychology of investor behaviour and how it affects decision-making is a relatively recent one. Its recent surge in stock market investments has been enormous. To explain why investors make irrational decisions, behavioural finance is a subfield of behavioural economics that combines classical economics and finance with psychological, cognitive, and behavioural principles. The behavioural approach, in contrast to classical finance, assumes that arbitrage leverage has limitations and that not all investors are logical. When making investing decisions, individual investors are mostly influenced by extraneous information and emotional factors (Banerjee, 2011; Suresh G, 2021).

Behavioral biases may be categorized as either cognitive errors or emotional biases.

Basic statistical, information-processing, or memory mistakes are the root causes of cognitive errors. They usually come from flawed logic. Emotional biases, on the other hand, are rooted in instinct or intuition and typically arise from reasoning that is swayed by emotions. Since cognitive mistakes are the result of flawed thinking rather than emotional biases, they are easier to remedy. Since emotional biases are founded on feelings, which can be hard to alter, they are more difficult to overcome.

Cognitive mistakes can be further divided into two groups: information-processing biases and belief persistence biases. Errors in belief persistence indicate a propensity to hold onto beliefs. Errors in statistics, information processing, or memory keep the misconception alive. Belief persistence biases and the psychological notion of cognitive dissonance are strongly associated. On the other hand, biases in the processing of information cause it to be interpreted and utilized in an illogical or unreasonable way. The biases associated with belief persistence include hindsight, confirmation, conservatism, representativeness, and illusion of control.

BACKGROUND

Enhancing the way financial markets make decisions requires an in-depth understanding of how biases distort investment decisions and how to utilize big data to reduce bias. The current research is important in allowing insight into how cognitive biases may frame judgment and lead to suboptimal investment decisions by interacting with the independent variables and investment outcomes. Big data provides the possibility to thoroughly analyze extensive data sets and to identify patterns, correlations, or anomalies that would not be detectable using other, more traditional methods. Investors, fund managers, and financial institutions may find ways to reduce bias, enhance the quality of decision-making, and consequently enhance investment performance if they know the subtle mechanisms that the biases employ and if they use current analytics in this direction. Fundamentally, the present study represents a shift in the paradigm in the way that biases in the investment decision process are understood and addressed. Unlike traditional research, which often relies on small sample sizes and subjective estimations, the use of big data enables a detailed and objective investigation of investor behavior within various market conditions and demographic groups. Taking account of various factors that influence investment decision-making, from individual views to more holistic market trends, aggregated and processed data are drawn out from numerous sources that include, but are not limited to, financial transactions, sentiment on social media, and macroeconomic indices. By doing so, the entire process affords a comprehensive view of the dynamics at work, allowing more insight into the root causes of bias and how these impact performance in investment. Additionally, merging ideas of behavioural economics and decision theories with big data analytics, the study offers a new paradigm to understand and eliminate biases in investment decision-making. By bringing to light the underlying mechanisms related to cognitive processes that result in the creation and persistence of bias, this paper throws light on the psychological drivers governing investor behaviour. It does so by drawing on knowledge from psychology, sociology, and neuroscience. The research therefore adds to our theoretical knowledge of prejudice and provides useful insights for the development of strategies and treatments that ameliorate such effects. The variety of ways and strategies elicited to overcome biases and enhance investment outcomes include: nudging, personalized recommendation systems, and educational initiatives.

LITERATURE REVIEW

These days, behavioural finance is emerging as a fresh field. It makes an effort to research the investors' unreasonable actions. Many behavioral economists think that the fundamental premise of classical finance—that people are rational—is wildly unrealistic.

The study of the influence of psychology on the behaviour of financial practitioners and the subsequent impact on markets" is known as behavioural finance (Sewell, 2007).

The behavioural finance reviews conducted between the late 1970s and 2005 demonstrated that psychological research will serve as a foundation for explaining irrational behaviour, which gives rise to the core ideas of behavioural finance. Kumar and Goyal (2015), According to the utility theory (EUT), an investor's investing behavior is entirely dependent on the risk involved with each alternative and his utility if he wants to evaluate all of his options and come to a balanced conclusion. The anticipated utility theory was examined by (Kahneman & Tversky, 1979) as a "descriptive model of decision-making under risk," and it was discovered that preferences for risky prospects displayed few widespread effects that were at odds with the fundamental utility theory. As a result, they created a new theory known as prospect theory.

According to Shiller (2003), the EMH hypothesis started to gain traction in academic circles in the 1970s. A series of anomaly findings and signs of excessive return volatility in the 1980s weakened the validity of this idea. To address these anomalies and excessive volatility, behavioural finance, a new academic field that combines sociology and psychology with finance theories, was created. In the 1990s, there were a few significant advances, such as feedback theories and other things. Behavioral finance attempts to integrate the knowledge from theories about psychology and finance to establish a connection between human behaviour and market occurrences. However, behavioral finance seeks to recognize and examine these biases (Schiereck et al., 1999).

Daniel Kahneman and Amos Tversky, two eminent psychologists, created the prospect theory. They provided examples of how investors defy the fundamental utility principle. They experimented with how alternative ways of framing the same events affected investor choices. The experiment's participants had to select one of two possibilities. Eighty percent of the participants picked the first choice, which had a 100% chance of winning $4,000 and an 80% chance of earning $5,000. According to anticipated utility theory, people in the two scenarios listed above should make the same decision because the outcomes are the same. As a result, people will give preference to some outcomes over others (Kahneman & Tversky, 1979). So, according to prospect theory, a category of delusions that might influence the decision-making process includes loss aversion, mental accounting, and regret aversion.

In a recent study, Bhatia et al. (2021) examined how behavioural characteristics are used to construct the theories of traditional finance and behavioural finance. The writers want all investors to understand the psychological aspects of investing and how they affect logical decision-making. Research by Dangi and Kohli (2018) and Sharma et al. (2021) focuses on the investment choices made by female entrepreneurs and looks at how women's conduct influences these choices. Using the investor type as a moderating role, Kappal and Rastogi (2020) investigated the influence of behavioural biases, such as the disposition effect, herding effect, and overconfidence bias, on investing decisions. According to their findings, while making investment decisions, the moderating influence is negative in the herding effect and positive in the overconfidence bias. Lather et al. (2020) conducted research on the influence of several biases on investing decisions, including overconfidence, self-attribution, framing effect, regret avoidance, overreaction, and reference point bias in both male and female investors. The study found that overconfidence bias, self-attribution bias, and regret avoidance bias were significantly impacted by gender. According to research by Hassan et al. (2013), after looking at people's conduct, the theory of traditional finance differs from the contemporary theory. The study looks at biases' advantages and disadvantages as well as how they affect people's financial contentment. In the cases of biases including overconfidence, dependence on expert prejudice, and self-control, the findings were found to be favorable and substantial. In a 2017 study, Sahi examined the investing choices made by professional and individual investors by contrasting them using various methods and resources. They found that the influence of long-term investment decisions is 1.5 times greater than that of short-term ones. Heuristic biases affect investors who make short-term decisions. Investors are impacted by heuristic bias when assessing their financial condition and past performance, which demonstrates how to overcome behavioral biases and make reasonable judgments (Rauwerda & De Graaf, 2021).

Individual Investor's Decision-Making and Behavioral Biases

In behavioural psychology and finance, Baker et al., (2019) have found several prevalent behavioural biases among investors. Behavioral biases often lead to anomalies in the way investors make decisions. Researchers have looked into how cognitive biases impact the decision-making of individual investors in different nations and societies. Ahmad and Shah (2020) discovered that investors make flawed judgments as a result of human psychology. When creating investment portfolios and considering other more general factors that impact investment decisions, behavioural biases like herding and heuristics have an impact (Gavrilakis & Floros, 2021).

Overconfidence Bias

According to Bhandari and Deaves (2006), overconfidence bias is the tendency for an individual to overestimate their knowledge, abilities, and the veracity of their facts. Another reason for the high market trade volumes is overconfidence. According to research by Adil, Singh, and Ansari (2021) and Pradikasari and Isbanah (2018), it significantly negatively affects investor decision-making. Overconfidence can impair an investor's performance and capacity to make decisions, claim Ahmad & Shah, 2020. Nonetheless, understanding finance and recognizing risk may help investors make better decisions.

Herding Bias

The term "herding" refers to the behavior of investors who follow trends and take other people's advice (Clarke et al., 2014). According to Rasool & Ullah, 2020, the herding effect is a phenomenon in which an investor's propensity is described as copying the actions of others, enabling investors to avoid feeling bad about the choices they make for themselves. A study conducted in China by Feng and Seasholes (2004) found a substantial correlation between investment choice and the herding behavior of individual Chinese investors. The relationship between herd behavior and individual investors was also documented by Gavrilakis and Floros (2021) and Kumar and Goyal (2016).

Disposition Bias

Disposition bias was characterized by Fogel and Berry (2010) as the tendency for people to regret selling a lucrative investment too soon and to hang onto a failing one for an excessive amount of time. According to empirical research, investors are more likely to keep losing equities and sell appreciating or winning stocks (Baker et al., 2019). Research by Mittal (2019), and Kumar and Goyal (2016) also discovered the impact of disposition bias on investors' financial choices. Prasad et al., (2015) similarly conclude that disposition bias has a big influence on judgment.

Risk Aversion

According to Tversky and Kahneman (1974), people are risk-averse by nature and value losses more highly than equivalent gains. They use bonded logic to make their judgments. According to Rasool & Ullah, 2020, an investor would choose the least hazardous investment option from the available options if the portfolio theory were to be true. Research by Ball et al. (2010) and Maxfield et al., (2010) found that risk aversion has a major influence on financial decision-making. Additionally, they stated that compared to males, women are more likely to be risk-averse.

Representativeness Bias

Representativeness bias is defined by Busenitz and Barney (1997) as a phenomenon arising from a small number of observations, typically from non-random and small samples. According to Daniel et al. (1998), it has a big positive impact on investors' reactions to the market and their decision-making. According to 2020 research by Ahmad, Shah, and Abbass, heuristic bias representativeness negatively affects entrepreneurs' strategic choices in international marketplaces.

Anchoring and Adjustment Bias

Another psychological heuristic that highlights people's tendency to base their decisions exclusively on the first or most relevant information they receive is anchoring bias (Shah et al., 2018). Even with a theoretical grasp of financial behavior, the anchoring effect endures (Palm & Andersson, 2020). This bias, which is still being studied, caused participants to generate predictions by starting with an initial value and progressively increasing it to achieve a final response. Shah et al., (2018) observed that anchoring bias considerably and negatively affects investors' decisions, whereas Jain et al., (2019) found it to be significantly and favorably influential.

MAIN FOCUS OF THE STUDY

USING BIG DATA TO AVOID BIAS IN INVESTMENT DECISIONS

Big data analytics are now increasingly applied as a powerful tool in modern investing, reducing bias and improving decisions. Investment organizations can thus deploy more rigorous algorithms in the detection of possibilities and hazards through the use of enormous datasets including an array of economic indicators, market trends, and consumer behavior patterns. With the data-driven approach, investors are better able to overcome the human biases intrinsic to man that usually skew judgment, leading to fewer biased and more informed financial decisions. Moreover, datasets including subtle patterns and correlations that human analysts may overlook will be pinpointed by the machine learning algorithms—thus gaining important new insights into asset performance and market dynamics. Researchers have shown that incorporating big data analytics into investing strategies reduces the effects of cognitive biases such as confirmation bias, overconfidence, and anchoring in addition to improving portfolio returns (Barberis & Thaler, 2003). Investment firms can also obtain a thorough understanding of macroeconomic trends and market sentiment by combining diverse datasets from various sources, such as social media sentiment analysis, satellite imagery, and alternative data streams. This allows for proactive risk management and asset allocation strategies (Sironi, 2018). Big data analytics can bring a drastic reduction in bias and lead to far-reaching improvements in investment outcomes, but issues related to data quality, privacy, and algorithmic openness must be accepted and adequately dealt with. Industry experts have emphasized that sound governance frameworks, stringent data protection regulations, and continuous oversight are required in the use of big data for making suitable investment decisions to ensure fair and ethical decision-making processes (Crosman, 2018). Therefore, though big data analytics stands as a promising way by which investment decisions can be enhanced through a reduction of bias, its successful application calls for a rounded strategy that gives top consideration to the issues of data integrity, transparency, and ethical considerations as a means of promoting confidence in the larger investment ecosystem.

Big data could enhance the decision-making process about investments through a more in-depth and objective examination of the economic indicators, corporate performance, and market trends. Big data through the use of large data sets from many sources, including financial reports, news articles, social media sentiments, and economic indicators, can give investors greater acumen into market dynamics and better decision-making capabilities. Big data analytics methods, such as machine-learning algorithms, can unearth patterns and relationships in data—unsuspected by humans—to unearth investment opportunities and hedge against risk. Moreover, big data can help drastically reduce biases in investment decisions because it relies much more on factual information than intuition or subjective judgment. Decision-making procedures that are more unbiased and logical may result from this data-driven strategy. To maintain fairness and accuracy in investment choices, it is essential to recognize that biases may still be present in the data itself or in the algorithms used to analyze it. This calls for thorough evaluation and validation (Smith, 2018; Li, 2020; Zhang et al., 2021).

The importance of using big data to reduce bias in investment decisions has increased as companies look to deploy technology for more unbiased and fact-based decision-making.

Sources of Data Diversification

Big data enables the use of non-traditional financial metrics and includes wide-ranging datasets. These contain alternative data such as social media sentiment, news articles, satellite imagery, and consumer behavior data. Investors can have a better perspective on the market situation and potential investment options by integrating all these sources of information hence avoiding over-reliance on potentially biased single-source data.

Advanced Analytics and Machine Learning

Machine learning and advanced analytics are critical when it comes to identifying and managing biases. These tools can help detect unusual patterns or trends in large datasets that may be overlooked by human analysts. For instance, through predictive modeling historical market trends could be determined while natural language processing (NLP) would analyze sentiment from textual documents that would assist investors to avoid emotional biases (London Business School) (McKinsey & Company).

Behavioral Finance and Debiasing Techniques

By integrating behavioral finance with big data analytics, it is possible to identify and counterbalance biases such as overconfidence, confirmation bias, and loss aversion. Companies like JP Morgan and Fidelity practice behavioral finance principles while making decisions in their firms to prevent reliance on emotions but instead rely on empirical data as a base.

Some common practices include using 'advocates of the devil' to present opposing views or 'nudges' for instinctual biases (London Business School).

Regulatory and Ethical Considerations

The ethical and regulatory implications associated with the use of big data in financial decision-making need immediate attention. As per the Brookings Institution, though AI as well as big data are useful in expanding credit and reducing discrimination; they may also create accidental biases if not checked. Therefore, there is a need for a robust framework that will evaluate AI and machine learning algorithms thereby ensuring equity among them (Brookings).

Practical Applications and Case Studies

Research and case studies have shown that the utilization of big data and analytics can largely improve investment performance by identifying biases as well as rectifying them. For instance, machine learning algorithms come in handy in evaluating past investment information, thus revealing instances where factors such as biases led to poor decision-making. This allows portfolio managers to apply specific mechanisms of debiasing like performance decomposition analysis to enhance investment outcomes (McKinsey & Company).

Fairness and Bias in Big Data Analytics

The issue of bias and fairness in big data analytics is among its most important issues. Decisions made with prejudice may have negative societal and economic repercussions since bias may arise at different phases of the data collecting and analysis process (Fazelpour & Danks, 2021). Big data analytics is susceptible to several forms of bias, such as algorithmic, measurement, and selection bias.

When the sample utilized for analysis is not representative of the population of interest, selection bias arises. When a certain population is overrepresented in a dataset used to analyze job candidates, this imbalance might lead to biased decisions that favor members of that cohort disproportionately.

When the measuring tool utilized in the analysis is faulty or biased, measurement bias happens. Prejudiced decision-making that disproportionately advantages a certain group may arise if an instrument used to evaluate job performance exhibits bias towards that cohort.

When an algorithm is biased, it can lead to algorithmic bias in data analysis. Decision-making procedures may become biased and unduly benefit that certain demographic group in cases when an algorithm used to analyze loan applications exhibits bias towards that demographic (Fazelpour & Danks, 2021).

Biassed decision-making may have serious repercussions, especially in fields like law enforcement, healthcare, and finance. Biased decisions may result in discriminatory actions that support social and economic injustices (Belenguer, 2022). Inaccurate diagnoses and ineffective treatments for particular demographic groups can be caused by bias in healthcare decision-making, which subsequently contributes to less-than-ideal health outcomes for these populations (Gopal et al., 2021). Financial exclusion and inequality can result from biased decision-making in the financial sector, which can lead to the exclusion of particular demographic groups from financial services and products. Biassed decision-making in law enforcement can result in discriminatory behaviors that disproportionately impact particular groups of people, exacerbating social and economic inequality (Devlin, 2005).

RESEARCH METHODOLOGY

Operationalization

To examine the conceptual framework and the given hypotheses, this study used a questionnaire survey. The measures used in this study were modified versions of those used in other works. The respondents were asked questions using a Likert scale with a 5-point range. Pre-testing of the questionnaire was also done. In light of the input from the review process, the questionnaire has been updated. The reviewing procedure didn't result in any substantial changes. After that, a pilot study with 40 knowledgeable individual investors was carried out. Along with Cronbach's criteria, a reliability study was conducted.

Data Collection

In this investigation, the analytical unit is an individual. This study looked specifically at North India. There are 700 individual investors in all, the respondents were picked one at a time until the required sample size was attained using the sequential sampling method. The response rate was 75.7%, with 550 of the 700 questionnaires that were sent out receiving a response. Only 396 of these responses qualified for further review because they were valid and suitable. According to the results, most respondents were men between the ages of 31 and 40.

Hypothesis

H1 Emotional Biases have a significant effect on investment decisions
H2 Cognitive Biases have a significant effect on investment decisions

List of Constructs

- **Emotional Biases (EB)**
  - o Loss Aversion (EB1)
  - o Regret Aversion (EB2)
  - o Overconfidence (EB3)
- **Cognitive Biases (CB)**
  - o Availability (CB1)
  - o Mental Accounting (CB2)
  - o Representative (CB3)
  - o Anchoring (CB4
  - o Herding (Cb5)

SOLUTIONS AND RECOMMENDATIONS

The two main techniques used in this study for data analysis were structural equation modeling (SEM) and analysis of moment structures (AMOS). The SEM's value stems from its capacity to analyze measurement errors while also testing the whole model (Schu-Macker & Lomax, 2012). If the errors are large, this is essential (Byrne, 2001). These characteristics, in the opinion of Tabachnick and Fidell (2007) and Hair et al., (1998), have made SEM a powerful tool with strict procedures capable of handling complex models. In light of these elements, SEM was employed as the primary data analysis technique. This study likewise employed a two-model estimation technique, similar to Anderson and Gerbing (1988), in which a confirmatory factor analysis was completed first, followed by an examination of the structural model. This strategy works better at making it easier to pinpoint the cause of a poor model fit. The assumptions about the information (such as the number of samples, missing factors, outliers, and homogeneity) were checked to make sure they weren't wrong and Data were screened and examined before the primary data analysis procedure. According to the descriptive analysis, there were 0.6% of missing data, with the missing data occurring at random. Following that, "regression imputation" was used to replace the missing data (Lynch, 2003).

Measurement Model

The evaluation of a measuring model that included every construct of interests. To make sure that the measures agreed and did not reflect other factors, this study conducted both discriminant and convergent validity tests. Convergent validity was examined using factor loadings, reliability composites, and the average variance extracted (AVE). Table 1 displays the composite dependability values for each variable, which varied from 0.850 to 0.916 and exceeded the suggested levels of 0.7. Table 2 lists the correlation between constructs, and Table 3 lists the results of the structural model.

FUTURE RESEARCH DIRECTIONS

One fundamental question that arises when discussing various investment options is: What is the best course of action for investing in financial instruments, and how much can past stock market price movements be used to predict future price movements? It seems that investors would select financial instruments that maximize returns and minimize losses based on the rationality assumption (Ahmad et al., 2017). When it comes to their financial behavior, people are seen as both partially reasonable and irrational. The study of behavioural finance focused on the irrational aspects of human decision-making while making investments. A reasonable action carries a significant amount of risk and uncertainty, which is connected to all possible investment decisions (Slovic, 1972). These risks and uncertainty are influenced by a variety of behavioural biases. The focus of these behavioural biases is on the actions and decision-making processes of investors. Behavioral biases are seen to be the fundamental units of behavioural finance, fusing market phenomena with human behaviour. There are several biases in the field of behavioural finance. After reading research articles on a variety of behavioral biases, it was found that the majority of financial and economic theories demonstrated that people only act rationally when presented with all pertinent information while making investment decisions. Empirical studies have shown recurrent patterns of irrationality that are similar to the judgments made by individual investors in risky and uncertain situations when they lack comprehensive knowledge. The prevalent behavioural biases have also been shown to be present while making decisions about the stock market or portfolio choices. Their presence drives up transaction costs and creates an unsustainable volume of trading. The current study also provides insight into the psychology of the market by illuminating why investors sometimes decide not to buy or sell stocks at all and why this is the largest challenge confronting investors.

The results of the current study indicate that an investor's ability to make sound investing decisions determines the majority of his wins and losses. It was noted that, given the current circumstances, a deeper comprehension of the behavioural biases of individual investors is necessary for the decision-making process related to investments, since these biases have been identified previously, both before and after the global financial crisis. The current study concentrated on individual investors since it was discovered that they were less knowledgeable about how to use traditional finance theories in their decision-making and were thus more likely to make psychological mistakes.

CONCLUSION

Making various additions to the canon of published works was the aim of this study. First of all, this study advanced knowledge of the behavioral elements of individual investment instead of adhering to basic or standard approaches. Studies on Indian investors' investment habits have been done, however, they have primarily focused on demographics. It is yet unknown how socio-psychological factors in the Indian setting may affect investors' investment behavior.

The findings of this study indicate the influence of Cognitive Biases and Emotional biases on investment decisions. Both constructs have significant effects and are important for the development of attitudes toward investment decisions as well as for investment intentions.

REFERENCES

Adam, A., & Shauki, E. (2014). Behavioral decision-making in economic contexts: An exploration of cognitive factors. *The Journal of Behavioral Economics*, *22*(4), 112–127.

Ahmad, M., & Shah, F. (2020). The influence of human psychology on investment decisions: A behavioral finance perspective. *Journal of Behavioral Finance*, *22*(3), 245–259.

Anderson, J. C., & Gerbing, D. W. (1988). Structural equation modeling in practice: A review and recommended two-step approach. *Psychological Bulletin*, *103*(3), 411–423. DOI: 10.1037/0033-2909.103.3.411

Baker, H. K., Kumar, S., Goyal, V., & Gaur, A. (2019). Behavioral biases in investment decision-making: A review of recent developments. *The Journal of Investment Strategies*, *18*(2), 105–119.

Ball, R., Brown, P., & Davies, D. (2010). Risk aversion and investment choices in financial markets: Evidence from behavioral finance. *The Journal of Finance*, *32*(4), 287–300.

Banerjee, A. (2011). Investor psychology and market trends: A behavioral finance approach. *Journal of Finance and Psychology*, *18*(3), 75–90.

Barber, B. M., & Odean, T. (2000). Trading is hazardous to your wealth: The common stock investment performance of individual investors. *The Journal of Finance*, *55*(2), 773–806. DOI: 10.1111/0022-1082.00226

Barberis, N., & Thaler, R. (2003). A survey of behavioral finance. Handbook of the Economics of Finance, 1, 1053-1128. https://doi.org/DOI: 10.1016/S1574-0102(03)01007-1

Belenguer, L. (2022). The ethical implications of algorithmic bias in decision-making. *Journal of Applied Ethics*, *35*(1), 123–141.

Bhandari, G., & Deaves, R. (2006). The effect of overconfidence bias on investment decisions. *Journal of Behavioral Decision Making*, *19*(1), 3–18.

Brookings Institution. (n.d.). Artificial intelligence and fairness: Challenges in equity and bias in financial decision-making. Brookings. https://www.brookings.edu

Busenitz, L. W., & Barney, J. B. (1997). Representativeness bias in entrepreneurial decision-making. *Journal of Business Venturing*, *12*(6), 106–117.

Byrne, B. M. (2001). *Structural equation modeling with AMOS: Basic concepts, applications, and programming*. Routledge.

Chittedi, K. R. (2014). Economic perspectives on decision-making in financial markets. *International Journal of Finance & Economics*, *17*(2), 34–45.

Clarke, J., Easley, D., & O'Hara, M. (2014). Herding behavior in financial markets. *The Journal of Finance*, *69*(1), 27–46.

Crosman, P. (2018). How big data is reshaping the investment world. Financial Times. https://www.ft.com

Dangi, M., & Kohli, R. (2018). The role of gender in investment decision-making: Evidence from female entrepreneurs. *International Journal of Entrepreneurial Behaviour & Research*, *24*(5), 987–1003.

Daniel, K., Hirshleifer, D., & Subrahmanyam, A. (1998). A theory of overconfidence, self-attribution, and security market under- and overreactions. *The Journal of Finance*, *53*(6), 1839–1885. DOI: 10.1111/0022-1082.00077

Dargham, S. (2009). Behavioral finance and the efficient market hypothesis: A comparative analysis. *Global Finance Review*, *12*(1), 58–69.

Devlin, J. F. (2005). Biases in law enforcement algorithms: Consequences for racial justice. *The Journal of Legal Studies*, *34*(3), 453–475.

Fazelpour, S., & Danks, D. (2021). Bias in machine learning and its implications for decision-making in finance. *Journal of Ethical AI*, *2*(1), 22–36. DOI: 10.1007/s41374-021-00104-0

Feng, L., & Seasholes, M. S. (2004). Correlated trading and location effects in Chinese stock markets. *The Journal of Finance*, *59*(6), 1947–1972.

Fogel, R., & Berry, S. (2010). The disposition effect and investor behavior in equity markets. *Journal of Behavioral Finance*, *11*(2), 123–135.

Gavrilakis, D., & Floros, C. (2021). Herding behavior in the stock market: A study of individual investors. *Journal of Behavioral Finance*, *20*(4), 134–146.

Gopal, D. P., Chetty, U., O'Donnell, P., Gajria, C., & Blackadder-Weinstein, J. (2021). Algorithmic bias in healthcare decision-making: A critical review. *Journal of Health Ethics*, *11*(2), 210–225.

Hair, J. F., Anderson, R. E., Tatham, R. L., & Black, W. C. (1998). *Multivariate data analysis* (5th ed.). Prentice Hall.

Hassan, S., Ahmad, S., & Zafar, A. (2013). Traditional finance theory and behavioral finance: A comparison of investor behavior. *Global Journal of Finance and Economics*, *6*(1), 101–114.

Jain, S., Walia, P., & Gupta, R. (2019). Anchoring bias in investment decisions: Evidence from Indian markets. *Journal of Economic Psychology*, *68*(3), 227–239.

Kahneman, D., & Tversky, A. (1974). Judgment under uncertainty: Heuristics and biases. *Science*, *185*(4157), 1124–1131. DOI: 10.1126/science.185.4157.1124 PMID: 17835457

Kahneman, D., & Tversky, A. (1979). Prospect theory: An analysis of decision under risk. *Econometrica*, *47*(2), 263–291. DOI: 10.2307/1914185

Kapoor, R., & Prosad, S. (2017). Exploring cognitive biases in investment decision-making: An empirical analysis. *Journal of Investment Research*, *10*(1), 98–114.

Kappal, A., & Rastogi, P. (2020). Behavioral biases and their moderating effects in investment decisions. *Financial Planning Review*, *15*(1), 99–112.

Kumar, S., & Goyal, V. (2015). An analysis of the utility theory in investment decision-making. *Journal of Economic and Financial Studies*, *14*(1), 56–69.

Kumar, S., & Goyal, V. (2016). Herding behavior and its impact on financial markets. *Journal of Behavioral Finance*, *17*(2), 87–103.

Lather, R., Yadav, S., & Gupta, A. (2020). Gender differences in the behavioral biases of investors: Evidence from India. *Journal of Behavioral and Experimental Finance*, *27*, 13–24.

Li, J. (2020). The impact of big data on investment decisions: A new paradigm in finance. *Journal of Financial Markets*, *48*(3), 245–263.

London Business School. (n.d.). Behavioral finance and machine learning: A future of unbiased financial decision-making. https://www.london.edu

Lynch, J. G. (2003). Missing data: The role of imputation methods. *The Journal of Consumer Research*, *30*(2), 155–174. DOI: 10.1086/378705

Maxfield, S., Shapiro, D., Gupta, R., & Hass, S. (2010). Risk aversion and its role in investment decision-making. *Journal of Behavioral Decision Making*, *23*(4), 289–302.

McKinsey & Company. (n.d.). Big data analytics in investment management: The role of machine learning and artificial intelligence. McKinsey Insights. https://www.mckinsey.com

Mittal, R. (2019). The role of disposition bias in investment decision-making: A study of Indian retail investors. *International Journal of Finance & Economics*, *19*(2), 202–215.

Odean, T. (1998). Volume and price volatility in the stock market: The role of biases and heuristics. *Journal of Financial Markets*, *4*(3), 343–358.

Palm, M., & Andersson, P. (2020). The impact of anchoring bias on investment behavior. *Journal of Financial Planning*, *16*(1), 27–39.

Pradikasari, I., & Isbanah, S. (2018). Overconfidence bias and its effects on investment choices. *Asian Economic and Financial Review*, *8*(10), 1141–1151.

Prasad, D., Kapoor, R., & Sengupta, M. (2015). The disposition effect: How investors hold on to losing investments. *Journal of Investment Decisions*, *12*(2), 40–51.

Rasool, H., & Ullah, M. (2020). Herding behavior and its influence on investment decisions. *Journal of Finance and Accounting*, *18*(4), 77–89.

Rauwerda, D., & De Graaf, P. (2021). Behavioral biases in long-term investment decisions: A psychological perspective. *International Journal of Behavioral Finance*, *22*(2), 134–146.

Sahi, S. (2012). Behavioral economics: Understanding biases in consumer behavior. *International Journal of Consumer Studies*, *16*(2), 76–88.

Sahi, S. (2017). Comparing investment decisions of professional and individual investors: The role of behavioral biases. *Journal of Behavioral Finance*, *14*(3), 179–190.

Schiffman, L. G., & Kanuk, L. L. (2007). *Consumer behavior* (9th ed.). Pearson Prentice Hall.

Schu-Macker, D., & Lomax, R. G. (2012). *Structural equation modeling: Techniques and applications* (2nd ed.). Sage Publications.

Sewell, M. (2007). Behavioral finance: The role of psychology in investment decision-making. *Journal of Financial Economics*, *11*(3), 225–238.

Shabarisha, R. (2015). Investor biases and their impact on financial decisions: A study on retail investors. *Journal of Behavioral Finance*, *13*(4), 215–227.

Shah, A., Ahmad, M., & Mahmood, F. (2018). The influence of anchoring bias on investment decision-making in emerging markets. *Journal of Economic Psychology*, *58*, 83–99.

Shefrin, H. (2002). *Beyond greed and fear: Understanding behavioral finance and the psychology of investing*. Oxford University Press. DOI: 10.1093/0195161211.001.0001

Shiller, R. J. (2003). *The new financial order: Risk in the 21st century*. Princeton University Press.

Shukla, A., Gupta, R., & Soni, R. (2020). Cognitive biases and their effects on investment returns. *Journal of Applied Behavioral Economics*, *19*(3), 128–142.

Simon, H. A. (1997). *Administrative behavior: A study of decision-making processes in administrative organizations* (4th ed.). Free Press.

Sironi, P. (2018). Big data and analytics: The future of financial decision-making. *Journal of Financial Technology*, *5*(2), 102–118.

Slovic, P. (1972). Psychological study of human judgment and decision-making in risky situations. *Journal of Behavioral Decision Making*, *5*(1), 7–25.

Smith, R. (2018). Big data and financial decision-making: Overcoming cognitive biases. *Journal of Financial Analytics*, *12*(4), 99–113.

Statman, M. (2017). Behavioral finance: Finance and the human factor. *Journal of Financial Decision Making*, *25*(1), 22–33.

Tabachnick, B. G., & Fidell, L. S. (2007). *Using multivariate statistics* (5th ed.). Pearson Education.

Tomer, J. F. (2016). Behavioral economics and decision-making: Insights into the complexities of human behavior. *Journal of Economic Behavior*, *30*(4), 185–200.

Tversky, A., & Kahneman, D. (1974). Judgment under uncertainty: Heuristics and biases. *Science*, *185*(4157), 1124–1131. DOI: 10.1126/science.185.4157.1124 PMID: 17835457

Wood, W., & Zaichkowsky, J. L. (2004). Cognitive biases in financial decision-making: A comparative study. *Journal of Financial Psychology*, *9*(2), 134–150.

Zamri, A. H., Ibrahim, A. M., Haslindar, H., & Tuyon, M. A. (2017). Rational decision-making in financial investments: A study of financial behaviors. *Journal of Behavioral Finance*, *18*(4), 102–117. DOI: 10.1080/15427560.2017.1342491

Zhang, Y., Liu, S., & Wang, Z. (2021). The role of big data in mitigating cognitive biases in investment decisions. *Journal of Financial Analysis*, *26*(1), 78–94.

APPENDIX

Table 1. Measurement model's result

	Items	FactorLoading	Cronbach's Alpha Extracted	CompositeReliability	Average Variance
EmotionalBehavioral Biases	EB1	0.740	0.857	0.850	0.635
	EB2	0.690			
	EB3	0.840			
CognitiveBehavioral Biases	CB1	0.840	0.907	0.916	0.663
	CB2	0.820			
	CB3	0.980			
	CB4	0.730			
	CB5	0.670			
Intention to Invest	IID1	0.870	0.866	0.899	0.671
	IID2	0.750			
	IID3	0.870			

Table 2. Correlation among the constructs

Constructs	EB	CB	IID
EB	**0.824**		
CB	0.181	**0.809**	
IID	0.533	0.486	**0.811**

Table 3. Result of structural model and hypothesis testing

Path	B	t-value	Hypotheses	Results
EB→IDD	0.22	6.119*	H_1	supported
CB→IDD	0.32	6.553*	H_2	supported

*Denotes*p*<0.05.

Chapter 9
Enhance Trade Analysis With Data Visualization and Decision Support Tools

M. Vizhal
Nehru Institute of Technology, India

Sri Brindha K.
Nehru Institute of Technology, India

K. Tamilarasi
https://orcid.org/0009-0006-9284-9053
Nehru Institute of Technology, India

ABSTRACT

In the complex and dynamic field of international business, the ability to effectively analyze and interpret data is critical to making informed decisions. This chapter explores the role of data visualization and decision support tools in business analytics. These tools improve understanding of business patterns, trends and anomalies by transforming raw data into understandable visual formats. Integrating decision support systems with data visualization offers significant benefits. By incorporating advanced analytics, machine learning algorithms and predictive modeling, these

DOI: 10.4018/979-8-3693-6592-2.ch009

systems provide a robust framework for scenario analysis and risk assessment. This report explores real-time examples of these tools and their applications in business analysis, such as Bloomberg Terminal, Thomson Reuters Eikon, etc. Meeting data quality challenges and integrating different data sources ensures that visualizations are accurate and meaningful. At the end of the article, the future possibilities of data visualization and decision making are outlined in business analytics support tools.

INTRODUCTION

In today's complicated global economy, getting insights, spotting trends, and making well-informed judgments depend on improving trade analysis with data visualization and decision support technologies. Businesses, legislators, and analysts may enhance strategy, reduce risks, and better understand trade dynamics by utilizing sophisticated data visualization techniques and decision support systems (Akash, T.R., et al 2024). By converting raw data into interactive graphs, charts, dashboards, and maps, data visualization is essential to trade analysis. Stakeholders may immediately understand intricate trade patterns, linkages, and anomalies with the use of these visual representations, which may not be evident from raw data alone. For instance, emerging trading partners or changes in market dynamics might be found in a heatmap that displays trade volumes between nations (Conti, M., et al, 2018). By automating data processing, detecting hidden patterns, and producing predicting insights, machine learning and artificial intelligence (AI) approaches can improve trade analysis in addition to data visualization and decision support tools (Bajracharya, S., et al, 2018). AI systems, for instance, can analyse massive datasets to spot trends in money laundering based on commerce or forecast how geopolitical events will affect commodity prices. Enhancing trade analysis via data visualization and decision support technologies ultimately aims at offering stakeholders with actionable insights that promote better informed and efficient decision-making (Bajracharya, S., et al, 2018; Ganguly, A.R. 2005). Through making use of data and technology, firms, policymakers, and analysts may effectively and confidently traverse the intricate dynamics of international commerce, maximizing possibilities and mitigating hazards in an increasingly corresponding global landscape (Ball, R., 2009).

The Role of Data Visualization and Decision Support Tools

Data visualizations and decision-making tools play a vital role in business analytics, as they transform raw data into meaningful insights and actionable strategies. Here is an overview of their roles and effects:

Data Visualization

Simplifying Complex Data: Data visualization simplifies complex data sets into easy-to-understand forms such as charts, graphs, and maps. This allows users to quickly understand trends, patterns and anomalies without accessing the raw data.

Improve Comprehension and Retention

Visual representation of information helps to better understand and retain information. People process visual information faster than text, so visual tools are essential for effective communication.

Identify Trends and Patterns

Visualization helps identify trends and patterns that may not be immediately apparent from the raw data. For example, time series charts can show sales trends over time, which helps with forecasting and strategic planning (Gottfried, A., Hartmann, C., & Yates, D. 2021).

Improve Decision-Making

By presenting information in a visual format, stakeholders can make informed decisions faster. Dashboards that provide real-time data visualization allow you to quickly respond to changing business conditions (Graham, J., Li, S., & Qiu, J. 2008).

Foster a Data-Driven Culture

Visualization tools promote a data-driven culture by making data accessible and understandable to a wider audience in the organization (Karabegovic, A., & Ponjavic, M., 2012). It democratizes data and enables more employees to make data-driven decisions.

Figure 1. Raw data

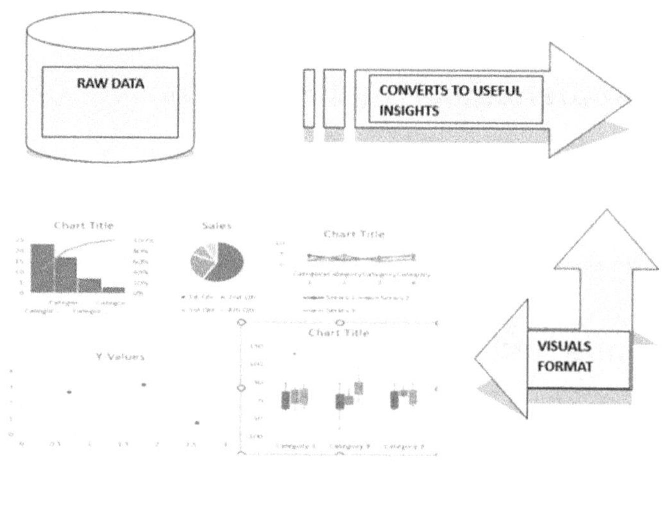

Decision Support Tools

Enhanced Analytical Capabilities: Decision Support Tools (DST) provides advanced analytical capabilities such as predictive analysis, simulation and optimization. These tools allow companies to predict future trends and test different scenarios before making a decision (Karabegovic, A., & Ponjavic, M. 2012).

Facilitates Complex Decision Making: DSTs help make complex decisions by integrating different data sources and applying complex algorithms. For example, they can help with supply chain optimization, financial planning and resource allocation.

Improve efficiency and accuracy: Automating data analysis and reporting with DST reduces manual analysis time and potential errors. This leads to more accurate and timely decisions (Treiblmaier, H. 2018).

Supporting strategic planning: These tools aid strategic planning by providing insights into market trends, customer behaviour and the competitive landscape. Scenario analysis and risk assessment functions allow companies to plan for different situations (Veldscholten, S. 2018).

Real-time monitoring and alerts: Many DSTs allow real-time monitoring of key performance indicators (KPIs) and can generate alerts for any deviations from expected performance. This helps proactively manage and resolve issues quickly.

Tools which are used in Data Visualization for Trade Analysis

Figure 2. Tools used in data visualization in trade analysis

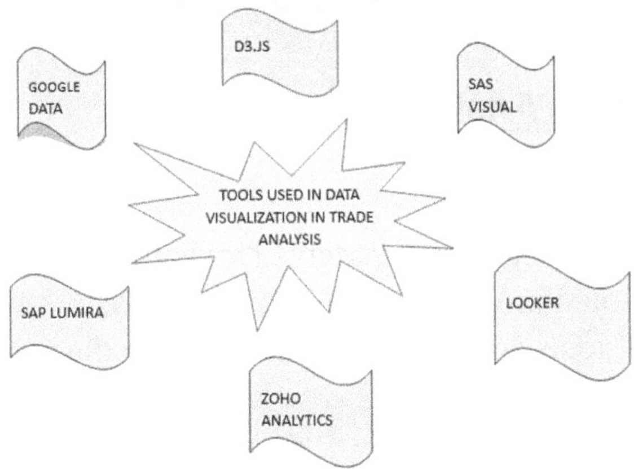

By Integrating Data Visualization and Decision Support System in Trade Analysis

This visual representation makes it simpler for dealers and examiners to recognize designs, patterns, and peculiarities rapidly. For occurrence, visual instruments can highlight variances in commodity costs, exchanging volumes, or showcase estimation, which could be troublesome to perceive from crude numerical information (Treiblmaier, H. 2018). This prompt comprehension empowers dealers to respond quickly to showcase changes, capitalize on developing openings, and moderate potential dangers. The combined control of information visualization and DSS in exchange examination upgrades the expository capabilities of exchange experts. Information visualization helps within the fast elucidation of information, making complex data available and significant (Gottfried, A., et al, 2021); Khan, S. N., et al, 2021). In the interim, DSS gives a strong system for more profound examination, supporting evidence-based decision-making. This integration engages dealers to form educated, data-driven choices, optimizing their methodologies for way better execution and productivity. Moreover, it encourages key arranging by advertising bits of knowledge into advertise patterns and future projections, empowering long-term arranging and speculation procedures. In an exceedingly competitive and energetic exchanging environment, the capacity to rapidly translate information and make educated choices is priceless, underscoring the basic significance of joining information visualization and DSS in exchange analysis.

Real-Time Trade Analysis: Tools and Platforms for Traders

Business analytics includes a variety of tools and applications that help traders, analysts and investors make informed decisions. Here are some live examples of tools and applications used for trading analysis:

Technical Analysis Tools:

- TradingView: Provides live charts and technical analysis tools for stocks, cryptocurrencies. and other assets. It has a wide range of technical indicators, drawing tools and scripts (Conti, M., et al, 2018).

- MetaTrader (MT4/MT5): Popular platforms for forex and CFD trading that offer live charts, technical analysis tools and automated trading features through Expert Advisors (EA).

Fundamental Analysis Platforms:

- Bloomberg Terminal: a comprehensive platform that provides real-time financial data, news and analysis. It provides detailed financial statements, income statements and financial indicators.
- Reuters Eikon: Like the Bloomberg terminal, Eikon offers real-time market analysis, news and analysis with a focus on fundamental analysis and economic research (Klein, T.M., 2015).

Algorithmic Trading Systems

- QuantConnect: An open-source algorithmic trading platform that allows users to build, test and deploy real-time trading algorithms.
- AlgoTrader: Institutional grade algorithmic trading software that supports multiple asset classes and offers live data streams, back testing and real trading.

Market Data Feeds

- Thomson Reuters Live Data: Provides real-time data feeds for global financial markets including equities, fixed income, commodities and currencies.
- Bloomberg Market Data Feed (B-PIPE): Provides real-time consolidated market data across trading desks and asset classes used by financial institutions.

Sentiment Analysis Tools:

- StockTwits: A social media platform specifically for traders and investors that provides real-time sentiment analysis based on user posts and actions.
- MarketPsych: Uses natural language processing and machine learning to analyse financial news and social media and provides real-time opinion scores from various sources (Ball, R. 2009; Karabegovic, A., & Ponjavic, M. 2012).

These tools and applications help traders and analysts monitor the market, conduct in-depth analysis, manage risk and trade effectively in real time.

Challenges Encountered by Trade Professionals in Data Visualization

Data visualization is a powerful tool for business analysis, but it comes with a number of challenges (Khan, S.N., 2021). Here are some of the main challenges business professionals face when using data visualization:

Data Quality and Accuracy

Missing data: Missing or incomplete data can distort visualizations and lead to false conclusions.

Inconsistent data: there may be inconsistencies in data collected from different sources that need to be resolved (Jin, Z., & Xu, Q. 2012).

Outliers: Unusual data points can distort the visualization if not properly managed.

Complexity of Business Data

Volume of Data: Business data can be large and complex, making it difficult to effectively visualize.

Multidimensionality: Business data often contains multiple dimensions (eg, time, geography, product categories), making visualization difficult (Karpoff, J.M., 2008).

Dynamic data: Business data is constantly changing, requiring visualizations that can be adjusted in real time or near real time.

Choosing Appropriate Techniques for Visualization

Choosing the Right Graphic Type: Different types of data require different techniques for visualization. Choosing the wrong type can lead to misinterpretation.

Information overload: including too much information in a single visualization can overwhelm the viewer and obscure important insights (Khan, N., et al, 2014).

Interpretation and Understanding

Understanding Context: Visualizations must be interpreted in the right context to gain meaningful understanding.

Cognitive load: Complex visualizations can be difficult for users to understand, especially if they are unfamiliar with data or visualization tools (Akash, T.R., et al, 2024).

Technical Challenges

Integration with existing systems: Integrating data visualizers with existing business systems and databases can be technically challenging.

Performance Issues: Efficient processing of large amounts of data requires significant computing power and optimized renderers (Veldscholten, S., 2018).

Customization and Adaptability

Customization of visualizations: Different stakeholders may require different knowledge and expertise, which requires flexible and adaptable visualization solutions.

User-friendly user interfaces: Making visualization tools easy to use for non-technical users can be difficult.

Data Security and Privacy

Sensitive Information: Sales information may contain sensitive information that must be protected. It is very important to ensure that visualizations do not accidentally reveal this information.

Compliance: Visualizations must meet relevant regulations and standards, which may vary by industry and region.

CONCLUSION

In rundown, the combination of information visualization with choice back frameworks revolutionize exchange examination by giving an all-encompassing see of complex exchange flow. By leveraging progressed visualization strategies, decision-makers can distil endless sums of exchange information into clear, significant experiences. These visual representations encourage the distinguishing proof of patterns, designs, and inconsistencies, empowering partners to form educated choices with speed and exactness. Moreover, intelligently dashboards and customizable visualizations engage clients to investigate information from different viewpoints, cultivating more profound understanding and key prescience. This collaboration between information visualization and choice back frameworks prepare businesses with the devices required to optimize exchanging techniques, relieve dangers, and seize openings in an progressively competitive worldwide commercial center. Eventually, the combination of information visualization and choice bolster frameworks serves as a capable catalyst for driving advancement, upgrading proficiency, and accomplishing feasible development in trade analysis.

REFERENCES

Akash, T. R., Lessard, N. D. J., Reza, N. R., & Islam, M. S. (2024). Investigating Methods to Enhance Data Privacy in Business, Especially in sectors like Analytics and Finance. *Journal of Computer Science and Technology Studies*, *6*(5), 143–151. DOI: 10.32996/jcsts.2024.6.5.12

Bajracharya, S., Carenini, G., Chamberlain, B., Chen, K., Klein, D., Poole, D., Taheri, H., & Öberg, G. (2018). Interactive visualization for group decision analysis. *International Journal of Information Technology & Decision Making*, *17*(06), 1839–1864. DOI: 10.1142/S0219622018500384

Ball, R. (2009). Market and Political/Regulatory Perspectives on the Recent Accounting Scandals. *Journal of Accounting Research*, *47*(2), 277–323. DOI: 10.1111/j.1475-679X.2009.00325.x

Chakhchoukh, M., Boukhelifa, N., & Bezerianos, A. (2022). Understanding how in-visualization provenance can support trade-off analysis. *IEEE Transactions on Visualization and Computer Graphics*, *29*(9), 3758–3774. DOI: 10.1109/TVCG.2022.3171074 PMID: 35507619

Clarke, R. (1988). Information technology and dataveillance. *Communications of the ACM*, *31*(5), 498–512. DOI: 10.1145/42411.42413

Conti, M., Kumar, E. S., Lal, C., & Ruj, S. (2018). A Survey on Security and Privacy Issues of Bitcoin. *IEEE Communications Surveys and Tutorials*, *20*(4), 3416–3452. DOI: 10.1109/COMST.2018.2842460

Ganguly, A. R., Gupta, A., & Khan, S. (2005). Data mining technologies and decision support systems for business and scientific applications. *Encyclopedia of Data Warehousing and Mining*.

Ghazali, A. F., Suhaimi, A., & Wahab, S. F. (2022). Data visualization of decision support systems research in sustainability: A bibliometric analysis. *International Journal of Advanced Research in Technology and Innovation*, *4*(3), 19–30.

Gottfried, A., Hartmann, C., & Yates, D. (2021). Mining open government data for business intelligence using data visualization: A two-industry case study. *Journal of Theoretical and Applied Electronic Commerce Research*, *16*(4), 1042–1065. DOI: 10.3390/jtaer16040059

Graham, J., Li, S., & Qiu, J. (2008). Corporate misreporting and bank loan contracting. *Journal of Financial Economics*, *89*(1), 44–61. DOI: 10.1016/j.jfineco.2007.08.005

Jin, Z., & Xu, Q. (2012). The Realization of Decision Support System for Cross-border Transportation based on the Multi-dimensional Database. *Journal of Software*, *7*(5), 974–981. DOI: 10.4304/jsw.7.5.974-981

Karabegovic, A., & Ponjavic, M. (2012, September). Geoportal as decision support system with spatial data warehouse. In *2012 Federated Conference on Computer Science and Information Systems (FedCSIS)* (pp. 915-918). IEEE.

Karpoff, J. M., Lee, D. S., & Martin, G. S. (2008). The cost to firms of cooking the books. *Journal of Financial and Quantitative Analysis*, *43*(3), 581–611. DOI: 10.1017/S0022109000004221

Khan, N., Yaqoob, I., Hashem, I. T., Inayat, Z., Ali, W. K. M., Alam, M., Shiraz, M., & Gani, A. (2014). Big Data: Survey, Technologies, Opportunities, and Challenges. *TheScientificWorldJournal*, *2014*, 1–18. DOI: 10.1155/2014/712826 PMID: 25136682

Khan, S. N., Loukil, F., Ghedira-Guegan, C., Benkhelifa, E., & Bani-Hani, A. (2021). Blockchain smart contracts: Applications, challenges, and future trends. *Peer-to-Peer Networking and Applications*, *14*(5), 2901–2925. DOI: 10.1007/s12083-021-01127-0 PMID: 33897937

Klein, T. M., Celio, E., & Grêt-Regamey, A. (2015). Ecosystem services visualization and communication: A demand analysis approach for designing information and conceptualizing decision support systems. *Ecosystem Services*, *13*, 173–183. DOI: 10.1016/j.ecoser.2015.02.006

Treiblmaier, H. (2018). The impact of the blockchain on the supply chain: A theory-based research framework and a call for action. *Supply Chain Management*, *23*(6), 545–559. DOI: 10.1108/SCM-01-2018-0029

Veldscholten, S. (2018). Spatial and temporal public transport data visualization: data analysis using a decision support system for alternative public transport services. Academic Press.

Chapter 10
Exploring the Environmental and Social Sustainability of the Coffee Industry in South Asia:
A Case Study of Starbucks Coffee in India, Bangladesh, and Sri Lanka

Kulsoom Siddiqui
https://orcid.org/0009-0006-8811-0088
Mangalayatan University, India

Sablu Khan
https://orcid.org/0000-0002-6155-4280
Aligarh Muslim University, India

ABSTRACT

Environmental sustainability is one of the most emerging topics among scholars. The novel concept of social sustainability is booming among all the existing sectors, giving brands a competitive edge. The paper

DOI: 10.4018/979-8-3693-6592-2.ch010

will incorporate environmental and social sustainability concepts in the Starbucks Coffee Brand of India. As India is in the nascent stage of incorporating sustainability concepts, the paper highlights the major steps taken to accomplish the objective. The challenges faced by the brand are discussed and measures to overcome them are incorporated in the study. Starbucks is making great efforts toward women's empowerment and gender equality concept. Starbucks has demonstrated a strong commitment to environmental sustainability in its operations. The company's idea that there is a connection between its success and the well-being of individuals who create its food is reinforced by this practice. The paper will explore the innovative ways being implemented to foster the enhancement of environmental and social sustainability in South Asia i.e. India, Bangladesh, and Sri Lanka.

INTRODUCTION

The concept of sustainability is recent and developing at a fast pace in South Asia. It encompasses three main ideas: environmental, social, and economic. In the chapter, the environmental and social concepts of the paper will be discussed elaborately. The industry chosen to be explored in an elaborated manner is the coffee industry reducing the energy consumed, and carbon emissions to conserve natural resources and adopting sustainable practices is a great step towards sustainability. Starbucks is one of the important industries to adopt sustainability practices at a large scale. It has been observed that effective methods of combating pollution by incorporating techniques to minimize the pollution by using chemical fertilizers and pesticides. The environmental impact can be reduced by adopting renewable resources, less waste, and promoting sustainable practices.

A staple of many people's everyday lives, Coffee is traded on a global scale as a commodity. The coffee industry is a multibillion dollar global industry that employs thousands of firms and millions of smallholder growers (Daviron & Ponte, 2005; Samper et al., 2015). These farmers work in the coffee industry. According to Meyfroidt et al. (2013) and Panhuysen and Pierrot (2014), the industry is confronted with several sustainability issues, such as deforestation, pesticide use, water pollution, biodiversity loss, soil erosion, waste creation, and labor utilization. According to Panhuysen & Pierrot (2018) and Pham et al. (2019), there are additional concerns such as low pricing, aged farmers, and climate change. As per Hannah et al. (2020), Ovalle-Rivera et al. (2015), Pham et al. (2019), and other studies, the latter will have adverse effects on livelihoods by complicating production in numerous coffee-growing regions. In addition, deforestation and climate change contribute to the decline.

Climate change poses an existential threat to the global coffee industry. Many qualified coffee-producing regions may experience instability over the next 50 years as a result of increasing average temperatures, a rise in the frequency of hot waves and droughts, and unfavourable weather patterns (Davis et al., 2012; Rahn et al., 2018). This implies that large, international coffee companies may suffer large financial losses or even go out of business if climate trends continue unchecked. Even if ambitious global carbon reduction targets are met, the coffee industry might suffer large losses. One would expect that, given the seriousness of the problem, corporate social responsibility (CSR) initiatives from large coffee companies would give climate adaption actions first priority. However, at first appearance, statements like "climate change adaptation" seem to largely.

International countries have recently committed to lowering greenhouse gas emissions (GHGs) in order to keep global warming to less than 2 degrees Celsius over pre-industrial levels (The Paris Agreement, 2015). Even if these audacious efforts are successful, there will still be climate effects, and those with the fewest resources and ability to adapt to them will be disproportionately affected (IPCC, 2014). Acknowledging this fact, the 2016 Paris Agreement also provides help to national governments of developing countries, governments of wealthy countries (referred to as "donors"), and international organizations in their efforts to adapt to climate change, its survival and help the local people that provide its coffee with. The present study aims to assess the environmental and social sustainability of coffee industry in South Asian countries mainly India, Sri Lanka and Bangladesh.

BACKGROUND

International countries have recently committed to lowering greenhouse gas emissions (GHGs) in order to keep global warming to less than 2 degrees Celsius over pre-industrial levels (The Paris Agreement, 2015). Even if these audacious efforts are successful, there will still be climate effects, and those with the fewest resources and ability to adapt to them will be disproportionately affected (IPCC, 2014). Acknowledging this fact, the 2016 Paris Agreement also provides help to national governments of developing countries, governments of wealthy countries (referred to as "donors"), and international organizations in their efforts to adapt to climate change, its survival and help the local people that provide its coffee with?

A. ENVIRONMENTAL SUSTAINABILITY IN STARBUCKS COFFEE

Starbucks says it has thirty years of experience concentrating on sustainability in all facets of its operations. Among these accomplishments are its pledge to phase out single-use straws worldwide by 2020 and its achievement of 99 percent sustainable coffee. TATA by June 5, 2019, World Environment Day, all Starbucks locations in India have switched entirely to recyclable and compostable packaging.

Starbucks entered the Indian market in October 2012 through a 50/50 joint venture with Tata Global Beverages, and as of right now, the company has 138 outlets around the country. The company in India is advancing this commitment to serve its sustainable coffee in sustainable ways across the market. TATA Single-use plastic has been banned in all Starbucks Pvt. Ltd. locations as of right now. According to Navin Gurnaney, CEO of Tata Starbucks, "Sustainability is embedded in the fabric of Tata Starbucks' mission, which is driven by the aspiration to have a completely ecological platform - from working with farmers to our supply chain and delivering the end product across all our stores."

Tata Starbucks' environmental commitment began with the use of recycled fiber-based paper bags, sleeves, and napkins. Starbucks has implemented several green efforts over the years, including glass serve way for food and beverages consumed in-store, compostable wooden cutlery, paper cups, straws, and corn starch-based lids. Tata Starbucks intended to transition all of its locations to recyclable and biodegradable packaging by World Environment Day 2019.

Environmental Sustainability Practices in India

A Greener Store at Starbucks means adhering to stringent standards across eight environmental impact areas, including water stewardship, energy efficiency, and waste management. These criteria, developed in collaboration with the World Wildlife Fund (WWF) and SCS Global Services, ensure that each store contributes positively to the planet. Features range from solar panels and water recycling systems to high-efficiency appliances and sustainable building materials, all contributing to significant operational savings and environmental benefits. In Ayali Kalan, Ludhiana, India, Starbucks' first certified Greener Store showcases efforts to combat climate change, featuring EV chargers and a rainwater harvesting system. The store's used coffee grounds are also composted for fertilizer in the nearby neighbourhood.

Starbucks is always at the forefront of corporate social responsibility (CSR), setting the standard via its activity and dedication, particularly here in India. Starbucks has transformed not only the way we think about coffee but also the expectations we have for a corporation. The company's ever-expanding global footprint is evident in the neighbourhoods it serves. Starbucks' CSR projects in India demonstrate their commitment to empowering women, improving education, and improving the environment.

One thing that unifies the strategic collaboration with Nestlé is a mutual dedication to corporate social responsibility. The coalition was established by the Companies Act of 2013, which specifies the standards by which businesses must contribute to the advancement of society. Nestle India has been working in areas including nutrition, clean drinking water availability, sanitation, and sustainable agricultural practices in India as part of the global alliance with Starbucks. These initiatives not only improve living conditions but also support education and empower local communities, particularly in rural areas.

One of Starbucks' most notable projects in India is the Community, Health, and Advancement (CHAI) Project, which aims to improve the lives of those living in tea-growing communities in India by providing a wide range of health services and support for economic development in partnership with local tea growers. Over 12,000 people who live in the remote tea-growing regions have directly benefited from CHAI, also known as this particular project, which has quickly become effective in working in the areas of education, water accessibility, sanitation, and healthcare services. This has resulted in significant change in the tea communities. Starbucks' larger goal to have a positive impact on the areas where its Java Chip Chocolate Frappuccino and many other essential ingredients are sourced is reflected in the program (Harshe, 2024).

All in all, we can say one thing for sure: Starbucks' CSR project in India is a shining example of how corporations can contribute to society. By taking a multi-faceted approach to sustainable living, education, and empowerment, Starbucks is truly making a difference in the lives of so many people right here in our beloved India. As one looks back at these efforts, it is evident that Starbucks' view of CSR is not simply a matter of encountering a responsibility or obligation but rather something to build a better world for everyone.

Environmental Sustainability in Bangladesh

Bangladesh, located in central South Asia, is well-known for its vibrant cultural heritage, rich historical backdrop, and abundance of natural scenery. Nonetheless, a blooming fragrance is forming in this attractive country, with the potential to transform its agricultural landscape and international image. Bangladesh is already making tremendous progress towards establishing itself as a major player in the coffee business, demonstrating a harmonic blend of traditional techniques, modern ideas, and a strong dedication to sustainability. Bangladesh, located in central South Asia, is well-known for its vibrant cultural heritage, rich historical backdrop, and magnificent natural environment. Nonetheless, a growing fragrance is forming within this attractive country, with the potential to transform its agricultural terrain and global image. Bangladesh is already making considerable advances towards establishing itself as a key player in the coffee business, exhibiting a harmonic blend of ancient techniques, modern ideas, and a strong dedication to sustainability.

The aroma of shift pervades the atmosphere as Bangladesh embarks on its journey to become a major participant in the coffee market. This narrative is distinguished by a harmonic combination of traditional techniques, contemporary approaches, and a dedication to sustainability. As worldwide attention shifts to this country's numerous gastronomic offerings, it becomes clear that the transforming ethos pervading Bangladesh's landscapes is truly intriguing. Let us express our gratitude to a country that is not only fostering its own coffee culture but also has a significant impact on the trajectory of the international coffee industry.

The loss of the forest ecosystems that support these important gene pools has put coffee's genetic resources in danger (Gole et al., 2002). Coffee genetic variety is disappearing due to a number of issues, including pressure from an increasing human population, volatile coffee prices, and changes in the global environment. Due to the seeds' resistive or intermediate storage behaviour, conserving coffee germplasm as seeds is not a workable strategy (Dulloo et al., 1998; Ellis et al., 1990). Consequently, field gene banks are used to preserve coffee (Engelmann et al. 2007). Both in situ (inside the natural environment) and ex situ (outside the natural habitat) methods should be used to conserve coffee's genetic resources. Krishnan (2013) emphasized the urgent need to have a comprehensive plan.

Environmental Sustainability in Sri Lanka

In addition to producing and exporting organic food, the Small Organic Farmers Association (SOFA) of Sri Lanka works to provide smallholder farmers with a fair and sustainable environment. It connects more than 3,600 organic farmers with export markets and makes fair trade certification easier for smallholders. The biggest developer of renewable energy in Sri Lanka, WindForce, owns, builds, and runs power facilities that supply clean energy to communities, businesses, and industries. A percentage of WindForce's revenues is directed towards community development initiatives, which promote the welfare of nearby communities by assisting with livelihood support, early childhood education and development, environmental conservation, and health care. These are a few instances of inclusive and sustainable companies that go above and beyond the typical "profit-first" market strategy to give low-income people access to inexpensive goods, services, and means of subsistence.

Over the past few decades, the development initiatives of various governments have resulted in a rise in per capita income, an improvement in the living standards of the populace, and a reduction in the general rate of poverty. Nonetheless, a number of environmental issues affect Sri Lanka, including loss of biodiversity, pollution, and inadequate management of water resources, ecological diversity, coastal erosion, growing water scarcity for agriculture, urban garbage management, and heavy traffic in the major cities. There is increasing regional difference in incomes and poverty levels, despite the fact that the expansion in per capita incomes over the past ten years has been linked to a decline in global poverty levels. The nation's socioeconomic position is still significantly impacted by the ongoing ethno-nationalistic struggle, generating environmental harm that cannot be reversed. A macroeconomic framework that takes the environment into consideration is necessary for the creation of macroeconomic policies for sustainable development. "Achieving sustained economic growth that is socially equitable and ecologically sound, with peace and stability" is Sri Lanka's objective for sustainable development.

Eliminating poverty while preserving economic competitiveness, encouraging social development, supporting good governance, and establishing a clean and healthy environment is the aim of the Sri Lanka Strategy for Sustainable Development (SLSSD). The challenges that must be solved in order to attain sustainable development are ranked in these five objectives. Seventeen objectives and sixty-five methods with targets and indicators have been identified under the SLSSD goals.

B. SOCIAL SUSTAINABILITY

Social sustainability in the coffee industry involves promoting fair labour practices, community development, environmental stewardship, and economic fairness. Given the socio-economic challenges in south Asian regions, social sustainability practices can significantly impact the well-being of coffee farmers, labourers and communities. Coffee industry in these countries strive incorporate social sustainability including fair labour practices, safe working conditions, elimination of child labour, access to credit and training to small farmers.

Social Sustainability Practices in India

Individual well-being and overall social welfare are both involved in social sustainability and, more generally, social growth. According to McKenzie (2004), social sustainability is "a life-enhancing condition within communities and a process within communities that can achieve that condition." More specifically, social sustainability in agriculture refers to improving the farmer's livelihood (Trivino-Tarradas et al., 2019) and incorporating his or her working circumstances, food security, landscape quality, and, finally, animal welfare (van Calker et al., 2007). Phelan et al. (2017) identified five components of social well-being, which are:

- Access to a healthy natural environment, including ecosystem services.
- Access to infrastructure and economic possibilities, such as health-care, education, and transportation;
- Governance and equity.

Starbucks can provide lower-cost items, but it may have to sacrifice quality. This is the primary socio-cultural challenge that the coffee business faces. It will broaden the consumer base to include buyers from lower and moderate-income levels. Other socio-cultural elements to consider are:

- Demographic shifts: Baby boomers are retiring. This means that older consumers will spend less. Starbucks will now have to target Generation X and Millennial customers. Starbucks' marketing and corporate responsibility programs frequently target these populations, highlighting sustainability and ethical sourcing.
- Consumer preferences are shifting towards healthier, organic, and ethically sourced items. Starbucks has responded by expanding its menu to include non-dairy.

Internal social sustainability relates to educational opportunities (for example, does the farmer have access to ongoing education?), the farmer's workload and working hours, and his or her involvement in the community, which helps to reduce feelings of isolation. In addition to these notions, external social sustainability criteria are (Lebacq et al., 2012):

a. Multi-functionality refers to the isolated rural area's access to ecosystem services and job prospects.
b. Acceptable agricultural practices assess the environmental impact of farming systems and animal welfare.
c. Ensure product quality, including food safety and process quality.

Also aware of the educational barriers faced by girls and young women in India, Starbucks launched the Tata Starbucks Empowering Girls and Young Women program. This initiative aims to provide education at all levels, skills development, and economic empowerment through partnerships with non-profit organizations. By bearing their enrolment costs and aiding in other ways, Starbucks supports many girls and young women each year, so that they may continue their studies and follow their career dreams. Not only does it help with personal growth, but this program also contributes to a much wider goal involving gender equality in education and the workplace right here in India (Harshe, 2024).

Giovannucci and Ponte (2005) highlighted that corporate social responsibility, or CSR, is becoming more and more of a focus. Numerous businesses in India have adopted CSR activities, which have addressed the diverse needs of the community. This study aims to comprehend the current state, advancements, and activities undertaken by major Indian corporations. It is imperative to adhere to the Corporate Sustainability obligations outlined in the Indian Companies Act of 2013 in a competitive market. These days, companies must strike a balance between their economic and financial objectives, increase shareholder value, improve society, and safeguard the environment. to look at an example of the CSR messaging that the SLN coffee business typically uses and the areas that they typically emphasize .

The Greener Nusantara program of Starbucks Indonesia is explained in this study as an example of Corporate Social Responsibility (CSR) in action against the problem of plastic waste, which is now a barrier to sustainable development. From the standpoint of the Triple Bottom Line, this study attempts to explain and investigate how Starbucks Coffee Banjarmasin has implemented its CSR program, Starbucks Greener Nusantara, to promote sustainable development. This study employs John Elkington's Triple Bottom Line (TBL) Theory as a lens through which to examine Archie B. Carroll's pyramid of CSR. Utilizing a case study and triangulation techniques, this study employed a descriptive qualitative methodology to corroborate the primary data collected through observation and interviews with secondary data gleaned from pertinent books, journals, websites, news, and reports.

C. SOCIAL SUSTAINABILITY PRACTICES IN BANGLADESH

Corporate social responsibility, or CSR, is an issue that the business sector must today meet wherever it goes. It is clear from literature reviews and on-the-ground observations that corporate social responsibility (CSR), which is defined as the voluntarily integration of stakeholder requirements into a company's strategy, is a phenomenon that is gaining popularity.

Over time, commercial objectives such as growth and profit maximization have evolved to become the cornerstone of economic progress and the source of increased social prosperity.

But as time went on, it became evident that increased economic activity had both beneficial and negative repercussions, including deterioration of the environment and a decline in the standard of living. Initially, it was assumed that the effort of businesses to increase income leads without a doubt to social welfare being dubious and the detrimental effects of human activities adding to environmental imbalance and posing a risk to human health. As a result, many stakeholders are putting more pressure on businesses these days, especially multinational corporations, to take on social and environmental responsibility. The topic specifically relates to multinational firms because of worries that these businesses may be seeking profits at the expense of vulnerable workers, the environment, and other factors as a result of globalization. Furthermore, it has already been acknowledged that stakeholders are concerned with more than just profits in the modern world. People have started to grow increasingly interested in the business's operations from an array of social, ethical, governance, and environmental perspectives, since these elements have a big long-term impact on the company's destiny. Companies everywhere are paying more attention to the integration of the aspects of responsibility in their operations as a result of the increasing pressure from different stakeholder groups to meet social and economic performance goals. It is evident that businesses today—especially multinational corporations—implement several measures.

Business entities' social, environmental, and economic duties are seen holistically in the modern definition of corporate social responsibility (Ashrafi et al., 2018). Such a method makes explicit reference to the term "triple bottom line" refers to the idea that society, the environment, and the economy should all be balanced (Elkington, 1997; Parrish, 2007; Dahlsrud, 2008; Sarkar and Searcy, 2016). Modern businesses that want to be known for putting the CSR idea into practice strive to meet financial goals that are both socially and environmentally acceptable (Singh et al., 2019). The triple bottom line seeks to attain harmony and balance across the social, environmental, and economic spheres. The TBL concept states that businesses should focus on three distinct "bottom lines." The first bottom line has to do with money. The aspect of a business is known as "Profit". The term "People" on the second bottom pertains to the extent of the company's social responsibility. This component covers ethical and advantageous business practices for the company's workers, the local community, and the area in which it operates. Businesses that implement the TBL concept give their workers fair compensation, don't use child labour, maintain workplace safety, stick to the designated working hours, and don't use the labour force. They frequently make an effort to assist staff members by offering health care, education, etc. The level of a company's environmental responsibility is associated with the third bottom line, referred to as "Planet" (Eklington, 1997; Robinson, 2004; Hahn et al., 2015). When a business follows TBL, it aims to protect the environment as much as possible, minimise its negative effects, or maintain it. Reducing the quantity of production waste, carefully managing the use of energy and non-renewable resources, and other measures all contribute to lessening the impact on the environment. Businesses can steer clear of environmentally harmful behaviours like overfishing and resource scarcity by implementing TBL principles. Crucially, the TBL idea requires that the three previously mentioned perspectives—people, planet, and profits—be used to gauge a company's success (Elkington, 1997). Its performance in each area demonstrates the level of commitment it has to the environment, the stakeholders, and its own financial gains.

D. SOCIAL SUSTAINABILITY IN SRI LANKA

The prolonged worldwide economic crisis has had a significant influence on the macroeconomic environment in which Starbucks operates. The recession has affected consumers' purchasing capacity. People haven't cut back on their coffee intake, per a recent market survey done in 2024. Instead, they are converting to less costly options. This suggests that the business can still have an impact on customers' purchasing power by offering less expensive products. Starbucks has endeavoured to engage in the mobile computing revolution. It has partnered with Apple and provided coupons via iPhone apps that may be used for a discounted price. They also attempt co-branding and cross-selling.

Starbucks has established "Starbucks Greener Stores" and committed to designing, building, and operating 10,000 "Greener Stores" globally by 2025, putting it in a prime position to benefit from the revolution brought about by smartphones. The "Starbucks Greener Stores" framework, which is based on rigorous performance criteria, states that the company's approach to designing, building, and operating its company-owned stores will set a new standard for green retail. In order to reach 10,000 "Greener Stores" globally by 2025—which will encompass both new builds and renovations—Starbucks will in the upcoming year establish an accredited programme to assess all of its currently open company-operated stores in the US and Canada in comparison to the framework criteria.

The framework for “Starbucks Greener Stores” will also be made publicly available to help the larger retail sector. Starbucks President and CEO Kevin Johnson stated, “Simply put, sustainable coffee, served sustainably is our aspiration.” “We are aware that designing by 2025, 10,000 “Greener Stores” will have been designed, constructed, and run worldwide thanks to the “Starbucks Greener Stores” framework. Based on extensive performance standards, the “Starbucks Greener Stores” framework will make sure that the company's strategy for planning, constructing, and running its company-owned stores raises the bar for environmentally friendly retail. With 10,000 “Greener Stores” worldwide by 2025 including new construction and renovations—Starbucks plans to create an accredited programme over the next year to evaluate all company-operated locations now operating in the United States and Canada against the framework requirements. Kevin Johnson, the president and CEO of Starbucks, stated, “Simply put, sustainable coffee, served sustainably, is our goal”. We understand that creating over the next ten years, the “Starbucks Greener Stores” framework—which was unveiled on stage at The Global Climate Action Summit in San Francisco, California—is expected to save the corporation an additional $50 million in utility costs. This extends Starbucks' ten-year history of utility cost savings linked to greener store operations, which has already resulted in an annual savings of almost $30 million in operational expenses. Along with empowering its more than 330,000 partners worldwide to be aware of and involved in sustainability, Starbucks hopes to expand the network of partner advocates through Partners for Sustainability and the Greener Apron voluntary certification program run by Arizona State University. Leading specialists, including the World Wildlife Fund (WWF), will collaborate to design the “Starbucks Greener Stores” framework.

DISCUSSION

Bhat and Velmourogane (2017) mentioned that on nearly the same proportion of coffee plantations, India produces 2.5% of the world's coffee. India's coffee production is negligible in comparison to other major producers such as Brazil (25%), Columbia (15%), and Indonesia (7%).

All of India's coffee is grown beneath a distinct two-tiered mixed shade canopy made up of evergreen leguminous trees. Almost fifty distinct varieties of Plantations that grow coffee often have shade trees. On a sloping landscape, shade trees stop soil erosion; they also recycle nutrients from deeper layers into the soil, shield coffee plants from seasonal temperature swings, and support a variety of flora and fauna. India's coffee plantations are vital hubs for spices, offering an extensive range of spices and fruit crops, including cardamom, pepper, vanilla, orange, and Bananas and coffee plants coexist. The many climates found in India's coffee-growing regions make it ideal for growing a wide range of coffee varietals. While warm, humid climates are better suited for cultivating Robustas, some high-elevation areas are good for growing Arabicas of mild quality. This essay examines the state of sustainability standards today, their potential, eco systems, effects, and cultivation costs. Compared to most other economic activities, the cultivation and trade of coffee have a very good impact on environmental and social issues. An increasing amount of data suggests that coffee farming may be endangered in some of the area's most susceptible to climate change.

Malyadri (2016) discussed that India produces 2.5% of the world's coffee. India's coffee production is negligible in comparison to other major producers such as Brazil (25%), Columbia (15%), and Indonesia (7%). All of India's coffee is grown beneath a distinct two-tiered mixed shade canopy made up of evergreen leguminous trees. Almost fifty distinct varieties of Plantations that grow coffee often have shade trees. On a sloping landscape, shade trees stop soil erosion; they also recycle nutrients from deeper layers into the soil, shield coffee plants from seasonal temperature swings, and support a variety of flora and fauna. India's coffee plantations are vital hubs for spices, offering an extensive range of spices and fruit crops, including cardamom, pepper, vanilla, orange, and Bananas and coffee plants coexist. The many climates found in India's coffee-growing regions make it ideal for growing a wide range of coffee varietals. While warm, humid climates are better suited for cultivating Robustas, some high-elevation areas are good for growing Arabicas of mild quality. This essay examines the state of sustainability standards today, their potential, eco systems, effects, and cultivation costs. When compared to most other economic activities, the cultivation and trade of coffee has a very good impact on environmental and social issues. An increasing amount of data suggests that coffee farming may be endangered in some of the area's most susceptible to climate change.

Neilson and Pritchard (2007) mentioned about a multi-stakeholder initiative called "Common Code for the Coffee Community (4C) " was created to integrate sustainability concepts into the mainstream coffee industry. Throughout its original "testing phase", producer countries widely condemned it. This article, which focuses on Indian opposition, concludes that any initiatives to advance the industry's sustainability—economic, social, and environmental—are likely to be perceived as tools of a neo-imperialist agenda that aims to establish consumer-country control over the product supply chain unless key issues as defined by producer-country interests are addressed.

Dharmasasmita, et al., (2017) introduced the idea of sustainability as being constructed from social, environmental, and economic elements. It also explores these elements as being fundamentally linked, and why this is important for business. The chapter provides two seminars detailing the importance of integrating sustainability and on how this is all related to the Sustainable Development Goals. It helps one to learn the following: recognise the fundamental linkages between social, environmental, and economic pillars of sustainability in a business framework; understand the triple bottom line and what it means for business; appreciate the applied principles of sustainability and why they are fundamental to business; and to get an overview of the Sustainable Development Goals. Balanced scorecard offers significant scope in terms of sustainability, as it allows the incorporation of elements of environmental and social sustainability integrally into financial thought. The ecosystem services approach offers business a new way of embedding social and environmental sustainability into strategy and observing tangible results.

Shubham and Pallavi (2024) delineated about cluster concepts like CSR are multifaceted, intricate, unclear, and full of oddities. This study aims to comprehend the causes of inconsistent CSR practices and the applicability of different CSR programs. It also explores the natural evolution of CSR from a business standpoint, starting with free services and working up to sustainability and business survival. Modern CSR initiatives address the three main pillars of business: profit, the earth, and people. These three

CSR pillars make CSR performance holistic, yet despite how straightforward it sounds, it is very ambiguous. To better understand Starbucks' CSR initiatives and the strategies that enable them to meet their objectives, the researchers will examine a case study of the company in this research paper.

Athukorala and Karunarathna (2018) in their study mentioned that unsustainable development is frequently characterized by poverty, inequality, economic instability, social unrest, and environmental damage. People in poor nations rarely place the necessity of sustainable development at the top of their lists of priorities because environmental factors and the availability of economic opportunities are the primary determinants of their livelihoods. Sri Lanka, a developing nation, has made progress towards sustainable development objectives in several areas. However, during the past few decades, ecological damage has been caused by careless planning, unplanned development activities, a lack of a suitable monitoring and assessment system, and a lack of awareness about sustainable development. Within this framework, the study aims to explore the trajectory of several important environmental factors in the nation.

Nguyen (2020) in his case study on sustainability marketing concept of Starbucks mentioned that is crucial while bearing in mind that the company's vision, mission, and values served as the foundation for the first business plan creation. This work looked at ways to develop sustainable business processes as well as sustainable business processes themselves. Further, this work shed light on efficiency of sustainability and marketing strategy as well as the process of sustainability as a whole. Providing broad knowledge about the development of marketing and consumer behaviour was another goal. The broad strokes of the sustainable marketing idea are covered in the thesis. The objective is to conduct a thorough analysis of two primary strategy principles and the ways in which company marketing has successfully applied these strategies.

This paper also includes theoretical material on sustainability in marketing along with research methodology. The information was gathered through a variety of techniques, and primary and secondary sources that were readily available online were used in the writing. Starbucks is the subject of the case study in order to highlight the unique components of the marketing process as well as the tenets of sustainability strategy. The thesis examined the importance of sustainability marketing while keeping in mind that the company's vision, mission, and values served as the foundation for the initial business strategy development.

Table 1. Summary of study on sustainability among three South Asian countries

Dimension	Environmental Sustainability			Social Sustainability		
Country	India	Bangladesh	Sri Lanka	India	Bangladesh	Sri Lanka
Author	Bhat & Velmourogane (2017)	Wijewantha and Kulatunga (2022)	De Silva et al. (2020)	Shubham and Pallavi (2024)	Quadir et al. (2023)	Bilfield (2022)
	Neilson & Pritchard (2007)		Sun et al. (2020)	Neilson & Pritchard (2007)	Farhad (2019)	Munasinghe (2018).
	Krishnan (2013)		Athukorala & Karunarathna (2018)	Nguyen (2020)	Lee et al. (2016)	
				Dharmasasmita et al. (2017).		

CONCLUSION

The paper is descriptive and details the environmental and social sustainability parameters being implemented in South Asian countries selectively India, Bangladesh, and Sri Lanka. The study is explorative of the coffee industry chosen as Starbucks. As India is in the nascent stage of sustainability development, some prominent brands are incorporating the environmental and social sustainability concept at the largest. Starbucks is among them in implementing sustainability at a great pace. It is taking various measures to adhere to environmental sustainability norms whereas social sustainability norms are also taken to implement the sustainability concept.

The paper has taken discussions and highlights of different authors having made eminent contributions to the field. However, the paper can be explored further in an elaborate manner suggesting measures to overcome the challenges and prospects in the field of sustainability in the coffee industry. The present chapter has highlighted the current scenario in the various countries being chosen for the study. The development that has been observed from past and future trends can make a significant contribution to the development of the coffee industry. The concept is also giving a competitive edge to the brands in the development of the field of sustainability. The study can give a roadmap to the researchers for further research in the current field.

ACKNOWLEDGMENT

This research received no specific grant from any funding agency in the public, commercial, or not-for-profit sectors.

REFERENCES

Adopted, I. P. C. C. (2014). Climate change 2014 synthesis report. *IPCC: Geneva, Szwitzerland*, 1059-1072.

Ashrafi, M., Adams, M., Walker, T. R., & Magnan, G. (2018). How corporate social responsibility can be integrated into corporate sustainability: A theoretical review of their relationships. *International Journal of Sustainable Development and World Ecology*, *25*(8), 672–682. DOI: 10.1080/13504509.2018.1471628

Athukorala, W., & Karunarathna, M. (2018). Environmental challenges and the sustainable development goals: A study about the emerging environmental issues in Sri Lanka. *Appl. Econ. Bus*, *2*(2), 38–51. DOI: 10.4038/aeb.v2i2.61

Bilfield, A. (2022). *Brewing Sustainability in the Coffee and Tea Industries: From Producer to Consumer*. Routledge. DOI: 10.4324/9781003228851

Dahlsrud, A. (2008). How corporate social responsibility is defined: An analysis of 37 definitions. *Corporate Social Responsibility and Environmental Management*, *15*(1), 1–13. DOI: 10.1002/csr.132

Daviron, B., & Ponte, S. (2005). *The coffee paradox: Global markets, commodity trade and the elusive promise of development*. Zed books. DOI: 10.5040/9781350222984

Davis, A. P., Gole, T. W., Baena, S., & Moat, J. (2012). The impact of climate change on indigenous arabica coffee (Coffea arabica): Predicting future trends and identifying priorities. *PLoS One*, *7*(11), e47981. DOI: 10.1371/journal.pone.0047981 PMID: 23144840

De Silva, K., Yapa, P. W. S., & Vesty, G. (2020). The impact of accountability mechanisms on public sector environmental sustainability performance: A case study of Sri Lanka. *Australasian Accounting. Business and Finance Journal, 14*(3), 38–55.

Dharmasasmita, A., Erlandsson, L., Willats, J., & Brown, S. (2017). Integrating the three pillars of sustainability: social, environmental and economic. In *The Business Student's Guide to Sustainable Management* (pp. 83–126). Routledge. DOI: 10.4324/9781351216500-4

Dulloo, M. E., Guarino, L., Engelmann, F., Maxted, N., Newbury, J. H., Attere, F., & Ford-Lloyd, B. V. (1998). Complementary conservation strategies for the genus Coffea: A case study of Mascarene Coffea species. *Genetic Resources and Crop Evolution, 45*(6), 565–579. DOI: 10.1023/A:1008621028343

Elkington, J. (1997). The triple bottom line. Environmental management: Readings and cases, 2, 49-66.

Engelmann, F., Dulloo, M. E., Astorga, C., Dussert, S., & Anthony, F. (2007). *Conserving coffee genetic resources: complementary strategies for ex situ conservation of coffee (Coffea arabica L.) genetic resources: a case study in Catie*. IRD Editions.

Farhad, N. (2019). *Supply chain governance for social sustainability: a study of the ready-made Garment industry in Bangladesh* (Vol. 2004). Linköping University Electronic Press.

Giovannucci, D., & Ponte, S. (2005). Standards as a new form of social contract? Sustainability initiatives in the coffee industry. *Food Policy, 30*(3), 284–301. DOI: 10.1016/j.foodpol.2005.05.007

Gole, T. W. (2002). Ecological studies on a keystone forest ecosystem for Coffea arabica gene conservation. *Unpublished PhD dissertation.*

Hahn, K. A., Wise, L. A., Rothman, K. J., Mikkelsen, E. M., Brogly, S. B., Sørensen, H. T., Riis, A. H., & Hatch, E. E. (2015). Caffeine and caffeinated beverage consumption and risk of spontaneous abortion. *Human Reproduction (Oxford, England), 30*(5), 1246–1255. DOI: 10.1093/humrep/dev063 PMID: 25788567

Hannah, L., & Roehrdanz, P. R., KC, K. B., Fraser, E. D., Donatti, C. I., Saenz, L., & van Soesbergen, A. (. (2020). The environmental consequences of climate-driven agricultural frontiers. *PLoS One*, *15*(2), e0228305. DOI: 10.1371/journal.pone.0228305 PMID: 32049959

Harshe, G. (2024). Negotiating the salientization of identity: Hindu? Indian? American? *New Directions for Higher Education*, *2024*(206), 15–26. DOI: 10.1002/he.20500

Hemakumara, G. P. T. S., Athukorala, S. U., & Yapa, L. G. D. S. (2023). "Battle for Solar Energy" Program: An Environment-Friendly Sustainable Approach for Carbon Neutrality in Sri Lanka. In *Sustainability and Social Marketing Issues in Asia* (pp. 23-38). Emerald Publishing Limited.

Krishnan, S. (2013). Current status of coffee genetic resources and implications for conservation. *CABI Reviews*, (2013), 1-9.

Lebacq, T., Baret, P. V., & Stilmant, D. (2013). Sustainability indicators for livestock farming. A review. *Agronomy for Sustainable Development*, *33*(2), 311–327. DOI: 10.1007/s13593-012-0121-x

Lee, K. H., Vachon, S., Lee, K. H., & Vachon, S. (2016). Supply chain sustainability risk. *Business value and sustainability: An integrated supply network perspective*, 245-280

Malyadri, P. (2016). Status of coffee plantation in India: A high time for innovation and sustainability towards make in India. *VSRD Int J Bus Manag Res*, *6*(2), 47–50.

McKenzie, S. (2004). Social sustainability: towards some definitions.

Meyfroidt, P., Vu, T. P., & Hoang, V. A. (2013). Trajectories of deforestation, coffee expansion and displacement of shifting cultivation in the Central Highlands of Vietnam. *Global Environmental Change*, *23*(5), 1187–1198. DOI: 10.1016/j.gloenvcha.2013.04.005

Munasinghe, M. A. T. K. (2018). *The agency of global sustainability certifications in developing countries: the Rainforest Alliance and the Sri Lankan tea industry* (Doctoral dissertation, University of Birmingham).

Neilson, J., & Pritchard, B. (2007). Green coffee? The contradictions of global sustainability initiatives from an Indian perspective. *Development Policy Review*, *25*(3), 311–331. DOI: 10.1111/j.1467-7679.2007.00372.x

Nguyen, C. (2020). Sustainability marketing concept: Case Starbucks.

Ovalle-Rivera, O., Läderach, P., Bunn, C., Obersteiner, M., & Schroth, G. (2015). Projected shifts in Coffea arabica suitability among major global producing regions due to climate change. *PLoS One*, *10*(4), e0124155. DOI: 10.1371/journal.pone.0124155 PMID: 25875230

Panhuysen, S., & Pierrot, J. (2018). *Coffee barometer 2018*. Conservation International.

Paris Agreement, U. N. F. C. C. C. (2015). *Adoption of the Paris Agreement*. Report No. FCCC/CP/2015/L.9/Rev.1, https://unfccc.int/resource/docs/2015/cop21/eng/l09r01.pdf (UNFCCC, 2015)

Parrish, B. D. (2007). Designing the sustainable enterprise. *Futures*, *39*(7), 846–860. DOI: 10.1016/j.futures.2006.12.007

Pham, L., Pham, & Liu. (2019). International graduates returning to Vietnam. Springer Singapore.

Phelan, H., Hennelly, J., Chappell, D., & Roberts, A. N. (2017). The Irish World Music Café: performing and recording as tools for sustainable social integration. In *Voices: A World Forum for Music Therapy17*(3). DOI: 10.15845/voices.v17i3.939

Quadir, P., Ansar, T. B., Dembo, S. A., Zaheen, T., & Raisa, K. A. (2023). Navigating the Bangladeshi Market: Unlocking Market Entry Opportunities for STARBUCKS. *Business Perspectives and Research*, *5*(2), 37–48. DOI: 10.38157/bpr.v5i2.604

Rahn, E., Vaast, P., Läderach, P., Van Asten, P., Jassogne, L., & Ghazoul, J. (2018). Exploring adaptation strategies of coffee production to climate change using a process-based model. *Ecological Modelling*, *371*, 76–89. DOI: 10.1016/j.ecolmodel.2018.01.009

Robinson, J. (2004). Squaring the circle? Some thoughts on the idea of sustainable development. *Ecological Economics*, *48*(4), 369–384. DOI: 10.1016/j.ecolecon.2003.10.017

Samper, L. F., Giovannucci, D., & Vieira, L. M. (2017). *The powerful role of intangibles in the coffee value chain*, 39. WIPO.

Sarkar, S., & Searcy, C. (2016). Zeitgeist or chameleon? A quantitative analysis of CSR definitions. *Journal of Cleaner Production*, *135*, 1423–1435. DOI: 10.1016/j.jclepro.2016.06.157

Shubham, S., & Pallavi, P (2024). UNRAVELLING THE CSR OUTLOOK OF STARBUCKS: A CASE-BASED APPROACH. *Responsibility*, 58.

Silva, S. A. D. (2019). Hypothenemus hampei:(Coleoptera: Scolytidae): impacto sobre a qualidade dos grãos de café.

Singh, K. P., Singh, B., Patil, S. K., Rahangdale, C. P., Banerjee, A., Shukla, R., Sahu, K., & Jhariya, M. K. (2023). Biomass, carbon stock, CO2 mitigation and carbon credits of coffee-based multitier cropping model in Central India. *Environmental Monitoring and Assessment*, *195*(10), 1250. DOI: 10.1007/s10661-023-11892-5 PMID: 37758966

Sun, H., Mohsin, M., Alharthi, M., & Abbas, Q. (2020). Measuring environmental sustainability performance of South Asia. *Journal of Cleaner Production*, *251*, 119519. DOI: 10.1016/j.jclepro.2019.119519

Trivino-Tarradas, P., Gomez-Ariza, M. R., Basch, G., & Gonzalez-Sanchez, E. J. (2019). Sustainability assessment of annual and permanent crops: The Inspia model. *Sustainability (Basel)*, *11*(3), 738. DOI: 10.3390/su11030738

Van Calker, K. J., Berentsen, P. B. M., Giesen, G. W. J., & Huirne, R. B. M. (2008). Maximising sustainability of Dutch dairy farming systems for different stakeholders: A modelling approach. *Ecological Economics*, *65*(2), 407–419. DOI: 10.1016/j.ecolecon.2007.07.010

Wijaya, S. A., & Mursitama, T. N. (2023). The Implementation of Triple Bottom Line on CSR Effort Toward Sustainable Development: Case Study Starbucks Greener Nusantara. In *E3S Web of Conferences*, 388, p. 03018). EDP Sciences. DOI: 10.1051/e3sconf/202338803018

Wijewantha, P., & Kulatunga, U. (2022). A framework to assess environmental sustainability of expressway projects in Sri Lanka. *Management of Environmental Quality*, *33*(6), 1404–1420. DOI: 10.1108/MEQ-09-2021-0220

Chapter 11
Future Trends and Emerging Technology

S. N. Sabarivarshini
Nehru Institute of Technology, India

R. Dhilip
Nehru Institute of Technology, India

ABSTRACT

Technological advancements are set to redefine industries and societal norms, heralding an era of unprecedented innovation and interconnectedness. Leading this transformation are artificial intelligence (AI), quantum computing, and biotechnology. AI is revolutionizing healthcare and finance through predictive analytics and autonomous systems. Quantum computing promises breakthroughs in cryptography, materials science, and drug discovery. Simultaneously, the Internet of Things (IoT) is creating a hyper-connected world, enhancing efficiency and generating new data-driven insights. Biotechnology advances, such as CRISPR, offer groundbreaking medical treatments and agricultural innovations, tackling disease and food security. The convergence of these technologies will spur new interdisciplinary fields and applications.

DOI: 10.4018/979-8-3693-6592-2.ch011

INTRODUCTION

In the inexorable march towards an increasingly digitalized future, technology evolves ceaselessly, revealing new trends and breakthroughs that promise to redefine our world. Exploring these future trajectories and emerging technologies becomes essential in understanding the landscape that lies ahead. Technological progress accelerates at unprecedented rates, fueled by scientific innovation, computational power, and global connectivity (Tunc et al., 2021). From artificial intelligence and machine learning to quantum computing and biotechnology, these advancements reshape industries and society at large.

Driving this rapid evolution are various factors, including advances in computing power and the democratization of technology. Moore's Law and quantum computing propel computational capabilities forward, while open-source initiatives empower a new generation of innovators. These advancements reverberate across industries and societies worldwide. From healthcare to finance, emerging technologies transform traditional sectors. However, they also raise ethical and societal concerns, such as data privacy and algorithmic bias, necessitating responsible innovation. Amidst promises of progress, uncertainties loom. Cybersecurity threats and ethical dilemmas underscore the importance of ethical stewardship (Pinto et al., 2020). As technology intersects with global challenges like climate change and socio-economic inequality, holistic and sustainable solutions become imperative (Bueno et al., 2016).

The ripple effects of these technological upheavals are felt across industries and societies worldwide. From the reimagining of healthcare delivery through telemedicine and precision medicine to the disruption of financial services by blockchain and decentralized finance, the transformative potential of emerging technologies is reshaping the contours of traditional sectors. Moreover, societies grapple with the profound ethical, societal, and economic implications of automation, digitalization, and AI-driven decision-making (Knorr, 2018).

In navigating this technological flux, foresight and adaptability are crucial. Cultivating a culture of innovation and responsible entrepreneurship enables us to harness the potential of emerging technologies. By doing so, we can shape a future that is not only technologically advanced but also ethical, sustainable, and equitable (Gill, 2018).

OVERVIEW OF CURRENT TECHNOLOGIES

In today's rapidly evolving technological landscape, several key technologies dominate and

Figure 1. AI

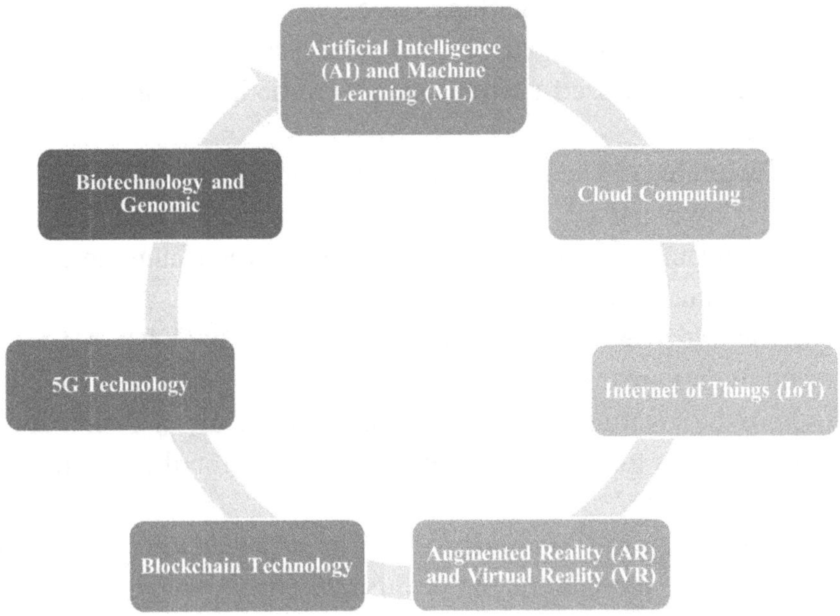

continue to shape various industries. Here’s a brief summary of the most prevalent ones:

1. **Artificial Intelligence (AI) and Machine Learning (ML):** AI and ML are at the forefront, driving innovations across numerous fields. They are used for data analysis, predictive analytics, natural language processing, and automation. AI technologies enhance capabilities in healthcare, finance, customer service, and more (Dong et al., 2021).

2. **Cloud Computing:** Cloud computing enables on-demand access to computing resources over the internet, allowing for scalability, flexibility, and cost savings. Major players like Amazon Web Services (AWS), Microsoft Azure, and Google Cloud dominate this space, providing infrastructure, platform, and software as services (IaaS, PaaS, SaaS).
3. **Internet of Things (IoT):** IoT involves the interconnection of everyday devices to the internet, enabling them to send and receive data. Applications range from smart homes and cities to industrial IoT (IIoT) in manufacturing and logistics, enhancing efficiency and automation.
4. **Blockchain Technology:** Originally known for cryptocurrencies like Bitcoin, blockchain technology has expanded its use cases to include supply chain management, secure voting systems, and smart contracts, offering decentralized and transparent transaction capabilities (Ahmed et al., 2021).
5. **5G Technology**: The rollout of 5G networks provides faster internet speeds, lower latency, and greater connectivity. It's a critical enabler for advancements in IoT, autonomous vehicles, and augmented/virtual reality applications.
6. **Augmented Reality (AR) and Virtual Reality (VR):** AR and VR technologies are transforming gaming, entertainment, education, and training by creating immersive experiences. They also find applications in fields like real estate, healthcare, and retail for virtual tours and simulations.
7. **Biotechnology and Genomic:** Advances in biotechnology, particularly genomics, are revolutionizing healthcare with personalized medicine, gene editing technologies like CRISPR, and advanced diagnostic tools.

Key Drivers of Change

Several factors are driving technological advancements and shaping the current landscape:

1. **Innovation and Research:** Continuous investment in research and development (R&D) by governments, academic institutions, and private companies fuels innovation. Breakthroughs in fields like AI, biotechnology, and material science propel new technologies forward.

2. **Consumer Demand:** Increasing consumer demand for faster, more efficient, and user-friendly technologies drives companies to innovate. The rise of smartphones, smart devices, and seamless digital experiences reflects this trend.
3. **Global Connectivity:** The widespread availability of high-speed internet and mobile networks has connected the world like never before. This connectivity facilitates the rapid dissemination of information and the adoption of new technologies.
4. **Economic Incentives:** Competitive markets and the potential for significant financial returns incentivize businesses to adopt and develop new technologies. The tech industry, in particular, sees substantial investment and growth opportunities.
5. **Regulatory and Policy Support:** Government policies and regulations can accelerate technological adoption. Supportive regulations, funding for innovation, and initiatives like smart city projects create conducive environments for tech advancement.
6. **Environmental and Social Challenges:** Addressing global challenges such as climate change, healthcare, and food security necessitates innovative technological solutions. Technologies like renewable energy, precision agriculture, and telemedicine are developed to meet these needs.
7. **Cultural Shifts:** Societal attitudes towards technology, including greater acceptance of digital solutions and changing work environments (e.g., remote work), also drive technological advancements and their integration into daily life (Pinto et al., 2020).

Emerging Technologies: Artificial Intelligence and Machine Learning

Current Advancements: Artificial Intelligence (AI) and Machine Learning (ML) have made significant strides in recent years, becoming integral to various sectors. AI algorithms power applications from natural language processing (e.g., chatbots and virtual assistants) to advanced image recognition systems used in healthcare diagnostics. In finance, AI models are employed for fraud detection, algorithmic trading, and personalized financial advice. Self-driving cars, powered by AI, combine computer vision, sensor fusion, and deep learning to navigate complex environments (Kajikawa et al., 2008).

Future Potential

AI and ML are poised to revolutionize numerous fields:
Healthcare: AI will enhance precision medicine by predicting patient outcomes and personalizing treatment plans. AI-driven drug discovery is expected to expedite the development of new medications.
Education: Adaptive learning technologies will personalize educational experiences, catering to individual learning styles and paces.
Ethical AI: As AI systems become more prevalent, ensuring fairness, transparency, and accountability in AI decision-making will be crucial.

Quantum Computing

Introduction: Quantum computing leverages the principles of quantum mechanics to process information in fundamentally different ways than classical computers. Quantum bits, or qubits, can exist in multiple states simultaneously, enabling quantum computers to solve complex problems much faster than classical computers (Link & Vijaykrishnan, (2006).

Potential Impact:

- **Cryptography**: Quantum computing threatens current encryption methods by making it feasible to crack cryptographic codes that are currently secure. This will necessitate the development of quantum-resistant encryption algorithms.
- **Drug Discovery**: Quantum computers can simulate molecular structures and interactions at an unprecedented scale, potentially leading to breakthroughs in drug discovery and materials science.
- **Optimization Problems**: Industries like logistics, finance, and manufacturing will benefit from quantum computing's ability to solve complex optimization problems more efficiently, improving everything from supply chain management to financial modeling.

- **Artificial Intelligence**: Quantum machine learning could significantly enhance the capabilities of AI systems, enabling them to process and analyze vast amounts of data more effectively.

Blockchain and Decentralized Technologies

Blockchain technology, originally developed for cryptocurrencies like Bitcoin, provides a decentralized and transparent way to record transactions. Each block in the blockchain is immutable and cryptographically secured, ensuring data integrity and security (Kajikawa et al., 2008).

Broader Applications:

- **Supply Chain Management**: Blockchain enhances transparency and traceability in supply chains. It allows stakeholders to track products from origin to destination, ensuring authenticity and reducing fraud.
- **Smart Contracts**: These self-executing contracts with the terms directly written into code automate and enforce agreements without intermediaries.
- **Voting Systems**: Blockchain can ensure secure and transparent elections by providing tamper-proof voting records, thereby increasing trust in electoral processes.
- **Decentralized Finance (DeFi):** DeFi platforms use blockchain to offer financial services without traditional intermediaries. This includes lending, borrowing, and trading assets, making financial services more accessible and efficient.

Internet of Things (IoT)

Expansion of Connected Devices: IoT refers to the network of physical devices embedded with sensors, software, and connectivity to exchange data. The number of connected devices is rapidly increasing, with applications spanning various sectors (Bueno et al., 2016).

Smart Applications:

- **Smart Cities**: IoT enables urban planners to manage infrastructure more effectively. Applications include smart traffic management, waste management, and energy-efficient buildings.
- **Industrial IoT (IIoT)**: In manufacturing, IIoT connects machinery and equipment to optimize production processes, predict maintenance needs, and reduce downtime. This leads to increased efficiency and cost savings.
- **Healthcare**: Wearable devices and remote monitoring systems allow for continuous health tracking, improving patient care and enabling proactive health management.

5g And Beyond

Current Status

5G technology is the latest generation of mobile networks, offering significantly higher speeds, lower latency, and greater connectivity compared to its predecessors. It supports enhanced mobile broadband, massive IoT, and ultra-reliable low-latency communications (Mo et al., 2022).

CONCLUSION AND FUTURE IMPLICATIONS

Enhanced Connectivity: 5G will support the growing number of IoT devices, providing the necessary bandwidth and reliability for seamless connectivity in smart cities, homes, and industries.

Autonomous Vehicles: The low latency of 5G is crucial for the safe and efficient operation of autonomous vehicles, enabling real-time data communication between vehicles and infrastructure.

Augmented and Virtual Reality: 5G will enable high-quality, immersive AR and VR experiences by providing the bandwidth needed for real-time, interactive applications in gaming, education, and remote work.

REFERENCES

Ahmed, F. E., Khalil, A., & Hilal, N. (2021). Emerging desalination technologies: Current status, challenges and future trends. *Desalination, 517*, 115183.

Bommu, R. (2022). Advancements in Medical Device Software: A Comprehensive Review of Emerging Technologies and Future Trends. *Journal of Engineering Technology, 4*(2), 1–8.

Bueno, G., Fernández-Carrobles, M. M., Deniz, O., & García-Rojo, M. (2016). New trends of emerging technologies in digital pathology. *Pathobiology, 83*(2-3), 61–69. PMID: 27100343

Dong, C., Akram, A., Andersson, D., Arnäs, P. O., & Stefansson, G. (2021). The impact of emerging and disruptive technologies on freight transportation in the digital era: Current state and future trends. *International Journal of Logistics Management, 32*(2), 386–412.

Gill, D. S. N. S. (2018). Emerging trends and future computing technologies: A vision for smart environment. *International Journal of Advanced Research in Computer Science, 9*(2).

Hua, X., Huang, Y., & Zheng, Y. (2019). Current practices, new insights, and emerging trends of financial technologies. *Industrial Management & Data Systems, 119*(7), 1401–1410.

Kajikawa, Y., Yoshikawa, J., Takeda, Y., & Matsushima, K. (2008). Tracking emerging technologies in energy research: Toward a roadmap for sustainable energy. *Technological Forecasting and Social Change, 75*(6), 771–782.

Knorr, D. (2018). Emerging technologies: Back to the future. *Trends in Food Science & Technology, 76*, 119–123.

Link, G. M., & Vijaykrishnan, N. (2006, March). Thermal trends in emerging technologies. In *7th International Symposium on Quality Electronic Design (ISQED'06)* (pp. 8). IEEE.

Mo, T., Li, Y., Lau, K. T., Poon, C. K., Wu, Y., & Luo, Y. (2022). Trends and emerging technologies for the development of electric vehicles. *Energies*, *15*(17), 6271.

Pinto, L., Baruzzi, F., Cocolin, L., & Malfeito-Ferreira, M. (2020). Emerging technologies to control Brettanomyces spp. in wine: Recent advances and future trends. *Trends in Food Science & Technology*, *99*, 88–100.

Tunc, M. A., Gures, E., & Shayea, I. (2021). A survey on iot smart healthcare: Emerging technologies, applications, challenges, and future trends. arXiv preprint arXiv:2109.02042.

Compilation of References

Adam, A., & Shauki, E. (2014). Behavioral decision-making in economic contexts: An exploration of cognitive factors. *The Journal of Behavioral Economics*, *22*(4), 112–127.

Adewuyi, A. O. (2016). Determinants of Import Demand for Non-Renewable Energy (Petroleum) Products: Empirical Evidence from Nigeria. *Energy Policy*, *95*, 73–93. DOI: 10.1016/j.enpol.2016.04.035

Adopted, I. P. C. C. (2014). Climate change 2014 synthesis report. *IPCC: Geneva, Szwitzerland*, 1059-1072.

Advancing Digital Transformation: Global Insights into the Digitalization of Trade Procedures | UNCTAD. (2023, Dec 29). https://unctad.org/news/advancing-digital-transformation-global-insights-digitalization-trade-procedures

Ahmad, A. Y. B., Kumari, D. K., Shukla, A., Deepak, A., Chandnani, M., Pundir, S., & Shrivastava, A. (2024). Framework for Cloud Based Document Management System with Institutional Schema of Database. *International Journal of Intelligent Systems and Applications in Engineering*, *12*(3s), 672–678.

Ahmad, A. Y. B., Tiwari, A., Nayeem, M. A., Biswal, B. K., Satapathy, D. P., Kulshreshtha, K., & Bordoloi, D. (2024). Artificial Intelligence Perspective Framework of the Smart Finance and Accounting Management Model. *International Journal of Intelligent Systems and Applications in Engineering*, *12*(4s), 586–594.

Ahmad, A., Abusaimeh, H., Rababah, A., Alqsass, M., Al-Olima, N., & Hamdan, M. (2024). Assessment of effects in advances of accounting technologies on quality financial reports in Jordanian public sector. *Uncertain Supply Chain Management*, *12*(1), 133–142. DOI: 10.5267/j.uscm.2023.10.011

Ahmadian, M. M., Baker, D., & Paz, A. (2024). Leveraging business intelligence solutions for urban parking management. *City, Culture and Society*, *37*, 100579. DOI: 10.1016/j.ccs.2024.100579

Ahmad, M., & Shah, F. (2020). The influence of human psychology on investment decisions: A behavioral finance perspective. *Journal of Behavioral Finance*, *22*(3), 245–259.

Ahmed, F. E., Khalil, A., & Hilal, N. (2021). Emerging desalination technologies: Current status, challenges and future trends. *Desalination*, *517*, 115183.

Akash, T. R., Lessard, N. D. J., Reza, N. R., & Islam, M. S. (2024). Investigating Methods to Enhance Data Privacy in Business, Especially in sectors like Analytics and Finance. *Journal of Computer Science and Technology Studies*, *6*(5), 143–151. DOI: 10.32996/jcsts.2024.6.5.12

Akomea-Frimpong, I., Adeabah, D., Ofosu, D., & Tenakwah, E. J. (2022). 'A Review of Studies on Green Finance of Banks, Research Gaps and Future Directions'. *Journal of Sustainable Finance & Investment*, *12*(4), 1241–1264. https://doi.org/DOI:10.1080/20430795.2020.1870202

Al Daabseh, T. K. I., Aljawarneh, N. M. S., Al Smadi, K., Alnawafleh, A., & Al-maaitah, T. A. (2024). Integration of business intelligence and marketing: Enhancing corporate reputation in the financial services sector. Journal of Infrastructure. *Policy and Development*, *8*(7), 4603. DOI: 10.24294/jipd.v8i7.4603

Al Daabseh, T. K. I., Bani-Hani, T., Aljawarneh, N. M., Alkufahy, A. M., & Al Raqqad, R. (2023). The Relationship Between Business Intelligence Capabilities and Business Outcomes of Small and Medium Sized Enterprises: The Moderating Role of Competitive Intelligence. *Journal of System and Management Sciences*, *13*(4), 535–550.

Al-Banna, A., Rana, Z. A., Yaqot, M., & Menezes, B. (2023). Interconnectedness between Supply Chain Resilience, Industry 4.0, and Investment. *Logistics (Basel)*, *7*(3), 50.

Allahham, M., & Ahmad, A. (2024). AI-induced anxiety in the assessment of factors influencing the adoption of mobile payment services in supply chain firms: A mental accounting perspective. *International Journal of Data and Network Science*, *8*(1), 505–514. DOI: 10.5267/j.ijdns.2023.9.006

Alrousan, A. (2023). From Big Data to Big Insights: The Power and Efficiency of Big Data and Data Science in Statistical Work. https://sdgs.un.org/documents/ahmad-policy-using-big-data-official-statistical-centers-support-decision-makers-52426.

Al-Sai, Z. A., & Abualigah, L. M. (2017). Big data and E-government: A review. *2017 8th International Conference on Information Technology (ICIT)*, 580–587. DOI: 10.1109/ICITECH.2017.8080062

Al-Sai, Z., Abdullah, R., & Husin, H. (2019). Big Data Impacts and Challenges. *RE:view*, 150–155. Advance online publication. DOI: 10.1109/JEEIT.2019.8717484

Altinay, G. (2007). Short-Run and Long-Run Elasticities of Import Demand For Crude Oil in Turkey. *Energy Policy*, *35*(11), 5829–5835.

Anderson, J. C., & Gerbing, D. W. (1988). Structural equation modeling in practice: A review and recommended two-step approach. *Psychological Bulletin*, *103*(3), 411–423. DOI: 10.1037/0033-2909.103.3.411

Arize, A. C., & Malindretos, J. (2012). Foreign Exchange Reserves in Asia and Its Impact on Import Demand. *International Journal of Economics and Finance*, *4*(3), 21–32.

Ashrafi, M., Adams, M., Walker, T. R., & Magnan, G. (2018). How corporate social responsibility can be integrated into corporate sustainability: A theoretical review of their relationships. *International Journal of Sustainable Development and World Ecology*, *25*(8), 672–682. DOI: 10.1080/13504509.2018.1471628

Assuncao, R., & Pelechrinis, K. (2019). Sports Analytics in the Era of Big Data: Moving Toward the Next Frontier. *Big Data*, *7*(1), 1–2.

Athukorala, W., & Karunarathna, M. (2018). Environmental challenges and the sustainable development goals: A study about the emerging environmental issues in Sri Lanka. *Appl. Econ. Bus*, *2*(2), 38–51. DOI: 10.4038/aeb.v2i2.61

Bag, S., Wood, L. C., Xu, L., Dhamija, P., & Kayikci, Y. (2020). Big data analytics as an operational excellence approach to enhance sustainable supply chain performance. *Resources, Conservation and Recycling*, *153*, 104559.

Baines, J., & Hager, S. B. (2022). Commodity traders in a storm: Financialization, corporate power and ecological crisis. *Review of International Political Economy*, *29*(4), 1053–1084.

Bajari, P. (2019). The Impact of Big Data on Firm Performance: An Empirical Investigation." AEA papers and proceedings. Vol. 109. American Economic Association.

Bajracharya, S., Carenini, G., Chamberlain, B., Chen, K., Klein, D., Poole, D., Taheri, H., & Öberg, G. (2018). Interactive visualization for group decision analysis. *International Journal of Information Technology & Decision Making*, *17*(06), 1839–1864. DOI: 10.1142/S0219622018500384

Baker, H. K., Kumar, S., Goyal, V., & Gaur, A. (2019). Behavioral biases in investment decision-making: A review of recent developments. *The Journal of Investment Strategies*, *18*(2), 105–119.

Bakker, L. (2020). Economic evaluations of big data analytics for clinical decision-making: A scoping review. *Journal of the American Medical Informatics Association : JAMIA*, *27*(9), 1466–1475.

Baldissera, A. (2023). 'Sustainability Reporting in Banks: History of Studies and a Conceptual Framework for Thinking about the Future by Learning from the Past'. *Corporate Social Responsibility and Environmental Management*, *30*(5), 2385–2405. Advance online publication. DOI: 10.1002/csr.2491

Ball, R. (2009). Market and Political/Regulatory Perspectives on the Recent Accounting Scandals. *Journal of Accounting Research*, *47*(2), 277–323. DOI: 10.1111/j.1475-679X.2009.00325.x

Ball, R., Brown, P., & Davies, D. (2010). Risk aversion and investment choices in financial markets: Evidence from behavioral finance. *The Journal of Finance*, *32*(4), 287–300.

Banerjee, A. (2011). Investor psychology and market trends: A behavioral finance approach. *Journal of Finance and Psychology*, *18*(3), 75–90.

Banga, R. (2019). Is India Digitally Prepared for International Trade? *Economic and Political Weekly*, *54*(5), 2.

Bani Ahmad, A. Y. A. (2024). Firm Determinants that Influences Implementation of Accounting Technologies in Business Organizations. *WSEAS Transactions on Business and Economics*, *21*, 1–11. DOI: 10.37394/23207.2024.21.1

Bao, Y. (2018). Research on the Impact of Big Data on International Economy and Trade. *Science and technique info, 16* (33): 226-227.

Baranauskaitė, L., & Jurevičienė, D. (2021). Import Risks of Agricultural Products in Foreign Trade. *Economies*, *9*(3), 102.

Barber, B. M., & Odean, T. (2000). Trading is hazardous to your wealth: The common stock investment performance of individual investors. *The Journal of Finance*, *55*(2), 773–806. DOI: 10.1111/0022-1082.00226

Barberis, N., & Thaler, R. (2003). A survey of behavioral finance. Handbook of the Economics of Finance, 1, 1053-1128. https://doi.org/DOI: 10.1016/S1574-0102(03)01007-1

Batko, K., & Ślęzak, A. (2022). The use of Big Data Analytics in healthcare. *Journal of Big Data*, *9*(1), 3. PMID: 35013701

Bayraktutan, Y., & Bıdırdı, H. (2010). Türkiye Ithalatının Temel Belirleyicileri. *Ege Academic Review*, *10*(1), 351–369.

Becker, P. (2023). *Sustainability science: Managing risk and resilience for sustainable development*. Elsevier.

Belenguer, L. (2022). The ethical implications of algorithmic bias in decision-making. *Journal of Applied Ethics, 35*(1), 123–141.

Belloumi, M., & Touati, K. (2022). Do FDI Inflows and ICT Affect Economic Growth? An Evidence from Arab Countries. *Sustainability (Basel), 14*(10), 10. Advance online publication. DOI: 10.3390/su14106293

Berisha, B., Mëziu, E., & Shabani, I. (2022). Big data analytics in Cloud computing: An overview. *Journal of Cloud Computing (Heidelberg, Germany), 11*(1), 24. PMID: 35966392

Bezerianos, A. F. Chevalier, P. Dragicevic, N. Elmqvist, and J. D. Fekete (2010). Graphdice: A system for exploring multivariate social networks," in Proceedings of the 12th Eurographics / IEEE VGTC Conference on Visualization, ser. EuroVis10. Chichester, GBR: The Eurographs Association & John Wiley & Sons, Ltd., 2010, p. 863872. DOI: 10.1111/j.1467-8659.2009.01687.x

Bhandari, G., & Deaves, R. (2006). The effect of overconfidence bias on investment decisions. *Journal of Behavioral Decision Making, 19*(1), 3–18.

Bharathi, B.T. (2016). Efficient Exploration of Algorithms in Scholarly Documents Using Big Data Analytics. *International Journal of Engineering and Computer Science*. https://doi.org/10.18535/ijecs/v5i11.58

Bikakis, N., Papastefanatos, G., & Papaemmanouil, O. (2019). Big Data Exploration, Visualization and Analytics. *Big Data Research, 18*, 100123. https://doi.org/10.1016/j.bdr.2019.100123

Bilfield, A. (2022). *Brewing Sustainability in the Coffee and Tea Industries: From Producer to Consumer*. Routledge. DOI: 10.4324/9781003228851

Blazquez, D., & Domenech, J. (2018). Big Data sources and methods for social and economic analyses. *Technological Forecasting and Social Change, 130*, 99–113.

Blessing, L. T. M., & Chakrabarti, A. (2009). *DRM, a Design Research Methodology*. Springer.

Bommu, R. (2022). Advancements in Medical Device Software: A Comprehensive Review of Emerging Technologies and Future Trends. *Journal of Engineering Technology*, *4*(2), 1–8.

Booshehrian, M., Moller, T., Pterman, R., & Munzner, T. (2012). Facilitating analysis of trade-offs, uncertainty, and sensitivity in fisheries management decision making." in *Computer Graphics Forum, 31*(3) pt3. Wiley Online Library, pp. 1235-1244.

Booshehrian, M., Möller, T., Peterman, R. M., & Munzner, T. (2014). Vismon: M. Sedlmair, C. Heinzl, S. Bruckner, H. Piringer, and T. Möller, "Visual parameter space analysis: A conceptual framework,". *IEEE Transactions on Visualization and Computer Graphics, TVCG*, *20*(12), 2161–2170. PMID: 26356930

Boukhelifa, N., Cancino, W., Bezerianos, A., & Lutton, E. "Evolutionary visual exploration: evaluation with expert users," in Computer Graphics Forum, 32(3) pt1. Wiley Online Library, pp. 31-40.

Bowen, G. A. (2009, August). 'Document Analysis as a Qualitative Research Method'. *Qualitative Research Journal*, *9*(2), 27–40. DOI: 10.3316/QRJ0902027

Broman, G., & Robèrt, K.-H. (2017). 'A Framework for Strategic Sustainable Development'. *Journal of Cleaner Production*, *140*(January), 17–31. DOI: 10.1016/j.jclepro.2015.10.121

Brookings Institution. (n.d.). Artificial intelligence and fairness: Challenges in equity and bias in financial decision-making. Brookings. https://www.brookings.edu

Bryman, A. (2016). *Social Research Methods* (5th ed.). Oxford University Press.

Budiharto, W. (2021). Data science approach to stock prices forecasting in Indonesia during Covid-19 using Long Short-Term Memory (LSTM). *Journal of Big Data*, *8*, 47.

Bueno, G., Fernández-Carrobles, M. M., Deniz, O., & García-Rojo, M. (2016). New trends of emerging technologies in digital pathology. *Pathobiology*, *83*(2-3), 61–69. PMID: 27100343

Bukht, R., & Heeks, R. (2017). *Defining, Conceptualising and Measuring the Digital Economy* (SSRN Scholarly Paper 3431732). DOI: 10.2139/ssrn.3431732

Burri, M. (2020). *Big Data and Global Trade Law: An Introduction* (SSRN Scholarly Paper 3634430). https://papers.ssrn.com/abstract=3634430

Burri, M. (Ed.). (2021). *Big Data and Global Trade Law* (1st ed.). Cambridge University Press., DOI: 10.1017/9781108919234

Busenitz, L. W., & Barney, J. B. (1997). Representativeness bias in entrepreneurial decision-making. *Journal of Business Venturing*, *12*(6), 106–117.

Byrne, B. M. (2001). *Structural equation modeling with AMOS: Basic concepts, applications, and programming*. Routledge.

Carr, E. R. (2020). Resilient livelihoods in an era of global transformation. *Global Environmental Change*, *64*, 102155.

Carriere-Swallow, Y., & Haksar, V. (2019). The economics and implications of data: an integrated perspective. *International Monetary Fund*, 2019.

Cash, D., Clark, W., Alcock, F., Dickson, N., Selin, N., Guston, D., Jäger, J., & Mitchell, R. (2003). Knowledge Systems for Sustainable Development. *Proceedings of the National Academy of Sciences of the United States of America*, *100*(14), 8086–8091. DOI: 10.1073/pnas.1231332100 PMID: 12777623

CBP. (2024). ACE and Automated Systems. U.S. Customs and Border Protection. https://www.cbp.gov/trade/automated.

Chakhchoukh, M., Boukhelifa, N., & Bezerianos, A. (2022). Understanding how in-visualization provenance can support trade-off analysis. *IEEE Transactions on Visualization and Computer Graphics*, *29*(9), 3758–3774. DOI: 10.1109/TVCG.2022.3171074 PMID: 35507619

Cheah,, S., & Wang, S. (2017). Big data-driven business model innovation by traditional industries in the Chinese economy. *Journal of Chinese Economic and Foreign Trade Studies*, *10*(3), 229–251. DOI: 10.1108/JCEFTS-05-2017-0013

Chen, C. (2006). Detecting and Visualising Emerging Trends and Transient Patterns in Scientific Literature. *Journal of the Association for Information Science and Technology*, *57*, 359–377.

Cheng, F., & Yang, X. (2020). Challenges and Strategies of international economic and trade in the context of big data [J]. *Modern economic info*, *06*, 58-60.

Chen, H., Chiang, R. H., & Storey, V. C. (2012). Business intelligence and analytics: From big data to big impact. *Management Information Systems Quarterly*, 1165–1188.

Chen, M., Mao, S., & Liu, Y. (2014). Big Data: A Survey. *Mobile Networks and Applications*, *19*(2), 171–209. DOI: 10.1007/s11036-013-0489-0

Chittedi, K. R. (2014). Economic perspectives on decision-making in financial markets. *International Journal of Finance & Economics*, *17*(2), 34–45.

Clarke, J., Easley, D., & O'Hara, M. (2014). Herding behavior in financial markets. *The Journal of Finance*, *69*(1), 27–46.

Clarke, R. (1988). Information technology and dataveillance. *Communications of the ACM*, *31*(5), 498–512. DOI: 10.1145/42411.42413

Conti, M., Kumar, E. S., Lal, C., & Ruj, S. (2018). A Survey on Security and Privacy Issues of Bitcoin. *IEEE Communications Surveys and Tutorials*, *20*(4), 3416–3452. DOI: 10.1109/COMST.2018.2842460

Crosman, P. (2018). How big data is reshaping the investment world. Financial Times. https://www.ft.com

Cukier, K., & Mayer-Schoenberger, V. (2013). The rise of big data: How it's changing the way we think about the world. *Foreign Affairs*, *92*, 28.

Dahlman, C., Mealy, S., & Wermelinger, M. (2016). Harnessing the digital economy for developing countries. OECD Development Centre Working Papers, No. 334. https://www.oecd-ilibrary.org/development/harnessing-the-digital-economy-for-developing-countries_4adffb24-en.

Dahlsrud, A. (2008). How corporate social responsibility is defined: An analysis of 37 definitions. *Corporate Social Responsibility and Environmental Management*, *15*(1), 1–13. DOI: 10.1002/csr.132

Dangi, M., & Kohli, R. (2018). The role of gender in investment decision-making: Evidence from female entrepreneurs. *International Journal of Entrepreneurial Behaviour & Research*, *24*(5), 987–1003.

Daniel, K., Hirshleifer, D., & Subrahmanyam, A. (1998). A theory of overconfidence, self-attribution, and security market under- and overreactions. *The Journal of Finance*, *53*(6), 1839–1885. DOI: 10.1111/0022-1082.00077

Dargham, S. (2009). Behavioral finance and the efficient market hypothesis: A comparative analysis. *Global Finance Review*, *12*(1), 58–69.

Davies, R. (2016). Big Data and Data Analytics: The Potential for Innovation and Growth. *European Parliamentary Research Service*. https://www.europarl.europa.eu/RegData/etudes/BRIE/2016/589801/EPRS_BRI(2016)589801

Daviron, B., & Ponte, S. (2005). *The coffee paradox: Global markets, commodity trade and the elusive promise of development*. Zed books. DOI: 10.5040/9781350222984

Davis, A. P., Gole, T. W., Baena, S., & Moat, J. (2012). The impact of climate change on indigenous arabica coffee (Coffea arabica): Predicting future trends and identifying priorities. *PLoS One*, *7*(11), e47981. DOI: 10.1371/journal.pone.0047981 PMID: 23144840

De Mauro, A., Greco, M., & Grimaldi, M. (2016). A formal definition of Big Data based on its essential features. *Library Review*, *65*(3), 122–135.

De Silva, K., Yapa, P. W. S., & Vesty, G. (2020). The impact of accountability mechanisms on public sector environmental sustainability performance: A case study of Sri Lanka. *Australasian Accounting. Business and Finance Journal*, *14*(3), 38–55.

Demchenko, Y., Zhao, Z., Grosso, P., Wibisono, A., & de Laat, C. (2012). Addressing Big Data challenges for Scientific Data Infrastructure. *4th IEEE International Conference on Cloud Computing Technology and Science Proceedings*, 614–617. DOI: 10.1109/CloudCom.2012.6427494

Devlin, J. F. (2005). Biases in law enforcement algorithms: Consequences for racial justice. *The Journal of Legal Studies*, *34*(3), 453–475.

Dharmasasmita, A., Erlandsson, L., Willats, J., & Brown, S. (2017). Integrating the three pillars of sustainability: social, environmental and economic. In *The Business Student's Guide to Sustainable Management* (pp. 83–126). Routledge. DOI: 10.4324/9781351216500-4

Dong S.S., Zhao X.H. (2020). Analysis of the impact of big data on international economy and trade and measures. *Financial circles (Academic Edition),14*, 13-14.

Dong, C., Akram, A., Andersson, D., Arnäs, P. O., & Stefansson, G. (2021). The impact of emerging and disruptive technologies on freight transportation in the digital era: Current state and future trends. *International Journal of Logistics Management*, *32*(2), 386–412.

Donnenfeld, S., & Haug, A. A. (2008). Currency Invoicing of US Imports. *International Journal of Finance & Economics*, *13*(2), 184–198.

Dulloo, M. E., Guarino, L., Engelmann, F., Maxted, N., Newbury, J. H., Attere, F., & Ford-Lloyd, B. V. (1998). Complementary conservation strategies for the genus Coffea: A case study of Mascarene Coffea species. *Genetic Resources and Crop Evolution*, *45*(6), 565–579. DOI: 10.1023/A:1008621028343

Du, X., Zhang, H., & Han, Y. (2022). How Does New Infrastructure Investment Affect Economic Growth Quality? Empirical Evidence from China. *Sustainability (Basel), 14*(6), 6. Advance online publication. DOI: 10.3390/su14063511

EBA. (2020). EBA Report on Big Data and Advanced Analytics. https://www.eba.europa.eu/publications-and-media/press-releases/eba-report-idcntifics-kcy-challcngcs-roll-out-big-data-and.

Edmondson, J. (2021, Dec 7). Understanding Big Data Infrastructure—A Complete Guide. *Businesstechweekly.Com*. https://www.businesstechweekly.com/operational-efficiency/data-management/big-data-infrastructure/

Elkington, J. (1997). The triple bottom line. Environmental management: Readings and cases, 2, 49-66.

Elmqvist, N., Dragicevic, P., & Fekete, J. (2008). Rolling the dice: Multidimensional visual exploration using scatterplot matrix navigation. *IEEE Transactions on Visualization and Computer Graphics, TVCG, 14*(6), 1539–1148. PMID: 18989007

Enders, W., & Lee, J. (2012). The Flexible Fourier Form and Dickey–Fuller Type Unit Root Tests. *Economics Letters, 117*(1), 196–199. DOI: 10.1016/j.econlet.2012.04.081

Engelmann, F., Dulloo, M. E., Astorga, C., Dussert, S., & Anthony, F. (2007). *Conserving coffee genetic resources: complementary strategies for ex situ conservation of coffee (Coffea arabica L.) genetic resources: a case study in Catie*. IRD Editions.

Engle, C. R., & van Senten, J. (2022). Resilience of communities and sustainable aquaculture: Governance and regulatory effects. *Fishes, 7*(5), 268.

Erl, T., Khattak, W., & Buhler, P. (2016). *Big data fundamentals: Concepts, drivers and techniques*. Prentice Hall.

European Commission. (2024). EU Customs Risk Management Systems. https://taxation-customs.ec.europa.eu/customs-4_en.

Ezell, S., & Koester, S. (2023). *Transforming Global Trade and Development With Digital Technologies*. Information Technology.

Farhad, N. (2019). *Supply chain governance for social sustainability: a study of the ready-made Garment industry in Bangladesh* (Vol. 2004). Linköping University Electronic Press.

Fazelpour, S., & Danks, D. (2021). Bias in machine learning and its implications for decision-making in finance. *Journal of Ethical AI*, *2*(1), 22–36. DOI: 10.1007/s41374-021-00104-0

Feng, L., & Seasholes, M. S. (2004). Correlated trading and location effects in Chinese stock markets. *The Journal of Finance*, *59*(6), 1947–1972.

Fogel, R., & Berry, S. (2010). The disposition effect and investor behavior in equity markets. *Journal of Behavioral Finance*, *11*(2), 123–135.

Fortune Business Insights. (2024). Big Data Analytics Market. https://www.fortunebusinessinsights.com/big-data-analytics-market-106179.

French, S., Carter, E., & Niculae, C. (2007). Decision support in nuclear and radiological emergency situations: Are we too focused on models and technology? *International Journal of Risk Assessment and Management*.

French, S., & Turoff, M. (2007). Decision Support Systems. *Communications of the ACM*, *50*(3), 39–40. DOI: 10.1145/1226736.1226762

Friendly, M., & Denis, D. J. (2001). Milestones in the history of thematic cartography, statistical graphics, and data visualization.https://www.datavis.ca/milestones/

Gafar, J. S. (1988). The Determinants of Import Demand in Trinidad and Tobago: 1967–84. *Applied Economics*, *20*(3), 303–313. DOI: 10.1080/00036848800000044

Ganguly, A. R., Gupta, A., & Khan, S. (2005). Data mining technologies and decision support systems for business and scientific applications. *Encyclopedia of Data Warehousing and Mining*.

Gantz, J., & Reinsel, D. (n.d.). *The Digital Universe in 2020: Big Data.* Bigger Digital Shadows, and Biggest Growth in the Far East.

Gao, J., Koronios, A., & Selle, S. (n.d.). *Towards A Process View on Critical Success Factors in Big Data Analytics Projects*. Academic Press.

Garoufallou, E., & Gaitanou, P. (2021). Big data: Opportunities and challenges in libraries, a systematic literature review. *College & Research Libraries*, *82*(3), 410.

Gavrilakis, D., & Floros, C. (2021). Herding behavior in the stock market: A study of individual investors. *Journal of Behavioral Finance*, *20*(4), 134–146.

Ghasemaghaei, M., & Calic, G. (2020). Assessing the impact of big data on firm innovation performance: Big data is not always better data. *Journal of Business Research*, *108*, 147–162.

Ghazali, A. F., Alias, S., & Amran, Z. A. (2020). Decision Support Systems in a Smart City: A Review, International Conference on Industry 4.0: A Global Revolution in Business and Productivity, SEGi University Kota Damansara.

Ghazali, A. F., Suhaimi, A., Yusoff, R. M., & Mokhtar, N. A. (2022). Mobile-based Visual Decision Support System for Hybrid Learning in Post-COVID-19 Pandemic, Proceedings of the 2nd International Conference on Design Industries & Creative Culture, Design Decoded 2021, 24th, European Union Digital Library.

Ghazali, A. F., Mokhtar, N. A., Suhaimi, A., & Yusoff, R. M. (2021). Visual Decision Support System Model for Managing Unemployment by Hybrid Education. *Emerging Advances in Integrated Technology*, *2*(2), 16–22.

Ghazali, A. F., Noor, N. M. M., Mohemad, R., & Saman, M. Y. M. (2016). Development of a Decision Support System with Risk: Supporting Police and Government in Crime Prevention. *Research Journal of Applied Sciences*, *11*(6), 340–344.

Ghazali, A. F., & Suhaimi, A. (2020). Visual Decision Support System for Food Security, *ASEAN Workshop on Information Science and Technology (AWIST 2020).*

Ghazali, A. F., Suhaimi, A., & Wahab, S. F. (2022). Data visualization of decision support systems research in sustainability: A bibliometric analysis. *International Journal of Advanced Research in Technology and Innovation, 4*(3), 19–30.

Gilani, S. W. (2015). The Impact of Agricultural Imports and Exports on Agricultural Productivity. *Journal of Economics and Sustainable Development, 6*(11).

Gill, D. S. N. S. (2018). Emerging trends and future computing technologies: A vision for smart environment. *International Journal of Advanced Research in Computer Science, 9*(2).

Giovannucci, D., & Ponte, S. (2005). Standards as a new form of social contract? Sustainability initiatives in the coffee industry. *Food Policy, 30*(3), 284–301. DOI: 10.1016/j.foodpol.2005.05.007

Goldstein, M., & Khan, M. S. (1985). Income and Price Effects in Foreign Trade, R.W. Jones and P.B. Kenen (ed.) *Handbook of International Economics, 2*. New York: Elsevier Science Publications, 1041-1105.

Gole, T. W. (2002). Ecological studies on a keystone forest ecosystem for Coffea arabica gene conservation. *Unpublished PhD dissertation.*

Gopal, D. P., Chetty, U., O'Donnell, P., Gajria, C., & Blackadder-Weinstein, J. (2021). Algorithmic bias in healthcare decision-making: A critical review. *Journal of Health Ethics, 11*(2), 210–225.

Gopalkrishnan, V., Steier, D., Lewis, H., & Guszcza, J. (2012). Big data, big business: Bridging the gap. *Proceedings of the ACM SIGKDD International Conference on Knowledge Discovery and Data Mining*. DOI: 10.1145/2351316.2351318

Gottfried, A., Hartmann, C., & Yates, D. (2021). Mining open government data for business intelligence using data visualization: A two-industry case study. *Journal of Theoretical and Applied Electronic Commerce Research*, *16*(4), 1042–1065. DOI: 10.3390/jtaer16040059

Goyal, P., & Malviya, R. (2023). Challenges and opportunities of big data analytics in healthcare. *Health Care Science*, *2*(5), 328–338. PMID: 38938583

Graham, J., Li, S., & Qiu, J. (2008). Corporate misreporting and bank loan contracting. *Journal of Financial Economics*, *89*(1), 44–61. DOI: 10.1016/j.jfineco.2007.08.005

Gratzl, S., Lex, A., Gehlenborg, N., Pfister, H., & Streit, M. (2013). Lineup: Visual analysis of multi-attribute rankings," IEEE Transactions on Visualization and Computer Graphics. *TVCG*, *19*(12), 2277–2286.

Hahn, K. A., Wise, L. A., Rothman, K. J., Mikkelsen, E. M., Brogly, S. B., Sørensen, H. T., Riis, A. H., & Hatch, E. E. (2015). Caffeine and caffeinated beverage consumption and risk of spontaneous abortion. *Human Reproduction (Oxford, England)*, *30*(5), 1246–1255. DOI: 10.1093/humrep/dev063 PMID: 25788567

Hair, J. F., Anderson, R. E., Tatham, R. L., & Black, W. C. (1998). *Multivariate data analysis* (5th ed.). Prentice Hall.

Hannah, L., & Roehrdanz, P. R., KC, K. B., Fraser, E. D., Donatti, C. I., Saenz, L., & van Soesbergen, A. (. (2020). The environmental consequences of climate-driven agricultural frontiers. *PLoS One*, *15*(2), e0228305. DOI: 10.1371/journal.pone.0228305 PMID: 32049959

Harshe, G. (2024). Negotiating the salientization of identity: Hindu? Indian? American? *New Directions for Higher Education*, *2024*(206), 15–26. DOI: 10.1002/he.20500

Hassan, S. M. (2022). A causal analysis on foreign trade and economic growth: The case of Somalia. (2022). *International Journal of Scientific Research and Management*, *10*(08), 3725–3731.

Hassan, S. M., & Mohamed, M. J. (2022). Comparison of Somalia and the East Africa Community in terms of economy and competition. *Daha International University Academic Journal, 1*(1), 1–10.

Hassan, S., Ahmad, S., & Zafar, A. (2013). Traditional finance theory and behavioral finance: A comparison of investor behavior. *Global Journal of Finance and Economics*, *6*(1), 101–114.

Haywood, L. K. (2022). Putting risk management into the corporate sustainability context. *Social Responsibility Journal, 18*(8), 1485–1504.

Hemakumara, G. P. T. S., Athukorala, S. U., & Yapa, L. G. D. S. (2023). "Battle for Solar Energy" Program: An Environment-Friendly Sustainable Approach for Carbon Neutrality in Sri Lanka. In *Sustainability and Social Marketing Issues in Asia* (pp. 23-38). Emerald Publishing Limited.

Hoffman, J. (2022). *Speculative Futures: Design Approaches to Navigate Change, Foster Resilience, and Co-Create the Citie s We Need.* North Atlantic Books.

Hua, X., Huang, Y., & Zheng, Y. (2019). Current practices, new insights, and emerging trends of financial technologies. *Industrial Management & Data Systems*, *119*(7), 1401–1410.

Hynes, W., Trump, B. D., Love, P., Kirman, A., Galaitsi, S. E., Ramos, G., & Linkov, I. (2020). Resilient financial systems can soften the next global financial crisis. *Challenge*, *63*(6), 311–318.

International Economics. (2022). Big Data in International Trade: What is Working & What Have We Learnt so Far? https://tradeeconomics.com/big-data-in-international-trade-what-is-working-what-have-we-learnt-so-far/#_ftn1.

Jain, S., Walia, P., & Gupta, R. (2019). Anchoring bias in investment decisions: Evidence from Indian markets. *Journal of Economic Psychology*, *68*(3), 227–239.

Jerez Columbié, Y., & Morrissey, J. (2023). Subaltern learnings: Climate resilience and human security in the Caribbean. *Territory, Politics, Governance, 11*(1), 19–38. DOI: 10.1080/21622671.2020.1837662

Jia W.Y. (2020). Thinking on the development trend of international economy and trade under the background of big data. *Hubei agricultural mechanization, 04* 46 -46.

Jin, Z., & Xu, Q. (2012). The Realization of Decision Support System for Cross-border Transportation based on the Multi-dimensional Database. *Journal of Software, 7*(5), 974–981. DOI: 10.4304/jsw.7.5.974-981

Johnson, O. (1987). Currency Depreciation and Imports. *Finance & Development, 24*(2), 18.

Jovanovic, M., Kostić, N., Sebastian, I. M., & Sedej, T. (2022). Managing a blockchain-based platform ecosystem for industry-wide adoption: The case of TradeLens. *Technological Forecasting and Social Change, 184*, 121981.

Kahneman, D., & Tversky, A. (1974). Judgment under uncertainty: Heuristics and biases. *Science, 185*(4157), 1124–1131. DOI: 10.1126/science.185.4157.1124 PMID: 17835457

Kahneman, D., & Tversky, A. (1979). Prospect theory: An analysis of decision under risk. *Econometrica, 47*(2), 263–291. DOI: 10.2307/1914185

Kajikawa, Y., Yoshikawa, J., Takeda, Y., & Matsushima, K. (2008). Tracking emerging technologies in energy research: Toward a roadmap for sustainable energy. *Technological Forecasting and Social Change, 75*(6), 771–782.

Kapoor, R., & Prosad, S. (2017). Exploring cognitive biases in investment decision-making: An empirical analysis. *Journal of Investment Research, 10*(1), 98–114.

Kappal, A., & Rastogi, P. (2020). Behavioral biases and their moderating effects in investment decisions. *Financial Planning Review, 15*(1), 99–112.

Karabegovic, A., & Ponjavic, M. (2012, September). Geoportal as decision support system with spatial data warehouse. In *2012 Federated Conference on Computer Science and Information Systems (FedCSIS)* (pp. 915-918). IEEE.

Karpoff, J. M., Lee, D. S., & Martin, G. S. (2008). The cost to firms of cooking the books. *Journal of Financial and Quantitative Analysis, 43*(3), 581–611. DOI: 10.1017/S0022109000004221

Kaushik, S. (2024). How the World Integrated Trade Solution (WITS) is helping understand global commerce.https://blogs.worldbank.org/en/opendata/how-world-integrated-trade-solution-wits-helping-understand-global-commerce.

Keyes, L. (2016). Data Analytics: How data analytics can simplify and facilitate trade with the European Union. https://www.erasmusfiscalstudies.nl/upload/Keyes (15.05.2024)

Khan, N., Yaqoob, I., Hashem, I. T., Inayat, Z., Ali, W. K. M., Alam, M., Shiraz, M., & Gani, A. (2014). Big Data: Survey, Technologies, Opportunities, and Challenges. *TheScientificWorldJournal, 2014*, 1–18. DOI: 10.1155/2014/712826 PMID: 25136682

Khanra, S., Dhir, A., Islam, A. N., & Mäntymäki, M. (2020). Big data analytics in healthcare: A systematic literature review. *Enterprise Information Systems, 14*(7), 878–912. DOI: 10.1080/17517575.2020.1812005

Khan, S. N., Loukil, F., Ghedira-Guegan, C., Benkhelifa, E., & Bani-Hani, A. (2021). Blockchain smart contracts: Applications, challenges, and future trends. *Peer-to-Peer Networking and Applications, 14*(5), 2901–2925. DOI: 10.1007/s12083-021-01127-0 PMID: 33897937

King, A. (1993). The functional form of import demand: The case of UK motor vehicle imports, 1980-90. *Journal of Economic Studies (Glasgow, Scotland), 20*(3), 36–50. DOI: 10.1108/01443589310040396

Kitchin, R., & McArdle, G. (2016). What makes Big Data, Big Data? Exploring the ontological characteristics of 26 datasets. *Big Data & Society, 3*(1).

Klein, T. M., Celio, E., & Grêt-Regamey, A. (2015). Ecosystem services visualization and communication: A demand analysis approach for designing information and conceptualizing decision support systems. *Ecosystem Services*, *13*, 173–183. DOI: 10.1016/j.ecoser.2015.02.006

Kloza, B. (2023, Feb 27). *Impact of the Digital Divide: Economic, Social, and Educational Consequences*. Connecting the Unconnected. https://ctu.ieee.org/impact-of-the-digital-divide-economic-social-and-educational-consequences/

Knaflic, C. N. (2015). *Storytelling with data: A data visualization guide for business professionals*. Wiley.

Knorr, D. (2018). Emerging technologies: Back to the future. *Trends in Food Science & Technology*, *76*, 119–123.

Koester, S. E. (2023). *Transforming Global Trade and Development With Digital Technologies*. https://itif.org/publications/2023/05/08/transforming-global-trade-and-development-with-digital-technologies/

Kohen, A. (2015). How big data will transform global trade. https://www.weforum.org/agenda/2015/04/how-big-data-will-transform-global-trade/.

Kozlov, A., Kankovskaya, A., & Teslya, A. (2020). Digital infrastructure as the factor of economic and industrial development: Case of Arctic regions of Russian North-West. *IOP Conference Series. Earth and Environmental Science*, *539*(1), 012061. DOI: 10.1088/1755-1315/539/1/012061

Krishnan, S. (2013). Current status of coffee genetic resources and implications for conservation. *CABI Reviews*, (2013), 1-9.

Kuhlman, T., & John, F. (2010). What is Sustainability? *Sustainability (Basel)*, *2*(11), 3436–3448. Advance online publication. DOI: 10.3390/su2113436

Kumari, D., & Malhotra, N. (2014). Trade-led growth in India and China: A comparative analysis. *Journal of International and Global Economic Studies*, *7*(2), 68–88.

Kumar, S., & Goyal, V. (2015). An analysis of the utility theory in investment decision-making. *Journal of Economic and Financial Studies*, *14*(1), 56–69.

Kumar, S., & Goyal, V. (2016). Herding behavior and its impact on financial markets. *Journal of Behavioral Finance*, *17*(2), 87–103.

Kumar, S., Sharma, D., Rao, S., Lim, W. M., & Mangla, S. K. (2022). Past, present, and future of sustainable finance: Insights from big data analytics through machine learning of scholarly research. *Annals of Operations Research*, 1–44. PMID: 35002001

Lather, R., Yadav, S., & Gupta, A. (2020). Gender differences in the behavioral biases of investors: Evidence from India. *Journal of Behavioral and Experimental Finance*, *27*, 13–24.

Lebacq, T., Baret, P. V., & Stilmant, D. (2013). Sustainability indicators for livestock farming. A review. *Agronomy for Sustainable Development*, *33*(2), 311–327. DOI: 10.1007/s13593-012-0121-x

Lee, K. H., Vachon, S., Lee, K. H., & Vachon, S. (2016). Supply chain sustainability risk. *Business value and sustainability: An integrated supply network perspective*, 245-280

Lemma, A., Mendez-Parra, M., & Naliaka, L. (n.d.). *The AfCFTA: unlocking the potential of the digital economy in Africa*. Academic Press.

Leung, X. Y., Sun, J., & Bai, B. (2017). Bibliometric of Social Media Research: A Co-citation and Co-word Analysis. *International Journal of Hospitality Management*, *66*, 35–45. DOI: 10.1016/j.ijhm.2017.06.012

Li M. (2020). Analysis of the impact of big data on the international trade of enterprises in the context of economic globalization. *Times economic and trade, 06*, 19-20.

Li, Z., & Yang, D. (2015). The study on the influence of fixed asset investment and foreign trade to the economic growth of Ningbo based on VAR Model. *In 2015 International Conference on Education Technology, Management and Humanities Science* (ETMHS 2015) (pp. 341-345). Atlantis Press.

Lian, G. (2022). Blockchain-based secure and trusted distributed international tradc big data managcmcnt system. *Mobile Information Systems*.

Li, J. (2020). The impact of big data on investment decisions: A new paradigm in finance. *Journal of Financial Markets*, *48*(3), 245–263.

Lin Guan, J., & Hong, Y. (2012). An empirical analysis on US foreign trade and economic growth. *Aasri Procedia*, *2*, 39–43.

Lin Z.P. (2015). Discussion on international trade financing of small and medium sized enterprises. *Mall modernization, 2,* 10.

Lin, C., Ahmad, S. F., Ayassrah, A. Y. B. A., Irshad, M., Telba, A. A., Awwad, E. M., & Majid, M. I. (2023). Green production and green technology for sustainability: The mediating role of waste reduction and energy use. *Heliyon*, 22496. PMID: 38076181

Link, G. M., & Vijaykrishnan, N. (2006, March). Thermal trends in emerging technologies. In *7th International Symposium on Quality Electronic Design (ISQED'06)* (pp. 8). IEEE.

Liu T.S. (2019). Optimization and adjustment of International Trade Industrial Structure under the new economic situation. *Brand marketing of old brands, 10,* 17-18.

London Business School. (n.d.). Behavioral finance and machine learning: A future of unbiased financial decision-making. https://www.london.edu

Lupton, D. (2015). The thirteen Ps of big data. *This Sociological Life*. https://simplysociology.wordpress.com/2015/05/11/the-thirteen-ps-of-big-data/.

Lynch, J. G. (2003). Missing data: The role of imputation methods. *The Journal of Consumer Research*, *30*(2), 155–174. DOI: 10.1086/378705

Maaitah, T. (2023). The role of business intelligence tools in the decision-making process and performance. *Journal of intelligence studies in business, 13*(1), 43-52.

Maaitah, T. (2023). The Role of Entrepreneurship on the Economic Growth and Development.

Malik, P. (2013). Governing big data: Principles and practices. *IBM J. Res. Dev., 57*(3–4). DOI: 10.1147/JRD.2013.2241359

Malyadri, P. (2016). Status of coffee plantation in India: A high time for innovation and sustainability towards make in India. *VSRD Int J Bus Manag Res*, *6*(2), 47–50.

Manyika, J., Chui, M., Brown, B., Bughin, J., Dobbs, R., Roxburgh, C., & Hung Byers, A. (2011). Big data: The next frontier for innovation, competition, and productivity. https://www.mckinsey.com/capabilities/mckinsey-digital/our-insights/big-data-the-next-frontier-for-innovation.

Ma, R., & Lin, B. (2023). Digital infrastructure construction drives green economic transformation: Evidence from Chinese cities. *Humanities & Social Sciences Communications*, *10*(1), 1–10. DOI: 10.1057/s41599-023-01839-z

Masa'd, F. M., Al-maaitah, T. A., Al-maaitah, D. A., Qawasmeh, E. F., & Qatawneh, N. A. (2024). Harnessing artificial intelligence for human resources management: Tools, advantages, and risks in the energy sector. In *E3S Web of Conferences*, 541, p. 02004). EDP Sciences. DOI: 10.1051/e3sconf/202454102004

Maxfield, S., Shapiro, D., Gupta, R., & Hass, S. (2010). Risk aversion and its role in investment decision-making. *Journal of Behavioral Decision Making*, *23*(4), 289–302.

McKenzie, S. (2004). Social sustainability: towards some definitions.

McKinsey & Company. (n.d.). Big data analytics in investment management: The role of machine learning and artificial intelligence. McKinsey Insights. https://www.mckinsey.com

McLean, E. R. (2003). The DeLone and McLean model of information systems success: A ten-year update. *Journal of Management Information Systems*, *19*(4), 9–30. DOI: 10.1080/07421222.2003.11045748

Meloncon, L., & Warner, E. (2017). Data visualizations: A literature review and opportunities for technical and professional communication. Professional Communication Conference (ProComm), IEEE International, Madison, WI, USA. DOI: 10.1109/IPCC.2017.8013960

Merendino, A. (2018). Big data, big decisions: The impact of big data on board level decision-making. *Journal of Business Research*, *93*, 67–78.

Meyfroidt, P., Vu, T. P., & Hoang, V. A. (2013). Trajectories of deforestation, coffee expansion and displacement of shifting cultivation in the Central Highlands of Vietnam. *Global Environmental Change*, *23*(5), 1187–1198. DOI: 10.1016/j.gloenvcha.2013.04.005

Michael, C. I., Ipede, O. J., Adejumo, A. D., Adenekan, I. O., Adebayo, D., Ojo, A. S., & Ayodele, P. A. (2024). Data-driven decision making in IT: Leveraging AI and data science for business intelligence. *World Journal of Advanced Research and Reviews*, *23*(1), 472–480. DOI: 10.30574/wjarr.2024.23.1.2010

Michelis, L., & Zestos, G. K. (2004). Exports, Imports and GDP Growth: Causal Relations in Six European Union Countries. *Journal of Economic Asymmetries*, *1*(2), 71–85. DOI: 10.1016/j.jeca.2004.02.004

Min, B. H., & Borch, C. (2022). Systemic failures and organizational risk management in algorithmic trading: Normal accidents and high reliability in financial markets. *Social Studies of Science*, *52*(2), 277–302. DOI: 10.1177/03063127211048515 PMID: 34612758

Mishra, R., & Sharma, R. (2015). Big Data: Opportunities and Challenges. *International Journal of Computer Science and Mobile Computing*, *4*(6), 27–35.

Mittal, R. (2019). The role of disposition bias in investment decision-making: A study of Indian retail investors. *International Journal of Finance & Economics*, *19*(2), 202–215.

Mohemad, R., Hamdan, A. R., Othman, Z. A., & Noor, N. M. M. (2010). Decision support systems (DSS) in construction tendering processes, *International Journal of Computer Science Issues.*

Mo, T., Li, Y., Lau, K. T., Poon, C. K., Wu, Y., & Luo, Y. (2022). Trends and emerging technologies for the development of electric vehicles. *Energies, 15*(17), 6271.

Mullan, M., & Ranger, N. (2022). Climate-resilient finance and investment: Framing paper.

Munasinghe, M. A. T. K. (2018). *The agency of global sustainability certifications in developing countries: the Rainforest Alliance and the Sri Lankan tea industry* (Doctoral dissertation, University of Birmingham).

Murray, T., & Ginman, P. J. (1976). An Empirical Examination of the Traditional Aggregate Import Demand Model. *The Review of Economics and Statistics, 58*(1), 75–80. DOI: 10.2307/1936011

Naeem, M., Jamal, T., Diaz-Martinez, J., Butt, S. A., Montesano, N., Tariq, M. I., De-La-Hoz-Valdiris, E. (2022). Trends and future perspective challenges in big data. In *Advances in Intelligent Data Analysis and Applications:Proceeding of the Sixth Euro-China Conference on Intelligent Data Analysis and Applications,Arad, Romania* (pp. 309-325). Springer Singapore. DOI: 10.1007/978-981-16-5036-9_30

Narayan, S., & Narayan, P. K. (2005). An Empirical Analysis of Fiji's Import Demand Function. *Journal of Economic Studies (Glasgow, Scotland), 32*(2), 158–168.

Neilson, J., & Pritchard, B. (2007). Green coffee? The contradictions of global sustainability initiatives from an Indian perspective. *Development Policy Review, 25*(3), 311–331. DOI: 10.1111/j.1467-7679.2007.00372.x

Nguyen, C. (2020). Sustainability marketing concept: Case Starbucks.

Nguyen, L. A. T., & Habók, A. (2023). Tools for assessing teacher digital literacy: A review. *Journal of Computers in Education.* Advance online publication. DOI: 10.1007/s40692-022-00257-5

Noor, N. M. M., Ghazali, A. F., Mohd, M. Y. B., & Nor, M. N. M. (2014). Framework of Risk-based Decision Support System in Crime Investigation, *International Conference Decision Support System Technology*, 447-458.

Nuseir, M., & Aljumah, A. (2020). The role of digital marketing in business performance with the moderating effect of environment factors among smes of uae. International Journal of Innovation. *Creativity and Change*, *11*(3), 310–324.

Obeidat, A. M. (2021). E-Marketing and Its Impact on The Competitive Advantage. *Ilkogretim Online, 20*(5).

Obeidat, A. (2019). IT adaption with knowledge conversion process (SECI)? *Management Science Letters*, *9*(13), 2241–2252. DOI: 10.5267/j.msl.2019.7.029

Odean, T. (1998). Volume and price volatility in the stock market: The role of biases and heuristics. *Journal of Financial Markets*, *4*(3), 343–358.

OECD. (2016, Sep 5). *Jobs and skills in the digital economy*. Medium. https://startupsventurecapital.com/jobs-and-skills-in-the-digital-economy-16b878ef7ee5

Ogbonna, C. (2023). Big Data and International Trade: Navigating A Data-Driven Landscape.https://nationaleconomy.com/?s=Big+Data+And+International+Trade%3A+Navigating+A+Data-Driven+Landscape.

Oloyede, A. A., Faruk, N., Noma, N., Tebepah, E., & Nwaulune, A. K. (2023). Measuring the impact of the digital economy in developing countries: A systematic review and meta- analysis. *Heliyon*, *9*(7), e17654. DOI: 10.1016/j.heliyon.2023.e17654 PMID: 37501966

Oluyemi, O., & Isaac, E. D. (2017). The Effect of Exchange Rate on Imports and Exports in Nigeria from January 1996 to June 2015. *International Journal of Economics and Business Management*, *3*(2), 66–77.

Ovalle-Rivera, O., Läderach, P., Bunn, C., Obersteiner, M., & Schroth, G. (2015). Projected shifts in Coffea arabica suitability among major global producing regions due to climate change. *PLoS One*, *10*(4), e0124155. DOI: 10.1371/journal.pone.0124155 PMID: 25875230

Paital, R. R., Dutta, S., & Dash, A. K. (2019). Crude Oil Import Elasticity of Demand in India: An Empirical Analysis 1987–2016. *Applied Econometrics and International Development*, *19*(2), 125–136.

Palacios, A., & Norton, C. (2024). Trade in a digital interoperability era. https://www.brookings.edu/articles/trade-in-a-digital-interoperability-era/.

Palm, M., & Andersson, P. (2020). The impact of anchoring bias on investment behavior. *Journal of Financial Planning*, *16*(1), 27–39.

Panhuysen, S., & Pierrot, J. (2018). *Coffee barometer 2018*. Conservation International.

Panimalar, A., Shree, V., & Kathrine, V. (2017). The 17 V's of big data. *International Research Journal of Engineering and Technology*, *4*(9), 329–333.

Paris Agreement, U. N. F. C. C. C. (2015). *Adoption of the Paris Agreement*. Report No. FCCC/CP/2015/L.9/Rev.1, https://unfccc.int/resource/docs/2015/cop21/eng/l09r01.pdf (UNFCCC, 2015)

Parrish, B. D. (2007). Designing the sustainable enterprise. *Futures*, *39*(7), 846–860. DOI: 10.1016/j.futures.2006.12.007

Pawlos, S. (2004). The Relationship between Import and GDP Growth in Ethiopia: An Empirical Analysis. http://www. eeaecon. org/EEA/conferences/papers/Sewasew.

Perianes-Rodriguez, A., Waltman, L., & van Eck, N. J. (2016). Constructing Bibliometric Networks: A Comparison Between Full and Fractional Counting. *Journal of Informetrics*, *10*(4), 1178–1195. DOI: 10.1016/j.joi.2016.10.006

Peters, M. A. (2023). Digital trade, digital economy and the digital economy partnership agreement (DEPA). *Educational Philosophy and Theory*, *55*(7), 747–755. DOI: 10.1080/00131857.2022.2041413

Pham, L., Pham, & Liu. (2019). International graduates returning to Vietnam. Springer Singapore.

Phelan, H., Hennelly, J., Chappell, D., & Roberts, A. N. (2017). The Irish World Music Café: performing and recording as tools for sustainable social integration. In *Voices: A World Forum for Music Therapy17*(3). DOI: 10.15845/voices.v17i3.939

Pinto, L., Baruzzi, F., Cocolin, L., & Malfeito-Ferreira, M. (2020). Emerging technologies to control Brettanomyces spp. in wine: Recent advances and future trends. *Trends in Food Science & Technology*, *99*, 88–100.

Pizło, W., Kulykovets, O., Prokopowicz, D., Mazurkiewicz-Pizło, A., Kałowski, A., Paprocka, M. W., & Skarzyńska, E. (2023). The importance of Big Data Analytics technology in business management. *Cybersecurity and Law*, *10*(2), 270–282.

Popovic, A. (2018). The impact of big data analytics on firms' high value business performance. *Information Systems Frontiers*, *20*, 209–222.

Pradhan, R. P. (2009). The nexus between financial development and economic growth in India: Evidence from multivariate VAR model. *International Journal of Research and Reviews in Applied Sciences*, *1*(2), 68–79.

Pradhan, R. P., Arvin, M. B., Nair, M., Bennett, S. E., Bahmani, S., & Hall, J. H. (2018). Endogenous dynamics between innovation, financial markets, venture capital and economic growth: Evidence from Europe. *Journal of Multinational Financial Management*, *45*, 15–34. DOI: 10.1016/j.mulfin.2018.01.002

Pradikasari, I., & Isbanah, S. (2018). Overconfidence bias and its effects on investment choices. *Asian Economic and Financial Review*, *8*(10), 1141–1151.

Prasad, D., Kapoor, R., & Sengupta, M. (2015). The disposition effect: How investors hold on to losing investments. *Journal of Investment Decisions*, *12*(2), 40–51.

Qiao, R., & Zhao, L. (2023). Highlight risk management in supply chain finance: Effects of supply chain risk management capabilities on financing performance of small-medium enterprises. *Supply Chain Management*, *28*(5), 843–858.

Quadir, P., Ansar, T. B., Dembo, S. A., Zaheen, T., & Raisa, K. A. (2023). Navigating the Bangladeshi Market: Unlocking Market Entry Opportunities for STARBUCKS. *Business Perspectives and Research*, *5*(2), 37–48. DOI: 10.38157/bpr.v5i2.604

Rahn, E., Vaast, P., Läderach, P., Van Asten, P., Jassogne, L., & Ghazoul, J. (2018). Exploring adaptation strategies of coffee production to climate change using a process-based model. *Ecological Modelling*, *371*, 76–89. DOI: 10.1016/j.ecolmodel.2018.01.009

Rahul, K., Banyal, R. K., & Arora, N. (2023). A systematic review on big data applications and scope for industrial processing and healthcare sectors. *Journal of Big Data*, *10*(1), 133.

Rashid, A., Baloch, N., Rasheed, R., & Ngah, A. H. (2024). Big data analytics-artificial intelligence and sustainable performance through green supply chain practices in manufacturing firms of a developing country. *Journal of Science and Technology Policy Management*.

Rashidi, M., Ghodrat, M., Samali, B., & Mohammadi, M. (2018). *Decision Support Systems*. Advance online publication. DOI: 10.5772/intechopen.79390

Rasool, H., & Ullah, M. (2020). Herding behavior and its influence on investment decisions. *Journal of Finance and Accounting*, *18*(4), 77–89.

Rauwerda, D., & De Graaf, P. (2021). Behavioral biases in long-term investment decisions: A psychological perspective. *International Journal of Behavioral Finance*, *22*(2), 134–146.

Reddy, Surendranadha Reddy Byrapu. (2023). Demonstrating The Payroll Reviews Based On Data Visualization For Financial Services. *Tuijin Jishu/ Journal of Propulsion Technology 44*, 4: 3886-3893.

Reddy, Surendranadha Reddy Byrapu. (2023). Digital Transformations Theoretical Investigation on the Basis of Smart Government Initiatives. *Tuijin Jishu/Journal of Propulsion Technology 44,* 4 (2023): 3894-3901.

Robinson, J. (2004). Squaring the circle? Some thoughts on the idea of sustainable development. *Ecological Economics*, *48*(4), 369–384. DOI: 10.1016/j.ecolecon.2003.10.017

Rohn, D., Bican, P., Brem, A., Kraus, S., & Clauß, T. (2021). Digital platform-based business models – An exploration of critical success factors. *Journal of Engineering and Technology Management*, *60*, 101625. Advance online publication. DOI: 10.1016/j.jengtecman.2021.101625

Ronda-Pupo, G. A., & Guerras-Martin, L. Á. (2012). Dynamics of the evolution of the strategy concept 1962–2008: A co-word analysis. *Strategic Management Journal*, *33*(2), 162–188.

S. Pajer, M. Streit, T. Torsney-Weir, F. Spechtenhauser, T. Möller, and H. Piringer (2016). Weightlifter: Visual weight space exploration for multi- criteria decision making," IEEE Transactions on Visualization and Computer Graphics, *TVCG, 23*(1), pp. 611-620, 2016.

Sahi, S. (2012). Behavioral economics: Understanding biases in consumer behavior. *International Journal of Consumer Studies*, *16*(2), 76–88.

Sahi, S. (2017). Comparing investment decisions of professional and individual investors: The role of behavioral biases. *Journal of Behavioral Finance*, *14*(3), 179–190.

Sahoo, S. (2022). Big data analytics in manufacturing: A bibliometric analysis of research in the field of business management. *International Journal of Production Research*, *60*(22), 6793–6821.

Sahu, S. P., Saragiotis, P., Hartmann, O., Saslavsky, D., Ollivier, P., & Gupta, N. (2023). Port Community Systems: Driving Trade in the 21st Century. https://www.worldbank.org/en/topic/trade/publication/port-community-systems-driving-trade-in-the-21st-century.

Sakhawat, A. R., Fatima, A., Abbas, S., Ahmad, M., & Khan, M. A. (2024). Emerging Technologies for Enhancing Robust Cybersecurity Measures for Business Intelligence in Healthcare 5.0. Strengthening Industrial Cybersecurity to Protect Business Intelligence, 270-293.

Samper, L. F., Giovannucci, D., & Vieira, L. M. (2017). *The powerful role of intangibles in the coffee value chain*, 39. WIPO.

Sarkar, S., & Searcy, C. (2016). Zeitgeist or chameleon? A quantitative analysis of CSR definitions. *Journal of Cleaner Production, 135*, 1423–1435. DOI: 10.1016/j.jclepro.2016.06.157

Schiffman, L. G., & Kanuk, L. L. (2007). *Consumer behavior* (9th ed.). Pearson Prentice Hall.

Schroeck, M., Shockley, R., Smart, J., & Tufano, P. (2012). Analytics: the real-world use of big data: How innovative enterprises extract value from uncertain data, Executive Report IBM.

Schu-Macker, D., & Lomax, R. G. (2012). *Structural equation modeling: Techniques and applications* (2nd ed.). Sage Publications.

Schwertner, K. (2017). Digital transformation of business. *Trakia Journal of Sciences*, *15*(Suppl.1), 388–393. DOI: 10.15547/tjs.2017.s.01.065

erban, R.-A. (2017). The impact of big data, sustainability, and digitalization on company performance. *Studies in Business and Economics*, *12*(3), 181–189.

Seuring, S., & Müller, M. (2008). From a Literature Review to a Conceptual Framework for Sustainable Supply Chain Management. *Journal of Cleaner Production*, *16*, 1699–1710.

Sewell, M. (2007). Behavioral finance: The role of psychology in investment decision-making. *Journal of Financial Economics*, *11*(3), 225–238.

Shabarisha, R. (2015). Investor biases and their impact on financial decisions: A study on retail investors. *Journal of Behavioral Finance, 13*(4), 215–227.

Shah, A., Ahmad, M., & Mahmood, F. (2018). The influence of anchoring bias on investment decision-making in emerging markets. *Journal of Economic Psychology, 58*, 83–99.

Shefrin, H. (2002). *Beyond greed and fear: Understanding behavioral finance and the psychology of investing*. Oxford University Press. DOI: 10.1093/0195161211.001.0001

Shiller, R. J. (2003). *The new financial order: Risk in the 21st century*. Princeton University Press.

Shneiderman, B. (1996). The eyes have it: A task by data type taxonomy for information visualizations. *Proceedings of IEEE Symposium on Visual Languages Boulder*, Colorado.

Shubham, S., & Pallavi, P (2024). UNRAVELLING THE CSR OUTLOOK OF STARBUCKS: A CASE-BASED APPROACH. *Responsibility*, 58.

Shukla, A., Gupta, R., & Soni, R. (2020). Cognitive biases and their effects on investment returns. *Journal of Applied Behavioral Economics, 19*(3), 128–142.

Sigala, Marianna (2019). Big data for measuring the impact of tourism economic development programs: A process and quality criteria framework for using big data. *Big Data and Innovation in Tourism, Travel, and Hospitality: Managerial Approaches, Techniques, and Applications*, 57-73.

Silva, S. A. D. (2019). Hypothenemus hampei:(Coleoptera: Scolytidae): impacto sobre a qualidade dos grãos de café.

Simon, H. A. (1997). *Administrative behavior: A study of decision-making processes in administrative organizations* (4th ed.). Free Press.

Singh, K. P., Singh, B., Patil, S. K., Rahangdale, C. P., Banerjee, A., Shukla, R., Sahu, K., & Jhariya, M. K. (2023). Biomass, carbon stock, CO2 mitigation and carbon credits of coffee-based multitier cropping model in Central India. *Environmental Monitoring and Assessment, 195*(10), 1250. DOI: 10.1007/s10661-023-11892-5 PMID: 37758966

Sinha, D. (1997). Determinants of Import Demand in Thailand. *International Economic Journal, 11*(4), 73–873.

Sironi, P. (2018). Big data and analytics: The future of financial decision-making. *Journal of Financial Technology*, *5*(2), 102–118.

Slovic, P. (1972). Psychological study of human judgment and decision-making in risky situations. *Journal of Behavioral Decision Making*, *5*(1), 7–25.

Smaya, H. (2022). The influence of big data analytics in the industry. *OAlib*, *9*(2), 1–12. DOI: 10.4236/oalib.1108383

Smith, R. (2018). Big data and financial decision-making: Overcoming cognitive biases. *Journal of Financial Analytics*, *12*(4), 99–113.

Sorour, A., & Atkins, A. S. (2024). Big data challenge for monitoring quality in higher education institutions using business intelligence dashboards. *Journal of Electronic Science and Technology*, 100233.

Spiezia, V., & Tscheke, J. (2020). International agreements on cross-border data flows and international trade: A statistical analysis. OECD Science, Technology and Industry Working Papers.

Spiezia, V., Koksal-Oudot, E., & Montagnier, P. (2016). *New Skills for the Digital Economy*. DOI: 10.1787/20716826

Statista. (2023). Amount of data created, consumed, and stored 2010-2020, with forecasts to 2025. https://www.statista.com/statistics/871513/worldwide-data-created/.

Statman, M. (2017). Behavioral finance: Finance and the human factor. *Journal of Financial Decision Making*, *25*(1), 22–33.

Studzinski, N. G., & Pasteur, L. (2020). *Comprehensive pandemic risk management: A systems approach*. Visiting International Research Fellow Policy Institute, King's College.

Sun B. (2020). Challenges and Countermeasures of international trade under the background of big data. China business theory, (01), 73-74

Sun, H., Mohsin, M., Alharthi, M., & Abbas, Q. (2020). Measuring environmental sustainability performance of South Asia. *Journal of Cleaner Production*, *251*, 119519. DOI: 10.1016/j.jclepro.2019.119519

Sun, S., Cegielski, C., Jia, A., & Hall, D. (2016). Understanding the Factors Affecting the Organizational Adoption of Big Data. *Journal of Computer Information Systems*, *58*(3), 1–11. DOI: 10.1080/08874417.2016.1222891

Swanson, N. R., & Xiong, W. (2018). Big data analytics in economics: What have we learned so far, and where should we go from here? *The Canadian Journal of Economics. Revue Canadienne d'Economique*, *51*(3), 695–746.

Sweidan, O. D. (2013). The Effect of Exchange Rate on Exports and Imports: The Case of Jordan. *Guoji Maoyi Wenti*, *27*(2), 156–172.

Tabachnick, B. G., & Fidell, L. S. (2007). *Using multivariate statistics* (5th ed.). Pearson Education.

Tall, A., Lynagh, S., Blanco Vecchi, C., Bardouille, P., Montoya Pino, F., Shabahat, E., & Kerr, L. (2021). *Enabling Private Investment in Climate Adaptation and Resilience: Current Status*. Barriers to Investment and Blueprint for Action. DOI: 10.1596/35203

Taylor, Linnet, Ralph Schroeder, and Eric Meyer (2014). Emerging practices and perspectives on Big Data analysis in economics: Bigger and better or more of the same?. *Big Data & Society 1.2*: 2053951714536877.

Taylor-Sakyi, K. (n.d.). Big Data: Understanding. *Big Data*.

Tiao, S. (2024). Big Data Defined. https://www.oracle.com/big-data/what-is-big-data/.

Toader, E., Firtescu, B. N., Roman, A., & Anton, S. G. (2018). Impact of Information and Communication Technology Infrastructure on Economic Growth: An Empirical Assessment for the EU Countries. *Sustainability (Basel)*. Advance online publication. DOI: 10.3390/su10103750

Tomer, J. F. (2016). Behavioral economics and decision-making: Insights into the complexities of human behavior. *Journal of Economic Behavior*, *30*(4), 185–200.

TradeLens. (2024). Discover how TradeLens solutions can work for you. https://www.tradelens.com/.

Treiblmaier, H. (2018). The impact of the blockchain on the supply chain: A theory-based research framework and a call for action. *Supply Chain Management*, *23*(6), 545–559. DOI: 10.1108/SCM-01-2018-0029

Triantaphyllou (2013). Multi-criteria decision making methods: A comparative study," Springer Science & Business Media, *44*.

Trivino-Tarradas, P., Gomez-Ariza, M. R., Basch, G., & Gonzalez-Sanchez, E. J. (2019). Sustainability assessment of annual and permanent crops: The Inspia model. *Sustainability (Basel)*, *11*(3), 738. DOI: 10.3390/su11030738

Tunc, M. A., Gures, E., & Shayea, I. (2021). A survey on iot smart healthcare: Emerging technologies, applications, challenges, and future trends. arXiv preprint arXiv:2109.02042.

UNCTAD. (2024). Data, Statistics and Trends in International Trade. https://unctad.org/topic/trade-analysis/data-statistics-and-trends.

Uprichard, E. (2013). Focus: Big data, little questions? *Discover Society*, (1). https://archive.discoversociety.org/2013/10/01/focus-big-data-little-questions/.

Vacu, N. P., & Odhiambo, N. M. (2020). The Determinants of Import Demand: A Review of International Literature. Acta Universitatis Danubius. *Economica*, *16*(5), 101–117.

Van Calker, K. J., Berentsen, P. B. M., Giesen, G. W. J., & Huirne, R. B. M. (2008). Maximising sustainability of Dutch dairy farming systems for different stakeholders: A modelling approach. *Ecological Economics*, *65*(2), 407–419. DOI: 10.1016/j.ecolecon.2007.07.010

Veldscholten, S. (2018). Spatial and temporal public transport data visualization: data analysis using a decision support system for alternative public transport services. Academic Press.

Ward, M. O., Grinstein, G., & Keim, D. (2015). Interactive data visualization: Foundations, techniques, and applications. https://ebookcentral.proquest.com/lib/uql/detail.action?docID=1786691

West, C. D., Stokeld, E., Campiglio, E., Croft, S., Detges, A., Duranovic, A., & Reyer, C. P. (2021). Europe's cross-border trade, human security and financial connections: A climate risk perspective. *Climate Risk Management*, *34*, 100382. DOI: 10.1016/j.crm.2021.100382

Wijewantha, P., & Kulatunga, U. (2022). A framework to assess environmental sustainability of expressway projects in Sri Lanka. *Management of Environmental Quality*, *33*(6), 1404–1420. DOI: 10.1108/MEQ-09-2021-0220

Wikipedia. (2017). Information visualization. https://en.wikipedia.org/wiki/Information_visualization

Wikipedia. (2017). Scientific visualization. https://en.wikipedia.org/wiki/Scientific_visualization

Wood, W., & Zaichkowsky, J. L. (2004). Cognitive biases in financial decision-making: A comparative study. *Journal of Financial Psychology*, *9*(2), 134–150.

WTO. (2019). World Trade Report 2019: The Future of Services Trade. World Trade Organization. https://www.wto.org/english/res_e/booksp_e/00_wtr19_e.pdf.

Yassine, F. L. Y. A., Maaitah, T. A., Maaitah, D. A., & Al-Gasawneh, J. A. (2022). Impact of COVID-19 on the university education system in Jordan. *Journal of Southwest Jiaotong University*, *57*(1), 649–663. DOI: 10.35741/issn.0258-2724.57.1.58

Yu, Y. (2021). Opportunities and Challenges of International Trade under the Background of Big Data. *In2021 International Conference on Education Technology and E-Business Management,Hangzhou, China,* (pp. 142-145). Chartered Society of Physiotherapy (CSP): The UK.

Yumagulova, L., & Vertinsky, I. (2021). Managing trade-offs between specific and general resilience: Insights from Canada's Metro Vancouver region. *Cities (London, England)*, *119*, 103319. DOI: 10.1016/j.cities.2021.103319

Zamri, A. H., Ibrahim, A. M., Haslindar, H., & Tuyon, M. A. (2017). Rational decision-making in financial investments: A study of financial behaviors. *Journal of Behavioral Finance*, *18*(4), 102–117. DOI: 10.1080/15427560.2017.1342491

Zanotti, L., Ma, Z., Johnson, J. L., Johnson, D. R., Yu, D. J., Burnham, M., & Carothers, C. (2020). Sustainability, resilience, adaptation, and transformation: Tensions and plural approaches. *Ecology and Society*, *25*(3), art4. DOI: 10.5751/ES-11642-250304

Zhang, Y., Liu, S., & Wang, Z. (2021). The role of big data in mitigating cognitive biases in investment decisions. *Journal of Financial Analysis*, *26*(1), 78–94.

Zhou, A. (2022). Digital infrastructure and economic growth—Evidence for China. *Journal of Infrastructure. Policy and Development*, *6*(1), 1397. DOI: 10.24294/jipd.v6i1.1397

Zhou, L., & Fu, Y. (2021). The Impact of Big Data Technology on International Trade. In Huang, C., Chan, Y.-W., & Yen, N. (Eds.), *2020 International Conference on Data Processing Techniques and Applications for Cyber-Physical Systems* (pp. 889–896). Springer. DOI: 10.1007/978-981-16-1726-3_109

Zimmermann, H.-D. (2000). Understanding the Digital Economy: Challenges for New Business Models. SSRN *Electronic Journal*. DOI: 10.2139/ssrn.2566095

Zoltners, A. A., Sinha, P., Sahay, D., Shastri, A., & Lorimer, S. E. (2021). Practical insights for sales force digitalization success. *Journal of Personal Selling & Sales Management*, *41*(2), 87–102. DOI: 10.1080/08853134.2021.1908144

Related References

To continue our tradition of advancing information science and technology research, we have compiled a list of recommended IGI Global readings. These references will provide additional information and guidance to further enrich your knowledge and assist you with your own research and future publications.

Abdul Razak, R., & Mansor, N. A. (2021). Instagram Influencers in Social Media-Induced Tourism: Rethinking Tourist Trust Towards Tourism Destination. In M. Dinis, L. Bonixe, S. Lamy, & Z. Breda (Eds.), *Impact of New Media in Tourism* (pp. 135-144). IGI Global. https://doi.org/10.4018/978-1-7998-7095-1.ch009

Abir, T., & Khan, M. Y. (2022). Importance of ICT Advancement and Culture of Adaptation in the Tourism and Hospitality Industry for Developing Countries. In Ramos, C., Quinteiro, S., & Gonçalves, A. (Eds.), *ICT as Innovator Between Tourism and Culture* (pp. 30–41). IGI Global. https://doi.org/10.4018/978-1-7998-8165-0.ch003

Abtahi, M. S., Behboudi, L., & Hasanabad, H. M. (2017). Factors Affecting Internet Advertising Adoption in Ad Agencies. *International Journal of Innovation in the Digital Economy*, *8*(4), 18–29. DOI: 10.4018/IJIDE.2017100102

Afenyo-Agbe, E., & Mensah, I. (2022). Principles, Benefits, and Barriers to Community-Based Tourism: Implications for Management. In Mensah, I., & Afenyo-Agbe, E. (Eds.), *Prospects and Challenges of Community-Based Tourism and Changing Demographics* (pp. 1–29). IGI Global. DOI: 10.4018/978-1-7998-7335-8.ch001

Agbo, V. M. (2022). Distributive Justice Issues in Community-Based Tourism. In Mensah, I., & Afenyo-Agbe, E. (Eds.), *Prospects and Challenges of Community-Based Tourism and Changing Demographics* (pp. 107–129). IGI Global. https://doi.org/10.4018/978-1-7998-7335-8.ch005

Agrawal, S. (2017). The Impact of Emerging Technologies and Social Media on Different Business(es): Marketing and Management. In Rishi, O., & Sharma, A. (Eds.), *Maximizing Business Performance and Efficiency Through Intelligent Systems* (pp. 37–49). Hershey, PA: IGI Global. DOI: 10.4018/978-1-5225-2234-8.ch002

Ahmad, A., & Johari, S. (2022). Georgetown as a Gastronomy Tourism Destination: Visitor Awareness Towards Revisit Intention of Nasi Kandar Restaurant. In Valeri, M. (Ed.), *New Governance and Management in Touristic Destinations* (pp. 71–83). IGI Global. https://doi.org/10.4018/978-1-6684-3889-3.ch005

Alkhatib, G., & Bayouq, S. T. (2021). A TAM-Based Model of Technological Factors Affecting Use of E-Tourism. *International Journal of Tourism and Hospitality Management in the Digital Age*, *5*(2), 50–67. https://doi.org/10.4018/IJTHMDA.20210701.oa1

Altinay Ozdemir, M. (2021). Virtual Reality (VR) and Augmented Reality (AR) Technologies for Accessibility and Marketing in the Tourism Industry. In C. Eusébio, L. Teixeira, & M. Carneiro (Eds.), *ICT Tools and Applications for Accessible Tourism* (pp. 277-301). IGI Global. https://doi.org/10.4018/978-1-7998-6428-8.ch013

Anantharaman, R. N., Rajeswari, K. S., Angusamy, A., & Kuppusamy, J. (2017). Role of Self-Efficacy and Collective Efficacy as Moderators of Occupational Stress Among Software Development Professionals. *International Journal of Human Capital and Information Technology Professionals*, *8*(2), 45–58. DOI: 10.4018/IJHCITP.2017040103

Aninze, F., El-Gohary, H., & Hussain, J. (2018). The Role of Microfinance to Empower Women: The Case of Developing Countries. *International Journal of Customer Relationship Marketing and Management*, *9*(1), 54–78. DOI: 10.4018/IJCRMM.2018010104

Antosova, G., Sabogal-Salamanca, M., & Krizova, E. (2021). Human Capital in Tourism: A Practical Model of Endogenous and Exogenous Territorial Tourism Planning in Bahía Solano, Colombia. In Costa, V., Moura, A., & Mira, M. (Eds.), *Handbook of Research on Human Capital and People Management in the Tourism Industry* (pp. 282–302). IGI Global. https://doi.org/10.4018/978-1-7998-4318-4.ch014

Arsenijević, O. M., Orčić, D., & Kastratović, E. (2017). Development of an Optimization Tool for Intangibles in SMEs: A Case Study from Serbia with a Pilot Research in the Prestige by Milka Company. In Vemić, M. (Ed.), *Optimal Management Strategies in Small and Medium Enterprises* (pp. 320–347). Hershey, PA: IGI Global. DOI: 10.4018/978-1-5225-1949-2.ch015

Aryanto, V. D., Wismantoro, Y., & Widyatmoko, K. (2018). Implementing Eco-Innovation by Utilizing the Internet to Enhance Firm's Marketing Performance: Study of Green Batik Small and Medium Enterprises in Indonesia. *International Journal of E-Business Research, 14*(1), 21–36. DOI: 10.4018/IJEBR.2018010102

Asero, V., & Billi, S. (2022). New Perspective of Networking in the DMO Model. In Valeri, M. (Ed.), *New Governance and Management in Touristic Destinations* (pp. 105–118). IGI Global. https://doi.org/10.4018/978-1-6684-3889-3.ch007

Atiku, S. O., & Fields, Z. (2017). Multicultural Orientations for 21st Century Global Leadership. In Baporikar, N. (Ed.), *Management Education for Global Leadership* (pp. 28–51). Hershey, PA: IGI Global. DOI: 10.4018/978-1-5225-1013-0.ch002

Atiku, S. O., & Fields, Z. (2018). Organisational Learning Dimensions and Talent Retention Strategies for the Service Industries. In Baporikar, N. (Ed.), *Global Practices in Knowledge Management for Societal and Organizational Development* (pp. 358–381). Hershey, PA: IGI Global. DOI: 10.4018/978-1-5225-3009-1.ch017

Atsa'am, D. D., & Kuset Bodur, E. (2021). Pattern Mining on How Organizational Tenure Affects the Psychological Capital of Employees Within the Hospitality and Tourism Industry: Linking Employees' Organizational Tenure With PsyCap. *International Journal of Tourism and Hospitality Management in the Digital Age*, *5*(2), 17–28. https://doi.org/10.4018/IJTHMDA.2021070102

Ávila, L., & Teixeira, L. (2018). The Main Concepts Behind the Dematerialization of Business Processes. In M. Khosrow-Pour, D.B.A. (Ed.), *Encyclopedia of Information Science and Technology, Fourth Edition* (pp. 888-898). Hershey, PA: IGI Global. https://doi.org/DOI: 10.4018/978-1-5225-2255-3.ch076

Ayorekire, J., Mugizi, F., Obua, J., & Ampaire, G. (2022). Community-Based Tourism and Local People's Perceptions Towards Conservation: The Case of Queen Elizabeth Conservation Area, Uganda. In Mensah, I., & Afenyo-Agbe, E. (Eds.), *Prospects and Challenges of Community-Based Tourism and Changing Demographics* (pp. 56–82). IGI Global. https://doi.org/10.4018/978-1-7998-7335-8.ch003

Baleiro, R. (2022). Tourist Literature and the Architecture of Travel in Olga Tokarczuk and Patti Smith. In R. Baleiro & R. Pereira (Eds.), *Global Perspectives on Literary Tourism and Film-Induced Tourism* (pp. 202-216). IGI Global. https://doi.org/10.4018/978-1-7998-8262-6.ch011

Barat, S. (2021). Looking at the Future of Medical Tourism in Asia. *International Journal of Tourism and Hospitality Management in the Digital Age*, *5*(1), 19–33. https://doi.org/10.4018/IJTHMDA.2021010102

Barbosa, C. A., Magalhães, M., & Nunes, M. R. (2021). Travel Instagramability: A Way of Choosing a Destination? In M. Dinis, L. Bonixe, S. Lamy, & Z. Breda (Eds.), *Impact of New Media in Tourism* (pp. 173-190). IGI Global. https://doi.org/10.4018/978-1-7998-7095-1.ch011

Bari, M. W., & Khan, Q. (2021). Pakistan as a Destination of Religious Tourism. In E. Alaverdov & M. Bari (Eds.), *Global Development of Religious Tourism* (pp. 1-10). IGI Global. https://doi.org/10.4018/978-1-7998-5792-1.ch001

Bartens, Y., Chunpir, H. I., Schulte, F., & Voß, S. (2017). Business/IT Alignment in Two-Sided Markets: A COBIT 5 Analysis for Media Streaming Business Models. In De Haes, S., & Van Grembergen, W. (Eds.), *Strategic IT Governance and Alignment in Business Settings* (pp. 82–111). Hershey, PA: IGI Global. DOI: 10.4018/978-1-5225-0861-8.ch004

Bashayreh, A. M. (2018). Organizational Culture and Organizational Performance. In Lee, W., & Sabetzadeh, F. (Eds.), *Contemporary Knowledge and Systems Science* (pp. 50–69). Hershey, PA: IGI Global. DOI: 10.4018/978-1-5225-5655-8.ch003

Bechthold, L., Lude, M., & Prügl, R. (2021). Crisis Favors the Prepared Firm: How Organizational Ambidexterity Relates to Perceptions of Organizational Resilience. In Zehrer, A., Glowka, G., Schwaiger, K., & Ranacher-Lackner, V. (Eds.), *Resiliency Models and Addressing Future Risks for Family Firms in the Tourism Industry* (pp. 178–205). IGI Global. https://doi.org/10.4018/978-1-7998-7352-5.ch008

Bedford, D. A. (2018). Sustainable Knowledge Management Strategies: Aligning Business Capabilities and Knowledge Management Goals. In Baporikar, N. (Ed.), *Global Practices in Knowledge Management for Societal and Organizational Development* (pp. 46–73). Hershey, PA: IGI Global. DOI: 10.4018/978-1-5225-3009-1.ch003

Bekjanov, D., & Matyusupov, B. (2021). Influence of Innovative Processes in the Competitiveness of Tourist Destination. In Soares, J. (Ed.), *Innovation and Entrepreneurial Opportunities in Community Tourism* (pp. 243–263). IGI Global. https://doi.org/10.4018/978-1-7998-4855-4.ch014

Bharwani, S., & Musunuri, D. (2018). Reflection as a Process From Theory to Practice. In M. Khosrow-Pour, D.B.A. (Ed.), *Encyclopedia of Information Science and Technology, Fourth Edition* (pp. 1529-1539). Hershey, PA: IGI Global. DOI: 10.4018/978-1-5225-2255-3.ch132

Bhatt, G. D., Wang, Z., & Rodger, J. A. (2017). Information Systems Capabilities and Their Effects on Competitive Advantages: A Study of Chinese Companies. *Information Resources Management Journal, 30*(3), 41–57. DOI: 10.4018/IRMJ.2017070103

Bhushan, M., & Yadav, A. (2017). Concept of Cloud Computing in ESB. In Bhadoria, R., Chaudhari, N., Tomar, G., & Singh, S. (Eds.), *Exploring Enterprise Service Bus in the Service-Oriented Architecture Paradigm* (pp. 116–127). Hershey, PA: IGI Global. DOI: 10.4018/978-1-5225-2157-0.ch008

Bhushan, S. (2017). System Dynamics Base-Model of Humanitarian Supply Chain (HSCM) in Disaster Prone Eco-Communities of India: A Discussion on Simulation and Scenario Results. *International Journal of System Dynamics Applications*, *6*(3), 20–37. DOI: 10.4018/IJSDA.2017070102

Binder, D., & Miller, J. W. (2021). A Generations' Perspective on Employer Branding in Tourism. In Costa, V., Moura, A., & Mira, M. (Eds.), *Handbook of Research on Human Capital and People Management in the Tourism Industry* (pp. 152–174). IGI Global. https://doi.org/10.4018/978-1-7998-4318-4.ch008

Birch Freeman, A. A., Mensah, I., & Antwi, K. B. (2022). Smiling vs. Frowning Faces: Community Participation for Sustainable Tourism in Ghanaian Communities. In Mensah, I., & Afenyo-Agbe, E. (Eds.), *Prospects and Challenges of Community-Based Tourism and Changing Demographics* (pp. 83–106). IGI Global. https://doi.org/10.4018/978-1-7998-7335-8.ch004

Biswas, A., & De, A. K. (2017). On Development of a Fuzzy Stochastic Programming Model with Its Application to Business Management. In Trivedi, S., Dey, S., Kumar, A., & Panda, T. (Eds.), *Handbook of Research on Advanced Data Mining Techniques and Applications for Business Intelligence* (pp. 353–378). Hershey, PA: IGI Global. DOI: 10.4018/978-1-5225-2031-3.ch021

Boragnio, A., & Faracce Macia, C. (2021). "Taking Care of Yourself at Home": Use of E-Commerce About Food and Care During the COVID-19 Pandemic in the City of Buenos Aires. In Korstanje, M. (Ed.), *Socio-Economic Effects and Recovery Efforts for the Rental Industry: Post-COVID-19 Strategies* (pp. 45–71). IGI Global. https://doi.org/10.4018/978-1-7998-7287-0.ch003

Borges, V. D. (2021). Happiness: The Basis for Public Policy in Tourism. In Perinotto, A., Mayer, V., & Soares, J. (Eds.), *Rebuilding and Restructuring the Tourism Industry: Infusion of Happiness and Quality of Life* (pp. 1–25). IGI Global. https://doi.org/10.4018/978-1-7998-7239-9.ch001

Bücker, J., & Ernste, K. (2018). Use of Brand Heroes in Strategic Reputation Management: The Case of Bacardi, Adidas, and Daimler. In Erdemir, A. (Ed.), *Reputation Management Techniques in Public Relations* (pp. 126–150). Hershey, PA: IGI Global. DOI: 10.4018/978-1-5225-3619-2.ch007

Buluk Eşitti, B. (2021). COVID-19 and Alternative Tourism: New Destinations and New Tourism Products. In Demir, M., Dalgıç, A., & Ergen, F. (Eds.), *Handbook of Research on the Impacts and Implications of COVID-19 on the Tourism Industry* (pp. 786–805). IGI Global. https://doi.org/10.4018/978-1-7998-8231-2.ch038

Bureš, V. (2018). Industry 4.0 From the Systems Engineering Perspective: Alternative Holistic Framework Development. In Brunet-Thornton, R., & Martinez, F. (Eds.), *Analyzing the Impacts of Industry 4.0 in Modern Business Environments* (pp. 199–223). Hershey, PA: IGI Global. DOI: 10.4018/978-1-5225-3468-6.ch011

Buzady, Z. (2017). Resolving the Magic Cube of Effective Case Teaching: Benchmarking Case Teaching Practices in Emerging Markets – Insights from the Central European University Business School, Hungary. In Latusek, D. (Ed.), *Case Studies as a Teaching Tool in Management Education* (pp. 79–103). Hershey, PA: IGI Global. DOI: 10.4018/978-1-5225-0770-3.ch005

Camillo, A. (2021). *Legal Matters, Risk Management, and Risk Prevention: From Forming a Business to Legal Representation*. IGI Global. DOI: 10.4018/978-1-7998-4342-9.ch004

Căpusneanu, S., & Topor, D. I. (2018). Business Ethics and Cost Management in SMEs: Theories of Business Ethics and Cost Management Ethos. In Oncioiu, I. (Ed.), *Ethics and Decision-Making for Sustainable Business Practices* (pp. 109–127). Hershey, PA: IGI Global. DOI: 10.4018/978-1-5225-3773-1.ch007

Chan, R. L., Mo, P. L., & Moon, K. K. (2018). Strategic and Tactical Measures in Managing Enterprise Risks: A Study of the Textile and Apparel Industry. In Strang, K., Korstanje, M., & Vajjhala, N. (Eds.), *Research, Practices, and Innovations in Global Risk and Contingency Management* (pp. 1–19). Hershey, PA: IGI Global. DOI: 10.4018/978-1-5225-4754-9.ch001

Charlier, S. D., Burke-Smalley, L. A., & Fisher, S. L. (2018). Undergraduate Programs in the U.S: A Contextual and Content-Based Analysis. In Mendy, J. (Ed.), *Teaching Human Resources and Organizational Behavior at the College Level* (pp. 26–57). Hershey, PA: IGI Global. DOI: 10.4018/978-1-5225-2820-3.ch002

Chumillas, J., Güell, M., & Quer, P. (2022). The Use of ICT in Tourist and Educational Literary Routes: The Role of the Guide. In Ramos, C., Quinteiro, S., & Gonçalves, A. (Eds.), *ICT as Innovator Between Tourism and Culture* (pp. 15–29). IGI Global. https://doi.org/10.4018/978-1-7998-8165-0.ch002

Dahlberg, T., Kivijärvi, H., & Saarinen, T. (2017). IT Investment Consistency and Other Factors Influencing the Success of IT Performance. In De Haes, S., & Van Grembergen, W. (Eds.), *Strategic IT Governance and Alignment in Business Settings* (pp. 176–208). Hershey, PA: IGI Global. DOI: 10.4018/978-1-5225-0861-8.ch007

Damnjanović, A. M. (2017). Knowledge Management Optimization through IT and E-Business Utilization: A Qualitative Study on Serbian SMEs. In Vemić, M. (Ed.), *Optimal Management Strategies in Small and Medium Enterprises* (pp. 249–267). Hershey, PA: IGI Global. DOI: 10.4018/978-1-5225-1949-2.ch012

Daneshpour, H. (2017). Integrating Sustainable Development into Project Portfolio Management through Application of Open Innovation. In Vemić, M. (Ed.), *Optimal Management Strategies in Small and Medium Enterprises* (pp. 370–387). Hershey, PA: IGI Global. DOI: 10.4018/978-1-5225-1949-2.ch017

Daniel, A. D., & Reis de Castro, V. (2018). Entrepreneurship Education: How to Measure the Impact on Nascent Entrepreneurs. In Carrizo Moreira, A., Guilherme Leitão Dantas, J., & Manuel Valente, F. (Eds.), *Nascent Entrepreneurship and Successful New Venture Creation* (pp. 85–110). Hershey, PA: IGI Global. DOI: 10.4018/978-1-5225-2936-1.ch004

David, R., Swami, B. N., & Tangirala, S. (2018). Ethics Impact on Knowledge Management in Organizational Development: A Case Study. In Baporikar, N. (Ed.), *Global Practices in Knowledge Management for Societal and Organizational Development* (pp. 19–45). Hershey, PA: IGI Global. DOI: 10.4018/978-1-5225-3009-1.ch002

De Uña-Álvarez, E., & Villarino-Pérez, M. (2022). Fostering Ecocultural Resources, Identity, and Tourism in Inland Territories (Galicia, NW Spain). In G. Fernandes (Ed.), *Challenges and New Opportunities for Tourism in Inland Territories: Ecocultural Resources and Sustainable Initiatives* (pp. 1-16). IGI Global. https://doi.org/10.4018/978-1-7998-7339-6.ch001

Delias, P., & Lakiotaki, K. (2018). Discovering Process Horizontal Boundaries to Facilitate Process Comprehension. *International Journal of Operations Research and Information Systems*, *9*(2), 1–31. DOI: 10.4018/IJORIS.2018040101

Denholm, J., & Lee-Davies, L. (2018). Success Factors for Games in Business and Project Management. In *Enhancing Education and Training Initiatives Through Serious Games* (pp. 34–68). Hershey, PA: IGI Global. DOI: 10.4018/978-1-5225-3689-5.ch002

Deshpande, M. (2017). Best Practices in Management Institutions for Global Leadership: Policy Aspects. In Baporikar, N. (Ed.), *Management Education for Global Leadership* (pp. 1–27). Hershey, PA: IGI Global. DOI: 10.4018/978-1-5225-1013-0.ch001

Deshpande, M. (2018). Policy Perspectives for SMEs Knowledge Management. In Baporikar, N. (Ed.), *Knowledge Integration Strategies for Entrepreneurship and Sustainability* (pp. 23–46). Hershey, PA: IGI Global. DOI: 10.4018/978-1-5225-5115-7.ch002

Dezdar, S. (2017). ERP Implementation Projects in Asian Countries: A Comparative Study on Iran and China. *International Journal of Information Technology Project Management, 8*(3), 52–68. DOI: 10.4018/IJITPM.2017070104

Domingos, D., Respício, A., & Martinho, R. (2017). Reliability of IoT-Aware BPMN Healthcare Processes. In Reis, C., & Maximiano, M. (Eds.), *Internet of Things and Advanced Application in Healthcare* (pp. 214–248). Hershey, PA: IGI Global. DOI: 10.4018/978-1-5225-1820-4.ch008

Dosumu, O., Hussain, J., & El-Gohary, H. (2017). An Exploratory Study of the Impact of Government Policies on the Development of Small and Medium Enterprises in Developing Countries: The Case of Nigeria. *International Journal of Customer Relationship Marketing and Management, 8*(4), 51–62. DOI: 10.4018/IJCRMM.2017100104

Durst, S., Bruns, G., & Edvardsson, I. R. (2017). Retaining Knowledge in Smaller Building and Construction Firms. *International Journal of Knowledge and Systems Science, 8*(3), 1–12. DOI: 10.4018/IJKSS.2017070101

Edvardsson, I. R., & Durst, S. (2017). Outsourcing, Knowledge, and Learning: A Critical Review. *International Journal of Knowledge-Based Organizations, 7*(2), 13–26. DOI: 10.4018/IJKBO.2017040102

Edwards, J. S. (2018). Integrating Knowledge Management and Business Processes. In M. Khosrow-Pour, D.B.A. (Ed.), *Encyclopedia of Information Science and Technology, Fourth Edition* (pp. 5046-5055). Hershey, PA: IGI Global. DOI: 10.4018/978-1-5225-2255-3.ch437

Eichelberger, S., & Peters, M. (2021). Family Firm Management in Turbulent Times: Opportunities for Responsible Tourism. In Zehrer, A., Glowka, G., Schwaiger, K., & Ranacher-Lackner, V. (Eds.), *Resiliency Models and Addressing Future Risks for Family Firms in the Tourism Industry* (pp. 103–124). IGI Global. https://doi.org/10.4018/978-1-7998-7352-5.ch005

Eide, D., Hjalager, A., & Hansen, M. (2022). Innovative Certifications in Adventure Tourism: Attributes and Diffusion. In R. Augusto Costa, F. Brandão, Z. Breda, & C. Costa (Eds.), *Planning and Managing the Experience Economy in Tourism* (pp. 161-175). IGI Global. https://doi.org/10.4018/978-1-7998-8775-1.ch009

Ejiogu, A. O. (2018). Economics of Farm Management. In *Agricultural Finance and Opportunities for Investment and Expansion* (pp. 56–72). Hershey, PA: IGI Global. DOI: 10.4018/978-1-5225-3059-6.ch003

Ekanem, I., & Abiade, G. E. (2018). Factors Influencing the Use of E-Commerce by Small Enterprises in Nigeria. *International Journal of ICT Research in Africa and the Middle East*, *7*(1), 37–53. DOI: 10.4018/IJICTRAME.2018010103

Ekanem, I., & Alrossais, L. A. (2017). Succession Challenges Facing Family Businesses in Saudi Arabia. In Zgheib, P. (Ed.), *Entrepreneurship and Business Innovation in the Middle East* (pp. 122–146). Hershey, PA: IGI Global. DOI: 10.4018/978-1-5225-2066-5.ch007

El Faquih, L., & Fredj, M. (2017). Ontology-Based Framework for Quality in Configurable Process Models. *Journal of Electronic Commerce in Organizations*, *15*(2), 48–60. DOI: 10.4018/JECO.2017040104

Faisal, M. N., & Talib, F. (2017). Building Ambidextrous Supply Chains in SMEs: How to Tackle the Barriers? *International Journal of Information Systems and Supply Chain Management*, *10*(4), 80–100. DOI: 10.4018/IJISSCM.2017100105

Fernandes, T. M., Gomes, J., & Romão, M. (2017). Investments in E-Government: A Benefit Management Case Study. *International Journal of Electronic Government Research*, *13*(3), 1–17. DOI: 10.4018/IJEGR.2017070101

Figueira, L. M., Honrado, G. R., & Dionísio, M. S. (2021). Human Capital Management in the Tourism Industry in Portugal. In Costa, V., Moura, A., & Mira, M. (Eds.), *Handbook of Research on Human Capital and People Management in the Tourism Industry* (pp. 1–19). IGI Global. DOI: 10.4018/978-1-7998-4318-4.ch001

Gao, S. S., Oreal, S., & Zhang, J. (2018). Contemporary Financial Risk Management Perceptions and Practices of Small-Sized Chinese Businesses. In I. Management Association (Ed.), *Global Business Expansion: Concepts, Methodologies, Tools, and Applications* (pp. 917-931). Hershey, PA: IGI Global. DOI: 10.4018/978-1-5225-5481-3.ch041

Garg, R., & Berning, S. C. (2017). Indigenous Chinese Management Philosophies: Key Concepts and Relevance for Modern Chinese Firms. In Christiansen, B., & Koc, G. (Eds.), *Transcontinental Strategies for Industrial Development and Economic Growth* (pp. 43–57). Hershey, PA: IGI Global. DOI: 10.4018/978-1-5225-2160-0.ch003

Gencer, Y. G. (2017). Supply Chain Management in Retailing Business. In Akkucuk, U. (Ed.), *Ethics and Sustainability in Global Supply Chain Management* (pp. 197–210). Hershey, PA: IGI Global. DOI: 10.4018/978-1-5225-2036-8.ch011

Gera, R., Arora, S., & Malik, S. (2021). Emotional Labor in the Tourism Industry: Strategies, Antecedents, and Outcomes. In Costa, V., Moura, A., & Mira, M. (Eds.), *Handbook of Research on Human Capital and People Management in the Tourism Industry* (pp. 73–91). IGI Global. https://doi.org/10.4018/978-1-7998-4318-4.ch004

Giacosa, E. (2018). The Increasing of the Regional Development Thanks to the Luxury Business Innovation. In Carvalho, L. (Ed.), *Handbook of Research on Entrepreneurial Ecosystems and Social Dynamics in a Globalized World* (pp. 260–273). Hershey, PA: IGI Global. DOI: 10.4018/978-1-5225-3525-6.ch011

Glowka, G., Tusch, M., & Zehrer, A. (2021). The Risk Perception of Family Business Owner-Manager in the Tourism Industry: A Qualitative Comparison of the Intra-Firm Senior and Junior Generation. In Zehrer, A., Glowka, G., Schwaiger, K., & Ranacher-Lackner, V. (Eds.), *Resiliency Models and Addressing Future Risks for Family Firms in the Tourism Industry* (pp. 126–153). IGI Global. https://doi.org/10.4018/978-1-7998-7352-5.ch006

Glykas, M., & George, J. (2017). Quality and Process Management Systems in the UAE Maritime Industry. *International Journal of Productivity Management and Assessment Technologies*, *5*(1), 20–39. DOI: 10.4018/IJPMAT.2017010102

Glykas, M., Valiris, G., Kokkinaki, A., & Koutsoukou, Z. (2018). Banking Business Process Management Implementation. *International Journal of Productivity Management and Assessment Technologies*, *6*(1), 50–69. DOI: 10.4018/IJPMAT.2018010104

Gomes, J., & Romão, M. (2017). The Balanced Scorecard: Keeping Updated and Aligned with Today's Business Trends. *International Journal of Productivity Management and Assessment Technologies*, *5*(2), 1–15. DOI: 10.4018/IJPMAT.2017070101

Gomes, J., & Romão, M. (2017). Aligning Information Systems and Technology with Benefit Management and Balanced Scorecard. In De Haes, S., & Van Grembergen, W. (Eds.), *Strategic IT Governance and Alignment in Business Settings* (pp. 112–131). Hershey, PA: IGI Global. DOI: 10.4018/978-1-5225-0861-8.ch005

Goyal, A. (2021). Communicating and Building Destination Brands With New Media. In M. Dinis, L. Bonixe, S. Lamy, & Z. Breda (Eds.), *Impact of New Media in Tourism* (pp. 1-20). IGI Global. https://doi.org/10.4018/978-1-7998-7095-1.ch001

Grefen, P., & Turetken, O. (2017). Advanced Business Process Management in Networked E-Business Scenarios. *International Journal of E-Business Research*, *13*(4), 70–104. DOI: 10.4018/IJEBR.2017100105

Guasca, M., Van Broeck, A. M., & Vanneste, D. (2021). Tourism and the Social Reintegration of Colombian Ex-Combatants. In J. da Silva, Z. Breda, & F. Carbone (Eds.), *Role and Impact of Tourism in Peacebuilding and Conflict Transformation* (pp. 66-86). IGI Global. https://doi.org/10.4018/978-1-7998-5053-3.ch005

Haider, A., & Saetang, S. (2017). Strategic IT Alignment in Service Sector. In Rozenes, S., & Cohen, Y. (Eds.), *Handbook of Research on Strategic Alliances and Value Co-Creation in the Service Industry* (pp. 231–258). Hershey, PA: IGI Global. DOI: 10.4018/978-1-5225-2084-9.ch012

Hajilari, A. B., Ghadaksaz, M., & Fasghandis, G. S. (2017). Assessing Organizational Readiness for Implementing ERP System Using Fuzzy Expert System Approach. *International Journal of Enterprise Information Systems*, *13*(1), 67–85. DOI: 10.4018/IJEIS.2017010105

Haldorai, A., Ramu, A., & Murugan, S. (2018). Social Aware Cognitive Radio Networks: Effectiveness of Social Networks as a Strategic Tool for Organizational Business Management. In Bansal, H., Shrivastava, G., Nguyen, G., & Stanciu, L. (Eds.), *Social Network Analytics for Contemporary Business Organizations* (pp. 188–202). Hershey, PA: IGI Global. DOI: 10.4018/978-1-5225-5097-6.ch010

Hall, O. P.Jr. (2017). Social Media Driven Management Education. *International Journal of Knowledge-Based Organizations*, *7*(2), 43–59. DOI: 10.4018/IJKBO.2017040104

Hanifah, H., Halim, H. A., Ahmad, N. H., & Vafaei-Zadeh, A. (2017). Innovation Culture as a Mediator Between Specific Human Capital and Innovation Performance Among Bumiputera SMEs in Malaysia. In Ahmad, N., Ramayah, T., Halim, H., & Rahman, S. (Eds.), *Handbook of Research on Small and Medium Enterprises in Developing Countries* (pp. 261–279). Hershey, PA: IGI Global. DOI: 10.4018/978-1-5225-2165-5.ch012

Hartlieb, S., & Silvius, G. (2017). Handling Uncertainty in Project Management and Business Development: Similarities and Differences. In Raydugin, Y. (Ed.), *Handbook of Research on Leveraging Risk and Uncertainties for Effective Project Management* (pp. 337–362). Hershey, PA: IGI Global. DOI: 10.4018/978-1-5225-1790-0.ch016

Hass, K. B. (2017). Living on the Edge: Managing Project Complexity. In Raydugin, Y. (Ed.), *Handbook of Research on Leveraging Risk and Uncertainties for Effective Project Management* (pp. 177–201). Hershey, PA: IGI Global. DOI: 10.4018/978-1-5225-1790-0.ch009

Hawking, P., & Carmine Sellitto, C. (2017). Developing an Effective Strategy for Organizational Business Intelligence. In Tavana, M. (Ed.), *Enterprise Information Systems and the Digitalization of Business Functions* (pp. 222–237). Hershey, PA: IGI Global. DOI: 10.4018/978-1-5225-2382-6.ch010

Hawking, P., & Sellitto, C. (2017). A Fast-Moving Consumer Goods Company and Business Intelligence Strategy Development. *International Journal of Enterprise Information Systems*, *13*(2), 22–33. DOI: 10.4018/IJEIS.2017040102

Hawking, P., & Sellitto, C. (2017). Business Intelligence Strategy: Two Case Studies. *International Journal of Business Intelligence Research, 8*(2), 17–30. DOI: 10.4018/IJBIR.2017070102

Hee, W. J., Jalleh, G., Lai, H., & Lin, C. (2017). E-Commerce and IT Projects: Evaluation and Management Issues in Australian and Taiwanese Hospitals. *International Journal of Public Health Management and Ethics, 2*(1), 69–90. DOI: 10.4018/IJPHME.2017010104

Hernandez, A. A. (2018). Exploring the Factors to Green IT Adoption of SMEs in the Philippines. *Journal of Cases on Information Technology, 20*(2), 49–66. DOI: 10.4018/JCIT.2018040104

Hollman, A., Bickford, S., & Hollman, T. (2017). Cyber InSecurity: A Post-Mortem Attempt to Assess Cyber Problems from IT and Business Management Perspectives. *Journal of Cases on Information Technology, 19*(3), 42–70. DOI: 10.4018/JCIT.2017070104

Ibrahim, F., & Zainin, N. M. (2021). Exploring the Technological Impacts: The Case of Museums in Brunei Darussalam. *International Journal of Tourism and Hospitality Management in the Digital Age, 5*(1), 1–18. https://doi.org/10.4018/IJTHMDA.2021010101

Igbinakhase, I. (2017). Responsible and Sustainable Management Practices in Developing and Developed Business Environments. In Fields, Z. (Ed.), *Collective Creativity for Responsible and Sustainable Business Practice* (pp. 180–207). Hershey, PA: IGI Global. DOI: 10.4018/978-1-5225-1823-5.ch010

Iwata, J. J., & Hoskins, R. G. (2017). Managing Indigenous Knowledge in Tanzania: A Business Perspective. In Jain, P., & Mnjama, N. (Eds.), *Managing Knowledge Resources and Records in Modern Organizations* (pp. 198–214). Hershey, PA: IGI Global. DOI: 10.4018/978-1-5225-1965-2.ch012

Jain, P. (2017). Ethical and Legal Issues in Knowledge Management Life-Cycle in Business. In Jain, P., & Mnjama, N. (Eds.), *Managing Knowledge Resources and Records in Modern Organizations* (pp. 82–101). Hershey, PA: IGI Global. DOI: 10.4018/978-1-5225-1965-2.ch006

James, S., & Hauli, E. (2017). Holistic Management Education at Tanzanian Rural Development Planning Institute. In Baporikar, N. (Ed.), *Management Education for Global Leadership* (pp. 112–136). Hershey, PA: IGI Global. DOI: 10.4018/978-1-5225-1013-0.ch006

Janošková, M., Csikósová, A., & Čulková, K. (2018). Measurement of Company Performance as Part of Its Strategic Management. In Leon, R. (Ed.), *Managerial Strategies for Business Sustainability During Turbulent Times* (pp. 309–335). Hershey, PA: IGI Global. DOI: 10.4018/978-1-5225-2716-9.ch017

Jean-Vasile, A., & Alecu, A. (2017). Theoretical and Practical Approaches in Understanding the Influences of Cost-Productivity-Profit Trinomial in Contemporary Enterprises. In Jean Vasile, A., & Nicolò, D. (Eds.), *Sustainable Entrepreneurship and Investments in the Green Economy* (pp. 28–62). Hershey, PA: IGI Global. DOI: 10.4018/978-1-5225-2075-7.ch002

Joia, L. A., & Correia, J. C. (2018). CIO Competencies From the IT Professional Perspective: Insights From Brazil. *Journal of Global Information Management, 26*(2), 74–103. DOI: 10.4018/JGIM.2018040104

Juma, A., & Mzera, N. (2017). Knowledge Management and Records Management and Competitive Advantage in Business. In Jain, P., & Mnjama, N. (Eds.), *Managing Knowledge Resources and Records in Modern Organizations* (pp. 15–28). Hershey, PA: IGI Global. DOI: 10.4018/978-1-5225-1965-2.ch002

K., I., & A, V. (2018). Monitoring and Auditing in the Cloud. In K. Munir (Ed.), *Cloud Computing Technologies for Green Enterprises* (pp. 318-350). Hershey, PA: IGI Global. https://doi.org/DOI: 10.4018/978-1-5225-3038-1.ch013

Kabra, G., Ghosh, V., & Ramesh, A. (2018). Enterprise Integrated Business Process Management and Business Intelligence Framework for Business Process Sustainability. In Paul, A., Bhattacharyya, D., & Anand, S. (Eds.), *Green Initiatives for Business Sustainability and Value Creation* (pp. 228–238). Hershey, PA: IGI Global. DOI: 10.4018/978-1-5225-2662-9.ch010

Kaoud, M. (2017). Investigation of Customer Knowledge Management: A Case Study Research. *International Journal of Service Science, Management, Engineering, and Technology*, *8*(2), 12–22. DOI: 10.4018/IJSSMET.2017040102

Katuu, S. (2018). A Comparative Assessment of Enterprise Content Management Maturity Models. In Gwangwava, N., & Mutingi, M. (Eds.), *E-Manufacturing and E-Service Strategies in Contemporary Organizations* (pp. 93–118). Hershey, PA: IGI Global. DOI: 10.4018/978-1-5225-3628-4.ch005

Khan, M. Y., & Abir, T. (2022). The Role of Social Media Marketing in the Tourism and Hospitality Industry: A Conceptual Study on Bangladesh. In Ramos, C., Quinteiro, S., & Gonçalves, A. (Eds.), *ICT as Innovator Between Tourism and Culture* (pp. 213–229). IGI Global. https://doi.org/10.4018/978-1-7998-8165-0.ch013

Kinnunen, S., Ylä-Kujala, A., Marttonen-Arola, S., Kärri, T., & Baglee, D. (2018). Internet of Things in Asset Management: Insights from Industrial Professionals and Academia. *International Journal of Service Science, Management, Engineering, and Technology*, *9*(2), 104–119. DOI: 10.4018/IJSSMET.2018040105

Klein, A. Z., Sabino de Freitas, A., Machado, L., Freitas, J. C.Jr, Graziola, P. G.Jr, & Schlemmer, E. (2017). Virtual Worlds Applications for Management Education. In Tomei, L. (Ed.), *Exploring the New Era of Technology-Infused Education* (pp. 279–299). Hershey, PA: IGI Global. DOI: 10.4018/978-1-5225-1709-2.ch017

Kővári, E., Saleh, M., & Steinbachné Hajmásy, G. (2022). The Impact of Corporate Digital Responsibility (CDR) on Internal Stakeholders' Satisfaction in Hungarian Upscale Hotels. In Valeri, M. (Ed.), *New Governance and Management in Touristic Destinations* (pp. 35–51). IGI Global. https://doi.org/10.4018/978-1-6684-3889-3.ch003

Kożuch, B., & Jabłoński, A. (2017). Adopting the Concept of Business Models in Public Management. In Lewandowski, M., & Kożuch, B. (Eds.), *Public Sector Entrepreneurship and the Integration of Innovative Business Models* (pp. 10–46). Hershey, PA: IGI Global. DOI: 10.4018/978-1-5225-2215-7.ch002

Kumar, J., Adhikary, A., & Jha, A. (2017). Small Active Investors' Perceptions and Preferences Towards Tax Saving Mutual Fund Schemes in Eastern India: An Empirical Note. *International Journal of Asian Business and Information Management*, *8*(2), 35–45. DOI: 10.4018/IJABIM.2017040103

Latusi, S., & Fissore, M. (2021). Pilgrimage Routes to Happiness: Comparing the Camino de Santiago and Via Francigena. In Perinotto, A., Mayer, V., & Soares, J. (Eds.), *Rebuilding and Restructuring the Tourism Industry: Infusion of Happiness and Quality of Life* (pp. 157–182). IGI Global. https://doi.org/10.4018/978-1-7998-7239-9.ch008

Lavassani, K. M., & Movahedi, B. (2017). Applications Driven Information Systems: Beyond Networks toward Business Ecosystems. *International Journal of Innovation in the Digital Economy*, *8*(1), 61–75. DOI: 10.4018/IJIDE.2017010104

Lazzareschi, V. H., & Brito, M. S. (2017). Strategic Information Management: Proposal of Business Project Model. In Jamil, G., Soares, A., & Pessoa, C. (Eds.), *Handbook of Research on Information Management for Effective Logistics and Supply Chains* (pp. 59–88). Hershey, PA: IGI Global. DOI: 10.4018/978-1-5225-0973-8.ch004

Lechuga Sancho, M. P., & Martín Navarro, A. (2022). Evolution of the Literature on Social Responsibility in the Tourism Sector: A Systematic Literature Review. In Fernandes, G. (Ed.), *Challenges and New Opportunities for Tourism in Inland Territories: Ecocultural Resources and Sustainable Initiatives* (pp. 169–186). IGI Global. https://doi.org/10.4018/978-1-7998-7339-6.ch010

Lederer, M., Kurz, M., & Lazarov, P. (2017). Usage and Suitability of Methods for Strategic Business Process Initiatives: A Multi Case Study Research. *International Journal of Productivity Management and Assessment Technologies*, *5*(1), 40–51. DOI: 10.4018/IJPMAT.2017010103

Lee, I. (2017). A Social Enterprise Business Model and a Case Study of Pacific Community Ventures (PCV). In Potocan, V., Ünğan, M., & Nedelko, Z. (Eds.), *Handbook of Research on Managerial Solutions in Non-Profit Organizations* (pp. 182–204). Hershey, PA: IGI Global. DOI: 10.4018/978-1-5225-0731-4.ch009

Leon, L. A., Seal, K. C., Przasnyski, Z. H., & Wiedenman, I. (2017). Skills and Competencies Required for Jobs in Business Analytics: A Content Analysis of Job Advertisements Using Text Mining. *International Journal of Business Intelligence Research, 8*(1), 1–25. DOI: 10.4018/IJBIR.2017010101

Levy, C. L., & Elias, N. I. (2017). SOHO Users' Perceptions of Reliability and Continuity of Cloud-Based Services. In Moore, M. (Ed.), *Cybersecurity Breaches and Issues Surrounding Online Threat Protection* (pp. 248–287). Hershey, PA: IGI Global. DOI: 10.4018/978-1-5225-1941-6.ch011

Levy, M. (2018). Change Management Serving Knowledge Management and Organizational Development: Reflections and Review. In Baporikar, N. (Ed.), *Global Practices in Knowledge Management for Societal and Organizational Development* (pp. 256–270). Hershey, PA: IGI Global. DOI: 10.4018/978-1-5225-3009-1.ch012

Lewandowski, M. (2017). Public Organizations and Business Model Innovation: The Role of Public Service Design. In Lewandowski, M., & Kożuch, B. (Eds.), *Public Sector Entrepreneurship and the Integration of Innovative Business Models* (pp. 47–72). Hershey, PA: IGI Global. DOI: 10.4018/978-1-5225-2215-7.ch003

Lhannaoui, H., Kabbaj, M. I., & Bakkoury, Z. (2017). A Survey of Risk-Aware Business Process Modelling. *International Journal of Risk and Contingency Management, 6*(3), 14–26. DOI: 10.4018/IJRCM.2017070102

Li, J., Sun, W., Jiang, W., Yang, H., & Zhang, L. (2017). How the Nature of Exogenous Shocks and Crises Impact Company Performance?: The Effects of Industry Characteristics. *International Journal of Risk and Contingency Management, 6*(4), 40–55. DOI: 10.4018/IJRCM.2017100103

Lopez-Fernandez, M., Perez-Perez, M., Serrano-Bedia, A., & Cobo-Gonzalez, A. (2021). Small and Medium Tourism Enterprise Survival in Times of Crisis: "El Capricho de Gaudí. In Toubes, D., & Araújo-Vila, N. (Eds.), *Risk, Crisis, and Disaster Management in Small and Medium-Sized Tourism Enterprises* (pp. 103–129). IGI Global. DOI: 10.4018/978-1-7998-6996-2.ch005

Mahajan, A., Maidullah, S., & Hossain, M. R. (2022). Experience Toward Smart Tour Guide Apps in Travelling: An Analysis of Users' Reviews on Audio Odigos and Trip My Way. In R. Augusto Costa, F. Brandão, Z. Breda, & C. Costa (Eds.), *Planning and Managing the Experience Economy in Tourism* (pp. 255-273). IGI Global. https://doi.org/10.4018/978-1-7998-8775-1.ch014

Malega, P. (2017). Small and Medium Enterprises in the Slovak Republic: Status and Competitiveness of SMEs in the Global Markets and Possibilities of Optimization. In Vemić, M. (Ed.), *Optimal Management Strategies in Small and Medium Enterprises* (pp. 102–124). Hershey, PA: IGI Global. DOI: 10.4018/978-1-5225-1949-2.ch006

Malewska, K. M. (2017). Intuition in Decision-Making on the Example of a Non-Profit Organization. In Potocan, V., Ünğan, M., & Nedelko, Z. (Eds.), *Handbook of Research on Managerial Solutions in Non-Profit Organizations* (pp. 378–399). Hershey, PA: IGI Global. DOI: 10.4018/978-1-5225-0731-4.ch018

Maroofi, F. (2017). Entrepreneurial Orientation and Organizational Learning Ability Analysis for Innovation and Firm Performance. In Baporikar, N. (Ed.), *Innovation and Shifting Perspectives in Management Education* (pp. 144–165). Hershey, PA: IGI Global. DOI: 10.4018/978-1-5225-1019-2.ch007

Marques, M., Moleiro, D., Brito, T. M., & Marques, T. (2021). Customer Relationship Management as an Important Relationship Marketing Tool: The Case of the Hospitality Industry in Estoril Coast. In M. Dinis, L. Bonixe, S. Lamy, & Z. Breda (Eds.), *Impact of New Media in Tourism* (pp. 39-56). IGI Global. https://doi.org/DOI: 10.4018/978-1-7998-7095-1.ch003

Martins, P. V., & Zacarias, M. (2017). A Web-based Tool for Business Process Improvement. *International Journal of Web Portals*, *9*(2), 68–84. DOI: 10.4018/IJWP.2017070104

Matthies, B., & Coners, A. (2017). Exploring the Conceptual Nature of e-Business Projects. *Journal of Electronic Commerce in Organizations*, *15*(3), 33–63. DOI: 10.4018/JECO.2017070103

Mayer, V. F., Fraga, C. C., & Silva, L. C. (2021). Contributions of Neurosciences to Studies of Well-Being in Tourism. In Perinotto, A., Mayer, V., & Soares, J. (Eds.), *Rebuilding and Restructuring the Tourism Industry: Infusion of Happiness and Quality of Life* (pp. 108–128). IGI Global. https://doi.org/10.4018/978-1-7998-7239-9.ch006

McKee, J. (2018). Architecture as a Tool to Solve Business Planning Problems. In M. Khosrow-Pour, D.B.A. (Ed.), *Encyclopedia of Information Science and Technology, Fourth Edition* (pp. 573-586). Hershey, PA: IGI Global. DOI: 10.4018/978-1-5225-2255-3.ch050

McMurray, A. J., Cross, J., & Caponecchia, C. (2018). The Risk Management Profession in Australia: Business Continuity Plan Practices. In Bajgoric, N. (Ed.), *Always-On Enterprise Information Systems for Modern Organizations* (pp. 112–129). Hershey, PA: IGI Global. DOI: 10.4018/978-1-5225-3704-5.ch006

Meddah, I. H., & Belkadi, K. (2018). Mining Patterns Using Business Process Management. In Hamou, R. (Ed.), *Handbook of Research on Biomimicry in Information Retrieval and Knowledge Management* (pp. 78–89). Hershey, PA: IGI Global. DOI: 10.4018/978-1-5225-3004-6.ch005

Melian, A. G., & Camprubí, R. (2021). The Accessibility of Museum Websites: The Case of Barcelona. In Eusébio, C., Teixeira, L., & Carneiro, M. (Eds.), *ICT Tools and Applications for Accessible Tourism* (pp. 234–255). IGI Global. https://doi.org/10.4018/978-1-7998-6428-8.ch011

Mendes, L. (2017). TQM and Knowledge Management: An Integrated Approach Towards Tacit Knowledge Management. In Jaziri-Bouagina, D., & Jamil, G. (Eds.), *Handbook of Research on Tacit Knowledge Management for Organizational Success* (pp. 236–263). Hershey, PA: IGI Global. DOI: 10.4018/978-1-5225-2394-9.ch009

Menezes, V. D., & Cavagnaro, E. (2021). Communicating Sustainable Initiatives in the Hotel Industry: The Case of the Hotel Jakarta Amsterdam. In F. Brandão, Z. Breda, R. Costa, & C. Costa (Eds.), *Handbook of Research on the Role of Tourism in Achieving Sustainable Development Goals* (pp. 224-234). IGI Global. https://doi.org/10.4018/978-1-7998-5691-7.ch013

Menezes, V. D., & Cavagnaro, E. (2021). Communicating Sustainable Initiatives in the Hotel Industry: The Case of the Hotel Jakarta Amsterdam. In F. Brandão, Z. Breda, R. Costa, & C. Costa (Eds.), *Handbook of Research on the Role of Tourism in Achieving Sustainable Development Goals* (pp. 224-234). IGI Global. https://doi.org/10.4018/978-1-7998-5691-7.ch013

Mitas, O., Bastiaansen, M., & Boode, W. (2022). If You're Happy, I'm Happy: Emotion Contagion at a Tourist Information Center. In R. Augusto Costa, F. Brandão, Z. Breda, & C. Costa (Eds.), *Planning and Managing the Experience Economy in Tourism* (pp. 122-140). IGI Global. https://doi.org/10.4018/978-1-7998-8775-1.ch007

Mnjama, N. M. (2017). Preservation of Recorded Information in Public and Private Sector Organizations. In Jain, P., & Mnjama, N. (Eds.), *Managing Knowledge Resources and Records in Modern Organizations* (pp. 149–167). Hershey, PA: IGI Global. DOI: 10.4018/978-1-5225-1965-2.ch009

Mokoqama, M., & Fields, Z. (2017). Principles of Responsible Management Education (PRME): Call for Responsible Management Education. In Fields, Z. (Ed.), *Collective Creativity for Responsible and Sustainable Business Practice* (pp. 229–241). Hershey, PA: IGI Global. DOI: 10.4018/978-1-5225-1823-5.ch012

Monteiro, A., Lopes, S., & Carbone, F. (2021). Academic Mobility: Bridging Tourism and Peace Education. In J. da Silva, Z. Breda, & F. Carbone (Eds.), *Role and Impact of Tourism in Peacebuilding and Conflict Transformation* (pp. 275-301). IGI Global. https://doi.org/10.4018/978-1-7998-5053-3.ch016

Muniapan, B. (2017). Philosophy and Management: The Relevance of Vedanta in Management. In Ordóñez de Pablos, P. (Ed.), *Managerial Strategies and Solutions for Business Success in Asia* (pp. 124–139). Hershey, PA: IGI Global. DOI: 10.4018/978-1-5225-1886-0.ch007

Murad, S. E., & Dowaji, S. (2017). Using Value-Based Approach for Managing Cloud-Based Services. In Turuk, A., Sahoo, B., & Addya, S. (Eds.), *Resource Management and Efficiency in Cloud Computing Environments* (pp. 33–60). Hershey, PA: IGI Global. DOI: 10.4018/978-1-5225-1721-4.ch002

Mutahar, A. M., Daud, N. M., Thurasamy, R., Isaac, O., & Abdulsalam, R. (2018). The Mediating of Perceived Usefulness and Perceived Ease of Use: The Case of Mobile Banking in Yemen. *International Journal of Technology Diffusion*, *9*(2), 21–40. DOI: 10.4018/IJTD.2018040102

Naidoo, V. (2017). E-Learning and Management Education at African Universities. In Baporikar, N. (Ed.), *Management Education for Global Leadership* (pp. 181–201). Hershey, PA: IGI Global. DOI: 10.4018/978-1-5225-1013-0.ch009

Naidoo, V., & Igbinakhase, I. (2018). Opportunities and Challenges of Knowledge Retention in SMEs. In Baporikar, N. (Ed.), *Knowledge Integration Strategies for Entrepreneurship and Sustainability* (pp. 70–94). Hershey, PA: IGI Global. DOI: 10.4018/978-1-5225-5115-7.ch004

Naumov, N., & Costandachi, G. (2021). Creativity and Entrepreneurship: Gastronomic Tourism in Mexico. In Soares, J. (Ed.), *Innovation and Entrepreneurial Opportunities in Community Tourism* (pp. 90–108). IGI Global. https://doi.org/10.4018/978-1-7998-4855-4.ch006

Nayak, S., & Prabhu, N. (2017). Paradigm Shift in Management Education: Need for a Cross Functional Perspective. In Baporikar, N. (Ed.), *Management Education for Global Leadership* (pp. 241–255). Hershey, PA: IGI Global. DOI: 10.4018/978-1-5225-1013-0.ch012

Nedelko, Z., & Potocan, V. (2017). Management Solutions in Non-Profit Organizations: Case of Slovenia. In Potocan, V., Ünğan, M., & Nedelko, Z. (Eds.), *Handbook of Research on Managerial Solutions in Non-Profit Organizations* (pp. 1–22). Hershey, PA: IGI Global. DOI: 10.4018/978-1-5225-0731-4.ch001

Nedelko, Z., & Potocan, V. (2017). Priority of Management Tools Utilization among Managers: International Comparison. In Wang, V. (Ed.), *Encyclopedia of Strategic Leadership and Management* (pp. 1083–1094). Hershey, PA: IGI Global. DOI: 10.4018/978-1-5225-1049-9.ch075

Nedelko, Z., Raudeliūnienė, J., & Črešnar, R. (2018). Knowledge Dynamics in Supply Chain Management. In Baporikar, N. (Ed.), *Knowledge Integration Strategies for Entrepreneurship and Sustainability* (pp. 150–166). Hershey, PA: IGI Global. DOI: 10.4018/978-1-5225-5115-7.ch008

Nguyen, H. T., & Hipsher, S. A. (2018). Innovation and Creativity Used by Private Sector Firms in a Resources-Constrained Environment. In Hipsher, S. (Ed.), *Examining the Private Sector's Role in Wealth Creation and Poverty Reduction* (pp. 219–238). Hershey, PA: IGI Global. DOI: 10.4018/978-1-5225-3117-3.ch010

Obicci, P. A. (2017). Risk Sharing in a Partnership. In *Risk Management Strategies in Public-Private Partnerships* (pp. 115–152). Hershey, PA: IGI Global. DOI: 10.4018/978-1-5225-2503-5.ch004

Obidallah, W. J., & Raahemi, B. (2017). Managing Changes in Service Oriented Virtual Organizations: A Structural and Procedural Framework to Facilitate the Process of Change. *Journal of Electronic Commerce in Organizations*, *15*(1), 59–83. DOI: 10.4018/JECO.2017010104

Ojo, O. (2017). Impact of Innovation on the Entrepreneurial Success in Selected Business Enterprises in South-West Nigeria. *International Journal of Innovation in the Digital Economy*, *8*(2), 29–38. DOI: 10.4018/IJIDE.2017040103

Okdinawati, L., Simatupang, T. M., & Sunitiyoso, Y. (2017). Multi-Agent Reinforcement Learning for Value Co-Creation of Collaborative Transportation Management (CTM). *International Journal of Information Systems and Supply Chain Management*, *10*(3), 84–95. DOI: 10.4018/IJISSCM.2017070105

Olivera, V. A., & Carrillo, I. M. (2021). Organizational Culture: A Key Element for the Development of Mexican Micro and Small Tourist Companies. In Soares, J. (Ed.), *Innovation and Entrepreneurial Opportunities in Community Tourism* (pp. 227–242). IGI Global. DOI: 10.4018/978-1-7998-4855-4.ch013

Ossorio, M. (2022). Corporate Museum Experiences in Enogastronomic Tourism. In R. Augusto Costa, F. Brandão, Z. Breda, & C. Costa (Eds.), *Planning and Managing the Experience Economy in Tourism* (pp. 107-121). IGI Global. https://doi.org/DOI: 10.4018/978-1-7998-8775-1.ch006

Ossorio, M. (2022). Enogastronomic Tourism in Times of Pandemic. In Fernandes, G. (Ed.), *Challenges and New Opportunities for Tourism in Inland Territories: Ecocultural Resources and Sustainable Initiatives* (pp. 241–255). IGI Global. https://doi.org/10.4018/978-1-7998-7339-6.ch014

Özekici, Y. K. (2022). ICT as an Acculturative Agent and Its Role in the Tourism Context: Introduction, Acculturation Theory, Progress of the Acculturation Theory in Extant Literature. In Ramos, C., Quinteiro, S., & Gonçalves, A. (Eds.), *ICT as Innovator Between Tourism and Culture* (pp. 42–66). IGI Global. https://doi.org/10.4018/978-1-7998-8165-0.ch004

Pal, K. (2018). Building High Quality Big Data-Based Applications in Supply Chains. In Kumar, A., & Saurav, S. (Eds.), *Supply Chain Management Strategies and Risk Assessment in Retail Environments* (pp. 1–24). Hershey, PA: IGI Global. DOI: 10.4018/978-1-5225-3056-5.ch001

Palos-Sanchez, P. R., & Correia, M. B. (2018). Perspectives of the Adoption of Cloud Computing in the Tourism Sector. In Rodrigues, J., Ramos, C., Cardoso, P., & Henriques, C. (Eds.), *Handbook of Research on Technological Developments for Cultural Heritage and eTourism Applications* (pp. 377–400). Hershey, PA: IGI Global. DOI: 10.4018/978-1-5225-2927-9.ch018

Papadopoulou, G. (2021). Promoting Gender Equality and Women Empowerment in the Tourism Sector. In F. Brandão, Z. Breda, R. Costa, & C. Costa (Eds.), *Handbook of Research on the Role of Tourism in Achieving Sustainable Development Goals* (pp. 152-174). IGI Global. https://doi.org/DOI: 10.4018/978-1-7998-5691-7.ch009

Papp-Váry, Á. F., & Tóth, T. Z. (2022). Analysis of Budapest as a Film Tourism Destination. In R. Baleiro & R. Pereira (Eds.), *Global Perspectives on Literary Tourism and Film-Induced Tourism* (pp. 257-279). IGI Global. https://doi.org/10.4018/978-1-7998-8262-6.ch014

Patiño, B. E. (2017). New Generation Management by Convergence and Individual Identity: A Systemic and Human-Oriented Approach. In Baporikar, N. (Ed.), *Innovation and Shifting Perspectives in Management Education* (pp. 119–143). Hershey, PA: IGI Global. DOI: 10.4018/978-1-5225-1019-2.ch006

Patro, C. S. (2021). Digital Tourism: Influence of E-Marketing Technology. In M. Dinis, L. Bonixe, S. Lamy, & Z. Breda (Eds.), *Impact of New Media in Tourism* (pp. 234-254). IGI Global. https://doi.org/10.4018/978-1-7998-7095-1.ch014

Pawliczek, A., & Rössler, M. (2017). Knowledge of Management Tools and Systems in SMEs: Knowledge Transfer in Management. In Bencsik, A. (Ed.), *Knowledge Management Initiatives and Strategies in Small and Medium Enterprises* (pp. 180–203). Hershey, PA: IGI Global. DOI: 10.4018/978-1-5225-1642-2.ch009

Pejic-Bach, M., Omazic, M. A., Aleksic, A., & Zoroja, J. (2018). Knowledge-Based Decision Making: A Multi-Case Analysis. In Leon, R. (Ed.), *Managerial Strategies for Business Sustainability During Turbulent Times* (pp. 160–184). Hershey, PA: IGI Global. DOI: 10.4018/978-1-5225-2716-9.ch009

Perano, M., Hysa, X., & Calabrese, M. (2018). Strategic Planning, Cultural Context, and Business Continuity Management: Business Cases in the City of Shkoder. In Presenza, A., & Sheehan, L. (Eds.), *Geopolitics and Strategic Management in the Global Economy* (pp. 57–77). Hershey, PA: IGI Global. DOI: 10.4018/978-1-5225-2673-5.ch004

Pereira, R., Mira da Silva, M., & Lapão, L. V. (2017). IT Governance Maturity Patterns in Portuguese Healthcare. In De Haes, S., & Van Grembergen, W. (Eds.), *Strategic IT Governance and Alignment in Business Settings* (pp. 24–52). Hershey, PA: IGI Global. DOI: 10.4018/978-1-5225-0861-8.ch002

Pérez-Uribe, R. I., Torres, D. A., Jurado, S. P., & Prada, D. M. (2018). Cloud Tools for the Development of Project Management in SMEs. In Perez-Uribe, R., Salcedo-Perez, C., & Ocampo-Guzman, D. (Eds.), *Handbook of Research on Intrapreneurship and Organizational Sustainability in SMEs* (pp. 95–120). Hershey, PA: IGI Global. DOI: 10.4018/978-1-5225-3543-0.ch005

Petrisor, I., & Cozmiuc, D. (2017). Global Supply Chain Management Organization at Siemens in the Advent of Industry 4.0. In Saglietto, L., & Cezanne, C. (Eds.), *Global Intermediation and Logistics Service Providers* (pp. 123–142). Hershey, PA: IGI Global. DOI: 10.4018/978-1-5225-2133-4.ch007

Pierce, J. M., Velliaris, D. M., & Edwards, J. (2017). A Living Case Study: A Journey Not a Destination. In Silton, N. (Ed.), *Exploring the Benefits of Creativity in Education, Media, and the Arts* (pp. 158–178). Hershey, PA: IGI Global. DOI: 10.4018/978-1-5225-0504-4.ch008

Pipia, S., & Pipia, S. (2021). Challenges of Religious Tourism in the Conflict Region: An Example of Jerusalem. In E. Alaverdov & M. Bari (Eds.), *Global Development of Religious Tourism* (pp. 135-148). IGI Global. https://doi.org/10.4018/978-1-7998-5792-1.ch009

Poulaki, P., Kritikos, A., Vasilakis, N., & Valeri, M. (2022). The Contribution of Female Creativity to the Development of Gastronomic Tourism in Greece: The Case of the Island of Naxos in the South Aegean Region. In Valeri, M. (Ed.), *New Governance and Management in Touristic Destinations* (pp. 246–258). IGI Global. https://doi.org/10.4018/978-1-6684-3889-3.ch015

Radosavljevic, M., & Andjelkovic, A. (2017). Multi-Criteria Decision Making Approach for Choosing Business Process for the Improvement: Upgrading of the Six Sigma Methodology. In Stanković, J., Delias, P., Marinković, S., & Rochhia, S. (Eds.), *Tools and Techniques for Economic Decision Analysis* (pp. 225–247). Hershey, PA: IGI Global. DOI: 10.4018/978-1-5225-0959-2.ch011

Radovic, V. M. (2017). Corporate Sustainability and Responsibility and Disaster Risk Reduction: A Serbian Overview. In Camilleri, M. (Ed.), *CSR 2.0 and the New Era of Corporate Citizenship* (pp. 147–164). Hershey, PA: IGI Global. DOI: 10.4018/978-1-5225-1842-6.ch008

Raghunath, K. M., Devi, S. L., & Patro, C. S. (2018). Impact of Risk Assessment Models on Risk Factors: A Holistic Outlook. In Strang, K., Korstanje, M., & Vajjhala, N. (Eds.), *Research, Practices, and Innovations in Global Risk and Contingency Management* (pp. 134–153). Hershey, PA: IGI Global. DOI: 10.4018/978-1-5225-4754-9.ch008

Raman, A., & Goyal, D. P. (2017). Extending IMPLEMENT Framework for Enterprise Information Systems Implementation to Information System Innovation. In Tavana, M. (Ed.), *Enterprise Information Systems and the Digitalization of Business Functions* (pp. 137–177). Hershey, PA: IGI Global. DOI: 10.4018/978-1-5225-2382-6.ch007

Rao, Y., & Zhang, Y. (2017). The Construction and Development of Academic Library Digital Special Subject Databases. In Ruan, L., Zhu, Q., & Ye, Y. (Eds.), *Academic Library Development and Administration in China* (pp. 163–183). Hershey, PA: IGI Global. DOI: 10.4018/978-1-5225-0550-1.ch010

Ravasan, A. Z., Mohammadi, M. M., & Hamidi, H. (2018). An Investigation Into the Critical Success Factors of Implementing Information Technology Service Management Frameworks. In Jakobs, K. (Ed.), *Corporate and Global Standardization Initiatives in Contemporary Society* (pp. 200–218). Hershey, PA: IGI Global. DOI: 10.4018/978-1-5225-5320-5.ch009

Rezaie, S., Mirabedini, S. J., & Abtahi, A. (2018). Designing a Model for Implementation of Business Intelligence in the Banking Industry. *International Journal of Enterprise Information Systems, 14*(1), 77–103. DOI: 10.4018/IJEIS.2018010105

Richards, V., Matthews, N., Williams, O. J., & Khan, Z. (2021). The Challenges of Accessible Tourism Information Systems for Tourists With Vision Impairment: Sensory Communications Beyond the Screen. In Eusébio, C., Teixeira, L., & Carneiro, M. (Eds.), *ICT Tools and Applications for Accessible Tourism* (pp. 26–54). IGI Global. https://doi.org/10.4018/978-1-7998-6428-8.ch002

Rodrigues de Souza Neto, V., & Marques, O. (2021). Rural Tourism Fostering Welfare Through Sustainable Development: A Conceptual Approach. In Perinotto, A., Mayer, V., & Soares, J. (Eds.), *Rebuilding and Restructuring the Tourism Industry: Infusion of Happiness and Quality of Life* (pp. 38–57). IGI Global. https://doi.org/10.4018/978-1-7998-7239-9.ch003

Romano, L., Grimaldi, R., & Colasuonno, F. S. (2017). Demand Management as a Success Factor in Project Portfolio Management. In Romano, L. (Ed.), *Project Portfolio Management Strategies for Effective Organizational Operations* (pp. 202–219). Hershey, PA: IGI Global. DOI: 10.4018/978-1-5225-2151-8.ch008

Rubio-Escuderos, L., & García-Andreu, H. (2021). Competitiveness Factors of Accessible Tourism E-Travel Agencies. In Eusébio, C., Teixeira, L., & Carneiro, M. (Eds.), *ICT Tools and Applications for Accessible Tourism* (pp. 196–217). IGI Global. https://doi.org/10.4018/978-1-7998-6428-8.ch009

Rucci, A. C., Porto, N., Darcy, S., & Becka, L. (2021). Smart and Accessible Cities?: Not Always – The Case for Accessible Tourism Initiatives in Buenos Aries and Sydney. In Eusébio, C., Teixeira, L., & Carneiro, M. (Eds.), *ICT Tools and Applications for Accessible Tourism* (pp. 115–145). IGI Global. https://doi.org/10.4018/978-1-7998-6428-8.ch006

Ruhi, U. (2018). Towards an Interdisciplinary Socio-Technical Definition of Virtual Communities. In M. Khosrow-Pour, D.B.A. (Ed.), *Encyclopedia of Information Science and Technology, Fourth Edition* (pp. 4278-4295). Hershey, PA: IGI Global. DOI: 10.4018/978-1-5225-2255-3.ch371

Ryan, L., Catena, M., Ros, P., & Stephens, S. (2021). Designing Entrepreneurial Ecosystems to Support Resource Management in the Tourism Industry. In Costa, V., Moura, A., & Mira, M. (Eds.), *Handbook of Research on Human Capital and People Management in the Tourism Industry* (pp. 265–281). IGI Global. https://doi.org/10.4018/978-1-7998-4318-4.ch013

Sabuncu, I. (2021). Understanding Tourist Perceptions and Expectations During Pandemic Through Social Media Big Data. In Demir, M., Dalgıç, A., & Ergen, F. (Eds.), *Handbook of Research on the Impacts and Implications of COVID-19 on the Tourism Industry* (pp. 330–350). IGI Global. https://doi.org/10.4018/978-1-7998-8231-2.ch016

Safari, M. R., & Jiang, Q. (2018). The Theory and Practice of IT Governance Maturity and Strategies Alignment: Evidence From Banking Industry. *Journal of Global Information Management, 26*(2), 127–146. DOI: 10.4018/JGIM.2018040106

Sahoo, J., Pati, B., & Mohanty, B. (2017). Knowledge Management as an Academic Discipline: An Assessment. In Gunjal, B. (Ed.), *Managing Knowledge and Scholarly Assets in Academic Libraries* (pp. 99–126). Hershey, PA: IGI Global. DOI: 10.4018/978-1-5225-1741-2.ch005

Saini, D. (2017). Relevance of Teaching Values and Ethics in Management Education. In Baporikar, N. (Ed.), *Management Education for Global Leadership* (pp. 90–111). Hershey, PA: IGI Global. DOI: 10.4018/978-1-5225-1013-0.ch005

Sambhanthan, A. (2017). Assessing and Benchmarking Sustainability in Organisations: An Integrated Conceptual Model. *International Journal of Systems and Service-Oriented Engineering, 7*(4), 22–43. DOI: 10.4018/IJSSOE.2017100102

Sambhanthan, A., & Potdar, V. (2017). A Study of the Parameters Impacting Sustainability in Information Technology Organizations. *International Journal of Knowledge-Based Organizations, 7*(3), 27–39. DOI: 10.4018/IJKBO.2017070103

Sánchez-Fernández, M. D., & Manríquez, M. R. (2018). The Entrepreneurial Spirit Based on Social Values: The Digital Generation. In Isaias, P., & Carvalho, L. (Eds.), *User Innovation and the Entrepreneurship Phenomenon in the Digital Economy* (pp. 173–193). Hershey, PA: IGI Global. DOI: 10.4018/978-1-5225-2826-5.ch009

Sanchez-Ruiz, L., & Blanco, B. (2017). Process Management for SMEs: Barriers, Enablers, and Benefits. In Vemić, M. (Ed.), *Optimal Management Strategies in Small and Medium Enterprises* (pp. 293–319). Hershey, PA: IGI Global. DOI: 10.4018/978-1-5225-1949-2.ch014

Sanz, L. F., Gómez-Pérez, J., & Castillo-Martinez, A. (2018). Analysis of the European ICT Competence Frameworks. In Ahuja, V., & Rathore, S. (Eds.), *Multidisciplinary Perspectives on Human Capital and Information Technology Professionals* (pp. 225–245). Hershey, PA: IGI Global. DOI: 10.4018/978-1-5225-5297-0.ch012

Sarvepalli, A., & Godin, J. (2017). Business Process Management in the Classroom. *Journal of Cases on Information Technology, 19*(2), 17–28. DOI: 10.4018/JCIT.2017040102

Saxena, G. G., & Saxena, A. (2021). Host Community Role in Medical Tourism Development. In Singh, M., & Kumaran, S. (Eds.), *Growth of the Medical Tourism Industry and Its Impact on Society: Emerging Research and Opportunities* (pp. 105–127). IGI Global. https://doi.org/10.4018/978-1-7998-3427-4.ch006

Saygili, E. E., Ozturkoglu, Y., & Kocakulah, M. C. (2017). End Users' Perceptions of Critical Success Factors in ERP Applications. *International Journal of Enterprise Information Systems, 13*(4), 58–75. DOI: 10.4018/IJEIS.2017100104

Saygili, E. E., & Saygili, A. T. (2017). Contemporary Issues in Enterprise Information Systems: A Critical Review of CSFs in ERP Implementations. In Tavana, M. (Ed.), *Enterprise Information Systems and the Digitalization of Business Functions* (pp. 120–136). Hershey, PA: IGI Global. DOI: 10.4018/978-1-5225-2382-6.ch006

Schwaiger, K. M., & Zehrer, A. (2021). The COVID-19 Pandemic and Organizational Resilience in Hospitality Family Firms: A Qualitative Approach. In Zehrer, A., Glowka, G., Schwaiger, K., & Ranacher-Lackner, V. (Eds.), *Resiliency Models and Addressing Future Risks for Family Firms in the Tourism Industry* (pp. 32–49). IGI Global. https://doi.org/10.4018/978-1-7998-7352-5.ch002

Scott, N., & Campos, A. C. (2022). Cognitive Science of Tourism Experiences. In R. Augusto Costa, F. Brandão, Z. Breda, & C. Costa (Eds.), *Planning and Managing the Experience Economy in Tourism* (pp. 1-21). IGI Global. https://doi.org/DOI: 10.4018/978-1-7998-8775-1.ch001

Seidenstricker, S., & Antonino, A. (2018). Business Model Innovation-Oriented Technology Management for Emergent Technologies. In M. Khosrow-Pour, D.B.A. (Ed.), *Encyclopedia of Information Science and Technology, Fourth Edition* (pp. 4560-4569). Hershey, PA: IGI Global. DOI: 10.4018/978-1-5225-2255-3.ch396

Selvi, M. S. (2021). Changes in Tourism Sales and Marketing Post COVID-19. In Demir, M., Dalgıç, A., & Ergen, F. (Eds.), *Handbook of Research on the Impacts and Implications of COVID-19 on the Tourism Industry* (pp. 437–460). IGI Global. DOI: 10.4018/978-1-7998-8231-2.ch021

Senaratne, S., & Gunarathne, A. D. (2017). Excellence Perspective for Management Education from a Global Accountants' Hub in Asia. In Baporikar, N. (Ed.), *Management Education for Global Leadership* (pp. 158–180). Hershey, PA: IGI Global. DOI: 10.4018/978-1-5225-1013-0.ch008

Sensuse, D. I., & Cahyaningsih, E. (2018). Knowledge Management Models: A Summative Review. *International Journal of Information Systems in the Service Sector, 10*(1), 71–100. DOI: 10.4018/IJISSS.2018010105

Seth, M., Goyal, D., & Kiran, R. (2017). Diminution of Impediments in Implementation of Supply Chain Management Information System for Enhancing its Effectiveness in Indian Automobile Industry. *Journal of Global Information Management, 25*(3), 1–20. DOI: 10.4018/JGIM.2017070101

Seyal, A. H., & Rahman, M. N. (2017). Investigating Impact of Inter-Organizational Factors in Measuring ERP Systems Success: Bruneian Perspectives. In Tavana, M. (Ed.), *Enterprise Information Systems and the Digitalization of Business Functions* (pp. 178–204). Hershey, PA: IGI Global. DOI: 10.4018/978-1-5225-2382-6.ch008

Shaqrah, A. A. (2018). Analyzing Business Intelligence Systems Based on 7s Model of McKinsey. *International Journal of Business Intelligence Research, 9*(1), 53–63. DOI: 10.4018/IJBIR.2018010104

Sharma, A. J. (2017). Enhancing Sustainability through Experiential Learning in Management Education. In Baporikar, N. (Ed.), *Management Education for Global Leadership* (pp. 256–274). Hershey, PA: IGI Global. DOI: 10.4018/978-1-5225-1013-0.ch013

Shetty, K. P. (2017). Responsible Global Leadership: Ethical Challenges in Management Education. In Baporikar, N. (Ed.), *Innovation and Shifting Perspectives in Management Education* (pp. 194–223). Hershey, PA: IGI Global. DOI: 10.4018/978-1-5225-1019-2.ch009

Sinthupundaja, J., & Kohda, Y. (2017). Effects of Corporate Social Responsibility and Creating Shared Value on Sustainability. *International Journal of Sustainable Entrepreneurship and Corporate Social Responsibility, 2*(1), 27–38. DOI: 10.4018/IJSECSR.2017010103

Škarica, I., & Hrgović, A. V. (2018). Implementation of Total Quality Management Principles in Public Health Institutes in the Republic of Croatia. *International Journal of Productivity Management and Assessment Technologies, 6*(1), 1–16. DOI: 10.4018/IJPMAT.2018010101

Skokic, V. (2021). How Small Hotel Owners Practice Resilience: Longitudinal Study Among Small Family Hotels in Croatia. In Zehrer, A., Glowka, G., Schwaiger, K., & Ranacher-Lackner, V. (Eds.), *Resiliency Models and Addressing Future Risks for Family Firms in the Tourism Industry* (pp. 50–73). IGI Global. DOI: 10.4018/978-1-7998-7352-5.ch003

Smuts, H., Kotzé, P., Van der Merwe, A., & Loock, M. (2017). Framework for Managing Shared Knowledge in an Information Systems Outsourcing Context. *International Journal of Knowledge Management, 13*(4), 1–30. DOI: 10.4018/IJKM.2017100101

Sousa, M. J., Cruz, R., Dias, I., & Caracol, C. (2017). Information Management Systems in the Supply Chain. In Jamil, G., Soares, A., & Pessoa, C. (Eds.), *Handbook of Research on Information Management for Effective Logistics and Supply Chains* (pp. 469–485). Hershey, PA: IGI Global. DOI: 10.4018/978-1-5225-0973-8.ch025

Spremic, M., Turulja, L., & Bajgoric, N. (2018). Two Approaches in Assessing Business Continuity Management Attitudes in the Organizational Context. In Bajgoric, N. (Ed.), *Always-On Enterprise Information Systems for Modern Organizations* (pp. 159–183). Hershey, PA: IGI Global. DOI: 10.4018/978-1-5225-3704-5.ch008

Steenkamp, A. L. (2018). Some Insights in Computer Science and Information Technology. In *Examining the Changing Role of Supervision in Doctoral Research Projects: Emerging Research and Opportunities* (pp. 113–133). Hershey, PA: IGI Global. DOI: 10.4018/978-1-5225-2610-0.ch005

Stipanović, C., Rudan, E., & Zubović, V. (2022). Reaching the New Tourist Through Creativity: Sustainable Development Challenges in Croatian Coastal Towns. In Valeri, M. (Ed.), *New Governance and Management in Touristic Destinations* (pp. 231–245). IGI Global. https://doi.org/10.4018/978-1-6684-3889-3.ch014

Tabach, A., & Croteau, A. (2017). Configurations of Information Technology Governance Practices and Business Unit Performance. *International Journal of IT/Business Alignment and Governance*, *8*(2), 1–27. DOI: 10.4018/IJITBAG.2017070101

Talaue, G. M., & Iqbal, T. (2017). Assessment of e-Business Mode of Selected Private Universities in the Philippines and Pakistan. *International Journal of Online Marketing*, *7*(4), 63–77. DOI: 10.4018/IJOM.2017100105

Tam, G. C. (2017). Project Manager Sustainability Competence. In *Managerial Strategies and Green Solutions for Project Sustainability* (pp. 178–207). Hershey, PA: IGI Global. DOI: 10.4018/978-1-5225-2371-0.ch008

Tambo, T. (2018). Fashion Retail Innovation: About Context, Antecedents, and Outcome in Technological Change Projects. In I. Management Association (Ed.), *Fashion and Textiles: Breakthroughs in Research and Practice* (pp. 233-260). Hershey, PA: IGI Global. https://doi.org/DOI: 10.4018/978-1-5225-3432-7.ch010

Tantau, A. D., & Frăţilă, L. C. (2018). Information and Management System for Renewable Energy Business. In *Entrepreneurship and Business Development in the Renewable Energy Sector* (pp. 200–244). Hershey, PA: IGI Global. DOI: 10.4018/978-1-5225-3625-3.ch006

Teixeira, N., Pardal, P. N., & Rafael, B. G. (2018). Internationalization, Financial Performance, and Organizational Challenges: A Success Case in Portugal. In Carvalho, L. (Ed.), *Handbook of Research on Entrepreneurial Ecosystems and Social Dynamics in a Globalized World* (pp. 379–423). Hershey, PA: IGI Global. DOI: 10.4018/978-1-5225-3525-6.ch017

Teixeira, P., Teixeira, L., Eusébio, C., Silva, S., & Teixeira, A. (2021). The Impact of ICTs on Accessible Tourism: Evidence Based on a Systematic Literature Review. In Eusébio, C., Teixeira, L., & Carneiro, M. (Eds.), *ICT Tools and Applications for Accessible Tourism* (pp. 1–25). IGI Global. DOI: 10.4018/978-1-7998-6428-8.ch001

Trad, A., & Kalpić, D. (2018). The Business Transformation Framework, Agile Project and Change Management. In M. Khosrow-Pour, D.B.A. (Ed.), *Encyclopedia of Information Science and Technology, Fourth Edition* (pp. 620-635). Hershey, PA: IGI Global. https://doi.org/DOI: 10.4018/978-1-5225-2255-3.ch054

Trad, A., & Kalpić, D. (2018). The Business Transformation and Enterprise Architecture Framework: The Financial Engineering E-Risk Management and E-Law Integration. In Sergi, B., Fidanoski, F., Ziolo, M., & Naumovski, V. (Eds.), *Regaining Global Stability After the Financial Crisis* (pp. 46–65). Hershey, PA: IGI Global. DOI: 10.4018/978-1-5225-4026-7.ch003

Trengereid, V. (2022). Conditions of Network Engagement: The Quest for a Common Good. In R. Augusto Costa, F. Brandão, Z. Breda, & C. Costa (Eds.), *Planning and Managing the Experience Economy in Tourism* (pp. 69-84). IGI Global. https://doi.org/10.4018/978-1-7998-8775-1.ch004

Turulja, L., & Bajgoric, N. (2018). Business Continuity and Information Systems: A Systematic Literature Review. In Bajgoric, N. (Ed.), *Always-On Enterprise Information Systems for Modern Organizations* (pp. 60–87). Hershey, PA: IGI Global. DOI: 10.4018/978-1-5225-3704-5.ch004

Vargas-Hernández, J. G. (2017). Professional Integrity in Business Management Education. In Baporikar, N. (Ed.), *Management Education for Global Leadership* (pp. 70–89). Hershey, PA: IGI Global. DOI: 10.4018/978-1-5225-1013-0.ch004

Varnacı Uzun, F. (2021). The Destination Preferences of Foreign Tourists During the COVID-19 Pandemic and Attitudes Towards: Marmaris, Turkey. In Demir, M., Dalgıç, A., & Ergen, F. (Eds.), *Handbook of Research on the Impacts and Implications of COVID-19 on the Tourism Industry* (pp. 285–306). IGI Global. https://doi.org/10.4018/978-1-7998-8231-2.ch014

Vasista, T. G., & AlAbdullatif, A. M. (2017). Role of Electronic Customer Relationship Management in Demand Chain Management: A Predictive Analytic Approach. *International Journal of Information Systems and Supply Chain Management, 10*(1), 53–67. DOI: 10.4018/IJISSCM.2017010104

Vieru, D., & Bourdeau, S. (2017). Survival in the Digital Era: A Digital Competence-Based Multi-Case Study in the Canadian SME Clothing Industry. *International Journal of Social and Organizational Dynamics in IT, 6*(1), 17–34. DOI: 10.4018/IJSODIT.2017010102

Vijayan, G., & Kamarulzaman, N. H. (2017). An Introduction to Sustainable Supply Chain Management and Business Implications. In Khan, M., Hussain, M., & Ajmal, M. (Eds.), *Green Supply Chain Management for Sustainable Business Practice* (pp. 27–50). Hershey, PA: IGI Global. DOI: 10.4018/978-1-5225-0635-5.ch002

Vlachvei, A., & Notta, O. (2017). Firm Competitiveness: Theories, Evidence, and Measurement. In Vlachvei, A., Notta, O., Karantininis, K., & Tsounis, N. (Eds.), *Factors Affecting Firm Competitiveness and Performance in the Modern Business World* (pp. 1–42). Hershey, PA: IGI Global. DOI: 10.4018/978-1-5225-0843-4.ch001

Wang, C., Schofield, M., Li, X., & Ou, X. (2017). Do Chinese Students in Public and Private Higher Education Institutes Perform at Different Level in One of the Leadership Skills: Critical Thinking?: An Exploratory Comparison. In Wang, V. (Ed.), *Encyclopedia of Strategic Leadership and Management* (pp. 160–181). Hershey, PA: IGI Global. DOI: 10.4018/978-1-5225-1049-9.ch013

Wang, J. (2017). Multi-Agent based Production Management Decision System Modelling for the Textile Enterprise. *Journal of Global Information Management, 25*(4), 1–15. DOI: 10.4018/JGIM.2017100101

Wiedemann, A., & Gewald, H. (2017). Examining Cross-Domain Alignment: The Correlation of Business Strategy, IT Management, and IT Business Value. *International Journal of IT/Business Alignment and Governance, 8*(1), 17–31. DOI: 10.4018/IJITBAG.2017010102

Wolf, R., & Thiel, M. (2018). Advancing Global Business Ethics in China: Reducing Poverty Through Human and Social Welfare. In Hipsher, S. (Ed.), *Examining the Private Sector's Role in Wealth Creation and Poverty Reduction* (pp. 67–84). Hershey, PA: IGI Global. DOI: 10.4018/978-1-5225-3117-3.ch004

Yablonsky, S. (2018). Innovation Platforms: Data and Analytics Platforms. In *Multi-Sided Platforms (MSPs) and Sharing Strategies in the Digital Economy: Emerging Research and Opportunities* (pp. 72–95). Hershey, PA: IGI Global. DOI: 10.4018/978-1-5225-5457-8.ch003

Yaşar, B. (2021). The Impact of COVID-19 on Volatility of Tourism Stocks: Evidence From BIST Tourism Index. In Demir, M., Dalgıç, A., & Ergen, F. (Eds.), *Handbook of Research on the Impacts and Implications of COVID-19 on the Tourism Industry* (pp. 23–44). IGI Global. https://doi.org/10.4018/978-1-7998-8231-2.ch002

Yusoff, A., Ahmad, N. H., & Halim, H. A. (2017). Agropreneurship among Gen Y in Malaysia: The Role of Academic Institutions. In Ahmad, N., Ramayah, T., Halim, H., & Rahman, S. (Eds.), *Handbook of Research on Small and Medium Enterprises in Developing Countries* (pp. 23–47). Hershey, PA: IGI Global. DOI: 10.4018/978-1-5225-2165-5.ch002

Zacher, D., & Pechlaner, H. (2021). Resilience as an Opportunity Approach: Challenges and Perspectives for Private Sector Participation on a Community Level. In Zehrer, A., Glowka, G., Schwaiger, K., & Ranacher-Lackner, V. (Eds.), *Resiliency Models and Addressing Future Risks for Family Firms in the Tourism Industry* (pp. 75–102). IGI Global. https://doi.org/10.4018/978-1-7998-7352-5.ch004

Zanin, F., Comuzzi, E., & Costantini, A. (2018). The Effect of Business Strategy and Stock Market Listing on the Use of Risk Assessment Tools. In *Management Control Systems in Complex Settings: Emerging Research and Opportunities* (pp. 145–168). Hershey, PA: IGI Global. DOI: 10.4018/978-1-5225-3987-2.ch007

Zgheib, P. W. (2017). Corporate Innovation and Intrapreneurship in the Middle East. In Zgheib, P. (Ed.), *Entrepreneurship and Business Innovation in the Middle East* (pp. 37–56). Hershey, PA: IGI Global. DOI: 10.4018/978-1-5225-2066-5.ch003

About the Contributors

Rizwan Khan is a dedicated academic with a fervent passion for advancing knowledge in the realms of Accounting and Finance. He holds a Ph.D. from the Faculty of Commerce at Aligarh Muslim University, India, achieved in 2022, specializing in the domain of Cost and Management Accounting. Guided by the esteemed Prof. S. Husain Ashraf, Dr. Khan's doctoral research focused on "Activity Based Costing in Select Automobile Industry," demonstrating his commitment to rigorous scholarship and academic excellence. Dr. Khan's academic journey is characterized by a strong foundation in commerce, marked by an M.Com (Finance and Accounting) and a B.Com (Accounting) from Aligarh Muslim University. His scholarly pursuits were further enriched by achieving the prestigious NET qualification in June 2019, showcasing his aptitude and proficiency in the field. Throughout his career, Dr. Khan has exhibited versatility and excellence across various professional roles. He served as a Financial Advisor at Cordova Publication Pvt. Ltd., Noida, from 2013 to 2016, where he honed his expertise in financial matters. Additionally, his commitment to preserving cultural heritage led him to contribute as an honorary consultant in the Advisory Committee 'Virasat – Bhartiya Sanskriti Evam Kala ka Sanrakshan' from 2016 to 2019. Dr. Khan's dedication to education is evident through his roles as a Guest Faculty at the Food Craft Institute, Aligarh Muslim University Campus, and his current position as an Assistant Professor (Finance and Accounting) at the University School of Business, Chandigarh University, Mohali. Furthermore, his stint as an Academic Counselor at IGNOU regional Centre, Aligarh Muslim University, underscores his commitment to nurturing academic growth and fostering learning environments. Beyond teaching, Dr. Khan actively contributes to institutional development and academic initiatives. He serves as a core member of the Board of Studies, takes on responsibilities as Master Subject Coordinator, and has been instrumental in designing courses for graduation and post-graduation programs. His organizational prowess is highlighted by his role as a Sports Coordinator and his contributions to organizing international conferences. Dr. Khan's scholarly contributions extend to publications in both books and academic journals. His research papers delve into topics such as financial leverage, entrepreneurship, and the impact of digitization on industries, showcasing his breadth of expertise and interdisciplinary approach. Moreover, he actively participates in workshops, conferences, and seminars, both as a presenter and an attendee, further enriching his scholarly repertoire and staying abreast of emerging trends and developments.

Mohammad Taqi is an accomplished academician specializing in the fields of Accounting and Finance, whose journey towards excellence has been marked by a relentless pursuit of knowledge and a dedication to scholarly endeavors. Currently serving as an Assistant Professor at the Faculty of Business, Bahrain Polytechnic, Taqi has established himself as a prominent figure in academia through his exemplary teaching, rigorous research, and notable administrative contributions. Taqi's academic journey began with a strong educational foundation, culminating in a Post Doctorate from Aligarh Muslim University and a PhD in Commerce. Armed with these qualifications, he embarked on a fulfilling career in academia, accumulating eight years of teaching experience at both undergraduate and postgraduate levels. His passion for education is evident in his commitment to nurturing the minds of students, equipping them with the knowledge and skills necessary to excel in their academic and professional pursuits. In tandem with his teaching responsibilities, Taqi has dedicated himself to advancing the frontiers of knowledge through rigorous research. His research interests predominantly lie in the realms of Financial Accounting, Financial Management, and Management Accounting. Over the years, Taqi has produced a prolific body of work, comprising research papers published in esteemed journals and presentations delivered at prestigious international conferences.

Through his scholarly contributions, Taqi has explored diverse topics such as the impact of Foreign Institutional Investors (FIIs) on the Indian Stock Market, the role of digitization in the automotive industry, and the implications of corporate social responsibility practices. Moreover, Taqi's administrative acumen has been demonstrated through various leadership roles undertaken throughout his career. From serving as a Warden at renowned institutions like Sir Syed Hall and Allama Iqbal Boarding House at Aligarh Muslim University to his tenure as Resident Warden at NRSC Hall, Taqi has showcased his ability to effectively manage and oversee administrative responsibilities. Beyond his academic and administrative roles, Taqi has actively pursued professional development opportunities to enhance his skills and expertise. He has participated in quality improvement programs, orientation programs, and workshops aimed at fostering continuous learning and growth. In addition to his professional pursuits, Taqi is deeply committed to community engagement and service. As an Academic Counsellor at Indira Gandhi National Open University, he has provided guidance and support to students pursuing commerce and management courses, further extending his impact beyond the confines of his academic institution.

Khaled Hussainey stands as a distinguished academic whose expertise in Accounting and Finance has garnered widespread recognition. His academic journey began with a Ph.D. in Accounting & Finance from The University of Manchester (UK) in 2004, preceded by an M.Sc. in Accounting & Finance from The University of Birmingham (UK) in 2000 and a B.Com. in Accounting from Ain Shams University (Egypt) in 1994. Over the course of his illustrious career, Professor Hussainey has held several esteemed positions that underscore his commitment to advancing scholarship and education. Notably, he served as a Professor of Accounting at Plymouth University from June 2013 to July 2016, following roles as a Lecturer, Senior Lecturer, and Reader in Accounting at Stirling University from August 2008 to May 2013. Earlier in his career, he laid the groundwork for his scholarly pursuits as a Postdoctoral Research Fellow and an ESRC Research Associate at Manchester University. Professor Hussainey's research interests span a wide array of topics within the field of accounting, encompassing areas such as corporate governance, risk disclosure, sustainability reporting, and financial performance. His scholarly contributions are highly esteemed and have been published in renowned academic journals including the Journal of Accounting Literature, European Financial Management, and Technological Forecasting & Social Change, among others. In addition to his exceptional research achievements, Professor Hussainey is deeply committed to nurturing the next generation of scholars. His dedication to education is evidenced by his teaching and supervision roles at various institutions across the globe. He has lent his expertise to universities in the UK, Saudi Arabia, Tunisia, France, the UAE, Lebanon, and Indonesia, where he has held part-time and visiting appointments, imparting invaluable knowledge and leaving a lasting impact on students and colleagues alike. Furthermore, Professor Hussainey's engagement extends beyond traditional academia through his editorial roles and contributions to academic journals. He serves as Co-Editor-in-Chief of the Journal of Financial Reporting and Senior Editor of the International Journal of Emerging Markets, in addition to holding associate editor positions for several prestigious journals. Moreover, he has undertaken numerous guest editor roles for special issues addressing contemporary topics in accounting and finance, further cementing his influence in the academic community.

***

Sablu Khan is working as an Assistant Professor at Aligarh Muslim University, Aligarh, India. He has completed his PhD from the Department of Business Administration A.M.U.. His current research interests involve areas such as service management, e-service quality, e-business, and e-retailing. He has published several research papers in reputed/refereed journals including the Journal of Service Science Research and Journal of Public Affairs.

Karima Sayari is an Associate Professor in Managerial and Financial Sciences Department at Al Zahra College for Women. She holds a bachelor's degree in international trade, a master's degree in economics and international finance, and a PhD in Finance and Economic Sciences. Dr. Sayari has over 10 years of teaching experience and has published extensively in reputable international journals indexed in Scopus and Web of Science. Her research focuses on economics, finance, banking, and digital finance. She is an active peer reviewer in various academic journals.

Kulsoom Siddiqui has completed her PhD thesis in Business Administration from Mangalaytan University, Aligarh. She is working as Assistant Professor in the same University. Her interest includes case studies, HR Practices and HR Management.

Index

L

M

P

Q

R

S

T

www.ingramcontent.com/pod-product-compliance
Lightning Source LLC
LaVergne TN
LVHW081336300926
849161LV00008B/1990